THE *Soups* of FRANCE

AVENUE BRILLAT-SAVARIN

CHARCUTERIE

CREPERIE TI SAOZON

THE *Soups* of FRANCE

Lois Anne Rothert

photographs by DON SMITH

CHRONICLE BOOKS

SAN FRANCISCO

Library of Congress Cataloging-in-Publication Data available.

ISBN 0-8118-3342-9

Manufactured in China

Designed by The Offices of Anne Burdick, Los Angeles
Typeset in Calvino, Mrs. Eaves, Filosofia

Distributed in Canada by Raincoast Books
9050 Shaughnessy Street
Vancouver, BC   V6P6E5

10 9 8 7 6 5 4 3 2 1

Chronicle Books LLC
85 Second Street
San Francisco, California 94105

www.chroniclebooks.com

ACKNOWLEDGMENTS

To my friends and colleagues throughout France, I thank you from the bottom of my heart. All of you have contributed immeasurably to this project—delicious bowls of soup, or honest recipes, or animated conversations. Sometimes all three.

In Alsace Lorraine, Marc Haeberlin of Auberge de L'Ille (Illhaeusern), Raymond Wir of Wir (Mulhouse), and Robert Husser of Le Cerf (Marlenheim); in the Auvergne, Guy Prouhèze of Grand Hotel Prouhèze (Aumont-Aubrac) and Michel Datessen of La Bateau Ivre (Le Puy); in le pays Basque, the Toyos family of Chez Mattin (Ciboure), Pascal Bassat of La Tourasse (St. Jean-de-Luz), and Firmin Arrambide of Les Pyrenees (St. Jean Pied-de-Port); in Bretagne, the Feunteun family of Grand Hotel (Carcarneau), Roger Tirel and Jan-Luc Guérin of Tirel-Guérin (La Gouesnière), Régis Mahé of Régis Mahé (Vannes), and M. Cabelguen of L'Escale (Locmariaquer); in Bourgogne, Dominique Lauriot of Hostellerie Bourguignonne (Verdun-sur-le-Doubs); in Champagne—le Nord, the makers of Le Creuset at Fresnoy-le-Grand and Jean-Pierre Dargent of La Faisanderie (Arras); on Corse, Paul Seta of Auberge Seta (Ajaccio); in the Dordogne, Charlou Reynal of Le Crémaillière (Brive-de-Gaillarde), Roland Mazère of Le Centenaire (Les Eyzies-de-Tayac), and Jean-Robert Hervé of Le Relais du Soleil d'Or (Montignac); in Franche-Comté, Pierre Michaud of Rôtisserie du Fier (Seyssel); in Languedoc, Alain Blanc of La Table du Alain (Montauban); in Normandie, M. Jouvin-Bessière of Lion d'Or (Bayeux) and Jean-Pierre Guéret of Le Quatre Saisons (Rouen).

In the Ile-de-France, there are many generous Parisians to thank: bookseller Mme Baudon of Librairie Gourmande, culinary historian Philip Hyman and Simone Bibillot; chefs, restaurateurs, and restauratrices of Paris; Françoise Meulier of Ambassade d'Auvergne; Andrée and Martian Persoons and Norbert Chich of Au Pied de Fouet; Martin Charriton of Auberge de Jarente; J.P. Egurreguy of Brasserie Balzar; Adrienne Biasin of Chez la Vieille; Colette Dejean of Chez Toutoune; Jean-Pierre Court of D'Chez Eux; M. Grolier of Guirlande de Julie; Jean-Marie Huclin of L'Oeillade; Marcel Baudin of L'Oulette; Mme Schweizer of La Providence; Alain Sainsard of La Truffière; Jacques Gellé of Champ de Mars; André Simon of Le Quercy; Alain Senderens of Lucas-Carton; Claude Udron of the former Pile ou Face; André Maillot of Polidor; Christiane Massia of Restaurant du Marché. In Provence, I thank Marc Chaminade of Le Patio (Fontvieille), Pierre and Jean-Michele Minguella of Miramar (Marseilles), and Etienne Sordello of Restaurant de Bacon (Cap d'Antibes); in the Rhone-Alpes, Alice Chamberod of Pot-au-Feu (Grenoble) and Jean-Claude Zorelle of Les Princes (Chambèry); in the Sud-ouest, Eric Mariottat of Le Parc (Agen), André Daguin of Hotel de France (Auch), Mme Cayrafourq of La Ferme Auberge (Pau), and Marie-Claude Gracia of the former La Belle Gasconne (Poudenas).

What I owe to Phyllis Wender, my steadfast agent, can never be adequately expressed. We began this circuitous journey over ten years ago and she has never wavered. Susie Cohen and Sonya Pabley, who assist Phyllis, are also utter professionals.

My relationships with the following people began professionally and grew into solid, comforting friendships. I need to convey my love and thanks to Lisa Wilber, my helpmate, who was integral to this book and the testing and tasting of recipes. Also of immense support has been Joe Vallone, creative chef and advisor. I am beholden to Todd Downs, once my gifted sous chef and now an eminent executive chef, for our long and rich association. I value the wit of George Mack, who always offers humor when I seem overcome. Jane Palajac, my confidante of twenty-two years, has been devoted to the success of this project.

And what would this book be without the photography of Smisse, also known as Don Smith? Both he and his wife, my good friend Susan Anderson, have added their talent, humor, and joie de vivre to my life and to this volume.

How can I thank the irrepressible Nick Malgiere? It was he who brought my project to the attention of my now editor, Bill LeBlond. And to Bill, as well, I am most appreciative. My deep thanks go to my able Chronicle colleagues, the estimable Amy Treadwell and copy editor sans pareil Sharon Silva. I am also grateful to editor Maria Guarnaschelli and William Morrow and Co. for their early interest in this project.

For their continued support for this cookbook, I must thank Dave Hirst, graphic designer Bill Bonnell, recipe testers Mike Robbins and Carrie Vallone, wine consultant Mike Yaney, and Needham and Mary Lou Hurst of Indianapolis. A number of diverse skills are needed to complete a manuscript and I would like to thank Gene Kraus for assisting me with online research to complete the bibliography, and to acknowledge Pamela Sandstrom of Indiana University for her illuminating bibliographical counsel.

No one ever works on a long-term project without the love and support of their family. My hard-working and talented sons, Jeff Hanselmann and John Hanselmann, were instrumental in helping me construct my Fort Wayne, Indiana, residence so I could return to the completion of this cookbook. Equally talented are my daughters, Jennifer Hanselmann and Julie Hanselmann Davies, who cosseted me with their enthusiasm, insights, and good-humored counsel.

And enfin, I'd like to thank my dear friend and companion, Jim Luckey, for saving the last dance for me.

In memory of Larsh Rothert

TABLE of CONTENTS

Preface

RAISON D'ÊTRE

I would like to discuss not so much my purpose in preparing this cookbook, but rather the book's own raison d'être. Never have I encountered a more appropriate moment for that classic French phrase. There is far more reason for the book's being than for my writing it. *The Soups of France* is more than a cookbook in the usual sense of the word. It is instead an essential work of safekeeping, a narrative of the great soups from all corners of France. These soups are significant because they are the basis of a cultural phenomenon unique to France, what ultimately became haute cuisine. Many of these ancestral soups, their origins obscure, are being lost, as the French, like the rest of the cosmos, move into the twenty-first century. I want to stem that tide. What were once believed to be enduring dishes are almost impossible to locate in restaurants, in private homes, and often even in cookbooks. Thus, a need to record French culinary history drives me to search out and document these dateless soups.

But that is not my sole reason for undertaking this project. Equally important is my enthusiastic enjoyment of delicious—and unusual—things to eat. Finding old soups is akin to discovering new dishes. When I discussed this project in Paris with a *restauratrice* who grew up in southwestern Toulouse, I mentioned the heady garlic soup, *tourin,* of that region. "Bah," huffed Mme Krinbarg, "no one in Paris knows about *tourin.*" I genuinely hope this record I'm tracing means food lovers everywhere will discover some wonderful soups of yesterday. To paraphrase French chef Alain Senderens on his mission at Archestrate, his first restaurant in Paris: "to make a journey into the past to discover recipes forgotten."

I have long been interested in the footprints of a language, so I have taken brief looks at how many of these soups were named. The linguistic expressions are often as revealing as the cookery. In the case of the ages-old regional dishes, the homespun soup designations resemble a quaint folk etymology. This tradition continued into classical French cuisine, as the christening of dishes, including soups, was derived from a system of honoring the distinguished people, places, and things.

SOUPS DU JOUR

It's hard even for me to understand why this ex-Hoosier living on a mountain ridge thousands of miles from France would find this project so absorbing. I suppose I laid the groundwork when I opened my restaurant, Du Jour, in 1980.

For seven unforgettable years, I was the owner-chef of a small café in Fort Wayne, Indiana, based on the simple idea that each day my staff and I would create a new menu. And we did. Every morning we prepared at least three new soups. We presented a lunch and dinner menu of those soups, plus four or five appetizers, six or seven main dishes, and four or five desserts. Creating new dishes based on the daily markets, various cooking techniques, and inventive concepts became addictive.

The kitchen staff enjoyed cooking, enjoyed creating, enjoyed one another. Not that we didn't take preparing top-flight dishes seriously—that was expected. But it was essential that we be innovative. We were in landlocked Indiana with lengthy winters and had to use long-hauled fresh seafood and produce. Occasionally these problems conspired to make our task a little trickier, but we did what we had hoped. We put together a fine little restaurant, with a passion for good food. Sandy, my good friend and manager, often referred to our activities as "cuisine by brinkmanship."

Stockpots were always going at full bore, and the format of a daily-changing menu insisted on the spirited search for new French soups, for our soups du jour. This collection of French soups is an extension of those creative, vibrant, and memorable days.

ARE YOU GOING TO FRANCE ON BUSINESS OR PLEASURE?

This engaging study of soups is a product of more than my years at Du Jour, however. I have tackled the subject in four additional ways: research, correspondence, travel, and, of course, cooking.

Documentation for the most venerable soups is available for the archaeological unearthing, so I tracked down old cookbooks written in French and now have my own collection of many of these treasures. I researched in libraries with extensive holdings in French-language cookbooks both in the United States and in France.

It was also essential that I establish a firsthand dialogue with cooks in France, through visits to their homes and restaurants and correspondence. This culinary portfolio grows daily as the French and U.S. postal systems somehow find me here in the Cascade Mountains, and I receive gracious, generous letters and recipes from unselfish and inspiring chefs who are proud of their rural heritage. They are flattered that French soups are in the spotlight.

I have had many culinary excursions to France over the last two decades, tasting traditional soups in every region of the country, and I have found many cooks who enjoyed preparing the authentic fare of their countryside. (Conversely, I have also found just the opposite—a good reason to continue my research.) To understand the essence of a French regional dish, one must taste it "at home," in its cultural habitat, at its hearth. When people ask me if I am going to France for business *or* pleasure, I am usually puzzled. Yes, I am going to France "to work," I say. But, after all, it *is* France.

FRENCH RECIPES AND AMERICAN COOKS

Optimally, a recipe should be a culinary formula, as precise as possible, so that the tasty outcome delivers on its descriptive name. On the other hand, translating recipes from French is often an exercise in second-guessing. Some instructions are surprisingly vague—*prenez quelque belles tomates* (take some beautiful tomatoes)—while others seem to give endearingly exact advise—*agitez avec une cuillière de bois* (stir with a wooden spoon). I have grown accustomed to reading recipes that ask for a *poignée* (handful) of this and a *poignée* of that. Sorrel and spinach maybe, but it's probably not a good idea to measure rice by the handful. Whose hand? It is extremely common for a French recipe to call for *un noix de beurre* (a nut of butter). By a Gallic twist this becomes *un noix comme un oeuf de beurre* (a nut like an egg of butter). One of my favorite measures is the recipe that requested celery *en grande quantité*. How much celery would you use?

To guarantee authenticity, I have several French sources for each of the recipes in this book, and I have translated all of the recipes from their original language. With some reluctance, it has been necessary to change the lyrical French to pragmatic English. I sincerely hope to illuminate the dim so that all the recipes have the requisite ingredient amounts and procedures. At the same time, I have retained that which makes the recipes characteristically French.

SOUPS THAT RESTORE

Many cooks interested in culinary history may remember the story of the Parisian, M. Boulanger, who, amid much controversy, opened a new kind of business to sell the broth *left over* from cooking meat. There was tonic, a pick-me-up, in a bowl of hot broth, M. Boulanger advertised. His sign, in Latin, concluded with the words "and I will restore you" (*et ego restaurabo vos*). What he opened was a *restaurant*—not an inn for travelers to rest and eat, or a café but an innovative establishment for eating in public.

Homemade soup is the one dish that can be made in any kitchen (or with a commercial slow cooker on a back porch or patio) and is guaranteed to give, in addition to something wonderful to eat, more refreshing pleasure than any other dish. When soup is on a burner, a family or guests feel well cared for, tended. We can hurry by a deli or any take-out food merchant and choose wonderful salads, fragrant loaves of bread, beautiful quiches, and perfect desserts. Seldom, if ever, can we "carry out" a soup that compares with one created at home.

Finally, two additional pleasures of preparing a batch of soup are its inherent frugality and the healthful nature of its components. Both your body and your checking account will feel restored.

Introduction

Of all the waiter-there's-something-in-my-soup jokes, my favorite is an old French chestnut: *Patron, patron, il y a une semelle dans la soupe. Ce n'est pas que ce soit sale, mais ce tient de la place!* Roughly translated, it reads: "Waiter, waiter, there's a shoe sole in my soup. It's not that it is dirty, but it takes up so much room!"

This may or may not tell us much about French humor, but it does reveal how the French feel about their soups. They have created soups on their farms and at their waterfronts. They have assembled soups from their rivers and from their mountainsides. They have composed ceremonial soups to honor their leaders and humble soups to salute their shepherds. It is my strong belief that more soups are found in France—in sheer number and variety—than in any other cuisine, including that of the American "melting pot." French soups span an astonishing range of styles, ingredients, interests, and attitudes. They sprawl horizontally across a variegated geography from seacoast to orchard to alpine meadow. They soar from the simplest farm-kitchen potage, like *potée bourguignonnne,* to the eminence of the presidential palace, like Paul Bocuse's *soupe aux truffes Élysée.*

As a soup devotee, I like to think that the soups of France stand as delicious metaphors for their entire cuisine, and I have conducted tasting searches to confirm this notion. Brillat-Savarin, *un fin gourmet,* wrote in the eighteenth century: "It is generally admitted that soup is never made so well as in France, and I have observed in my travels the truth of this statement confirmed . . . as soup is the basis of our French national diet." Following his lead, I have traveled throughout France to sample soups, from a rich, if conventional, gratinéed bowl of "French" onion to an unprecedented grass-green nettle soup.

In an attempt to make the study of the French language more interesting, teachers often point out to their students that France has a unique outline: it is *une hexagone.* The six-sided contour of the nation helps illustrate its general diversity. It is bounded by four ever-changing bodies of water: the Mediterranean, the Atlantic, the English Channel, and the North Sea. Three of these "sides" of France adjoin water: the North Sea and English Channel to the northwest, the Atlantic Ocean to the west, and the Mediterranean to the south. Consequently, at least half of France is coastal and a huge fishing industry has become an asset to the economy and to the gastronomy. Is it any wonder that seafood soups have a special prominence in the cooking of France? From the coastal waters of Brittany comes *cotriade,* a mélange of fresh fish, potatoes, and often a little vinegar. The fishermen's stew bouillabaisse is Mediterranean in origin and reflects the sun not only in the regional seafood it contains, but also in its tomatoes, garlic, and fennel. Perhaps not as well known (nor as controversial) is *bourride,* a soup of poached white fish enriched with the vigorous aioli, a garlicky mayonnaise.

The three remaining sides of hexagonal France border on countries with widely differing cultures and cuisines. Belgium and Luxembourg lie to the north, Germany and Switzerland to the east, and Italy and Spain to the southeast and southwest, respectively. It is at these borders that the boundaries are fixed politically but are blended culinarily. When close neighbors exist, there are always dishes that share flavors and concepts. The north *hochepot,* a thick soup with a wide variety of ingredients (yes, hodgepodge), is shared with Flanders. Robust dumplings are found in the soups enjoyed by the Alsatians and the adjacent Germans alike. The sunny *soupe au pistou* reflects the flavors of fresh basil, garlic, pasta, and beans of both Provence and Italy. Throughout all of France, in all her provinces, soups are a way of life.

In *Adam Bede,* author George Eliot has one of her rustics from England's Warwickshire countryside speak with the typical enmity of the British toward the French in Napoléon's time: "it's a big Frenchman as reaches five foot high, an' they live upon spoon-meat mostly." That rural gentleman may have been mistaken about the height of a Frenchman but not about the French preference for "spoon-meat," or soups.

Soups and Influences

Spirited Kettles: wine-warmed soups

A continuing debate surrounds the question of whether drinking wine with soup enhances the soup or, for that matter, the wine. Some think it odd to drink a liquid and eat a liquid at the same time. Many French soups are blessed by adding a good wine to the soup pot, however, which is no surprise in a nation that produces and so enthusiastically consumes its glorious wines, from *premier cru* to *vin ordinaire*. When wine is one of the ingredients of a soup, it adds a dimension that no other flavor can achieve. Soups in the following pages in which wine plays that role have been indicated with the "Spirited Kettles" icon.

The French have even created a lighthearted ceremony of pouring some of the wine they are drinking into the bottom of the bowl of soup they are finishing. They give the wine and soup a good swirl, and then they drink up the bracing broth. This lusty tradition, often called *faire chabrol*, is as practical as it is symbolic: wine and soup are good mates. As soups have become more elegant, the French (never ones to give up a tasty tradition) have modified this convention. At formal occasions, the wine that accompanies a soup (usually a clear consommé) is now commonly a sherry or, occasionally, a Madeira. In the spirit of the old country custom, a little sherry is added to warm the soup.

Some soups that I have included use wine or cider not as an enhancement, but as an essential ingredient—an element integral to the soup itself. If you can't get the specific wine or its close likeness, then you ought to postpone preparing the recipe.

Confluence of Flavors: soups of the borders

When I took a close look at the collection of soups I wished to include in this volume, it became obvious that many of them had culinary bonds with the countries that encircle France. Those neighborly contributions are important in the history of French cooking and should be noted. For all of the soups that are connected to the cuisine of a bordering nation, I have earmarked the recipe with the "Confluence of Flavors" icon, indicating the soup's twofold character, and have included which country shares the soup with France.

It takes a lot of tilting of swords and subsequent conference tables to determine the borders of a given nation. France is no exception. It is a desirable piece of land and has had to fight both offensive and defensive battles to establish what we know now as *la belle France*. Other than sheer political power, why would a body of non-French people wish to possess parts or all of this diverse country? The answer lies with its "best of all worlds" natural features. Within France are fertile lands, good climate, and endless waterways. Some have regarded it as an isthmus between the Mediterranean and the North Sea. Political instability and territorial conflict have been problems as long as the French can remember. With the exception of Belgium and Luxembourg, most of its frontiers are natural barriers (oceans, mountains, and the Rhine River) and have been in place since the sixteenth century. The current international borders were only settled in the mid-twentieth century, with Alsace-Lorraine in flux due to the wars with Germany.

The geography of France is conducive to creating wonderful things to eat. The long coastlines and their diverse waters provide enough seafood for an entire nation and then some. From the mountain masses that ripple across the country issue the waters that become the great navigable rivers, rivers that have traditionally carried seafood, produce, and new ideas into the heart of France. (These waterways, of course, greatly preceded the *train grande vitesse* and the *autoroute*.) There has been enough rich, fertile, and appropriate soil to support all the Norman orchards and cheese-producing dairy cattle, to sustain acres of vineyards, to cultivate productive vegetable and grain crops, and to raise healthy livestock.

The different regions bring great variations of climate, from the chillier and damper conditions of the northwest and Belgium borders to the hot and sunny Mediterranean frontiers with Italy. The cold winters of the eastern French Alps at the Swiss border contrast with the bright warmth of the southern Catalan region skirting Spain. No wonder there is a dramatic range of differences among the separate provinces. Perhaps it is more dramatic that there exists a strong, stable nation. In fact, it is one of the questions continually debated by political theorists. While it is true that some Basques and Corsicans and a few Bretons entertain separatists' movements, on the whole the inhabitants of France are arrogantly, obstinately, and unblushingly proud to be French. Humility is not a Gallic trait. Remember chauvinism originated in France.

HUMOR AND EPITHETS: NAMING OF FRENCH SOUPS AS FOLKLORE

HUMOR
AND
EPITHETS

I have always been intrigued with the manner in which the French language is used to express matters of the kitchen. I once arranged a meal for the guests of our restaurant in which each course comprised a dish whose name was, quite loosely, a French metaphor.

The main dish was called "the lamb that weeps" (*gigot qui pleure*), garlic-studded leg of lamb roasted on a rack placed over a bed of potatoes to catch the succulent drippings. We completed the meal with "eggs in the snow" (*oeufs à la neige*), poached meringues with English pouring custard. We accompanied and contrasted the soft, rich dessert with some fun: "cat's tongues" (*langues de chat*), thin, long butter cookies, and "pig's ears" (*oreilles de cochon*), deep-fried small pastry ovals. I realize that in the United States we also use a few names, like hush puppy and hot dog, that have an interesting linguistic history, and others such as green goddess salad dressing that are flights of fancy. But nothing here compares with the expressiveness with which the French use their language and cultural wit to name dishes.

Countless soups carry names that reflect the French amusement and mischief in calling up people, places, and things. A Lenten soup with vegetables but no meat is "meager soup" (*soupe maigre*), even though it is as nourishing and plentiful as possible. A substantive soup with a full measure of meat is the descriptive (and elusive) "wooden leg soup" (*soupe de jambe de bois*). To make it, the bone-in leg of beef is simmered in a huge kettle with vegetables until the meat is so completely and tenderly cooked that it falls off the bone. The bone is then placed across the top of the soup kettle as the long-awaited signal that "soup's on!" The famed Paul Bocuse even has a full account of this creation in one of his cookbooks, possibly because Bocuse and *jambe de bois* share the down-to-earth roots of Lyonnaise cuisine.

The French language is saturated with culinary terms: the art of eating (or talking about eating, or cooking, or shopping for cooking) is, for the French, a national diversion, perhaps an obsession. (Many writers quip that the French *talk* about *talking about* eating.) Our own

English language is enriched with the more elegant French terms, reportedly a consequence of the Norman conquest of England in 1066. The very word *restaurant* is French along with many restaurant-related words such as table d'hôte, à la carte, and maître d'hôtel. The witty Craig Claiborne once commented that the lovely French *pâte brisée* sounded much lighter and more delicate—as it should—than its counterpart in English, the leaden "pie dough." For the purposes of this book, it is fortunate that the French titles of potage, bouillon, consommé, and purée are the same in both languages. We are familiar with the link between our "supper" and French *soupe,* and few grown-ups in America do not understand at a glance *soupe du jour.*

In the days when a fire (*feu*) was at the center of family life—it represented both warmth and nourishment—all members of the family gathered in front of it. Over time and usage, this place became known as the *foyer.* The meaning of the word has changed slightly, but it is still the primary gathering place in a home or in a public building.

At that point in history, all cooking was done at the fire as well. The act of cooking and the place where the cooking is done are the same word in French, *la cuisine.*

It seems perfectly natural for the French, given their love of good food, to apply the language of the table to other arenas of living. For example, we Americans say, "Too many cooks spoil the broth," and the French say pretty much the same thing. In the same way, we say, "Good things come in small packages," and the French say, "The best soup is made in little pots." Thinking about another of their favorite pastimes, the French also offer, "It is in the old pots that one makes the best soup" (*C'est dans les vieux pots qu'on fait les meilleures soupes*), meaning that it is with women of experience that one can best settle down.

When there is no food in my house, "The cupboard is bare." In France, *La marmite est renversée* (The pot is upside down). I may "beat around the bush" in delaying a direct statement, but since the sixteenth century the French have used a form of *tourner autour du pot* (turn around the pot) to do the same thing. From the nineteenth century comes the French expression *être pot-au-feu* (to be a pot-on-the-fire), which is what we might call a homebody. The woman's domestic role in the French kitchen of our grandmother's day is made clear with the term *tâte-au-pot* (taste the pot), meaning a man who interfered with household affairs.

I have noted those soups that display a link between the soup and the metaphor the French have used to describe the dish with the "Humor and Epithets" icon.

SOUPE ANCIENNE   I would be remiss if I did not include a glimpse of the very oldest of the soups of France. While trying not to romanticize the past, I still think it is valuable to view the earliest soups prepared by an essentially rural and often impoverished people. As rustic traditions have nearly disappeared in France, these venerable soups may exist only in print—perhaps here in this book. Although obsolete, the *ancienne soupes* do carry stories of the past that bear telling today.

Champagne-le Nord

Normandie

Alsace Lorraine

Ile-de-France

Bretagne

Loire

Franche-Comté

Bourgogne

Atlantique-Bordeaux

Rhône-Alpes

Dordogne

Auvergne

Sud-ouest

Provence

Languedoc

le pays Basque

Corse

REGIONS AND INFLUENCES

 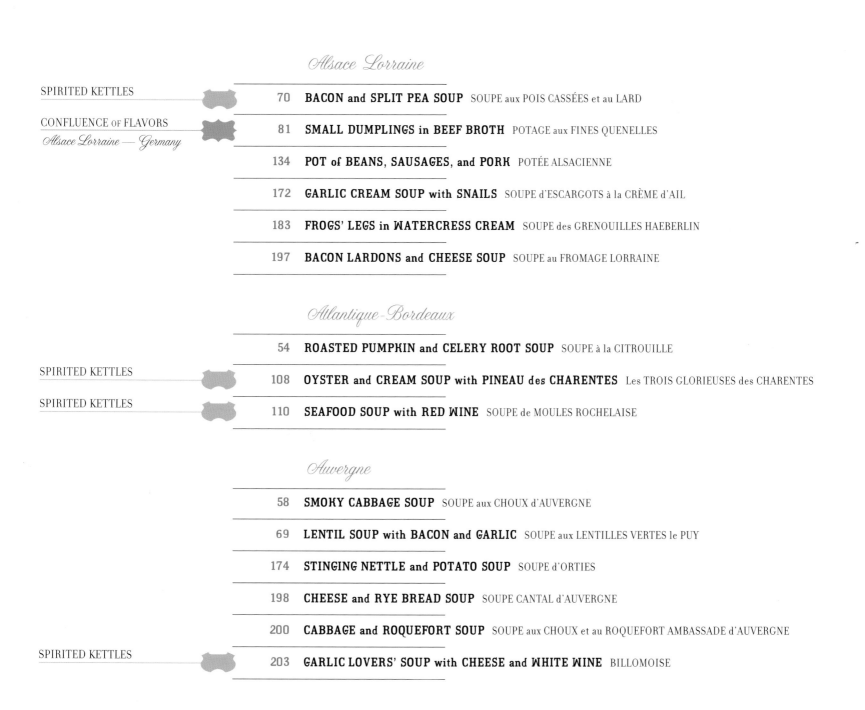

SPIRITED KETTLES

HUMOR AND EPITHETS

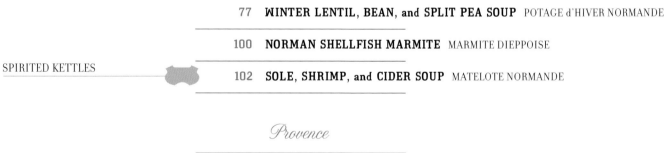

The Regions of France:
"The time and space of yesterday"

The recipes in this cookbook are organized into logical, user-friendly food groups. But the soups also need to be viewed within the context of the actual landscapes that have given them birth. It is the geography and climate of France that have driven its cooking, that have determined the lives of its people.

While larger mountain ranges (Pyrenees, Alps) have defined frontiers between France and neighboring countries, smaller ranges (Jura, Vosges, Massif Central) have shaped large regions within France itself. The network of rivers pouring out of the mountains has framed the smaller provincial domains. (These rivers have also served French farmers well, leaving most of the land well watered.) The climate is particularly varied: colder from Eastern Europe, more temperate from Atlantic oceanic air, and hot and dry from the Mediterranean—all of this in a nation smaller than Texas. Thus, mountains, rivers, and weather contrasts have bequeathed to France a patchwork of regions and localities, and each has developed its own personality and identity. In his book *Fragile Glory*, a look at contemporary France, journalist Richard Bernstein calls this characteristic of the French "the persistence of the parts."

Another unusual tendency pervades France, the playing out of Proust's "remembrance of times past." In rural areas—and there still are a great many—old customs and habits continue to endure, retaining what historian Fernand Braudel calls "the time and space of yesterday." France is a still a nation of small villages (even Paris is organized into "villages"), and staying close to home seems to be a French phenomenon. Even today, there still are some *paysans* who have not traveled beyond their hamlets.

In the following pages I offer a glimpse of seventeen French regions, a brief look that demonstrates that diversity is the key to French regional cuisine.

TO BEGIN

No finer words exist to begin this book than those of French writer and gastronome Robert Courtine. Introducing one of his cookbooks on regional French cooking, he wrote:

> *This is not a book of recipes but a lengthy and unconventional walk through the recipes. The recipes of a true cuisine, that is to say, bound intimately to geography, to history, in a word, to the soil.*

A TYPICAL TREE-LINED ROAD BEGINS THIS
JOURNEY THROUGH THE REGIONS OF FRANCE.

Alsace Lorraine

ALSATIANS CHOOSE WHIMSICAL WROUGHT-IRON SIGNS FOR THEIR BUSINESSES, SUCH AS THIS RESTAURANT IN PICTURESQUE KAYSERBERG.

Is there anything more agreeable in this lower world than to sit down with three or four old friends before a well-set table, in an antique, ancestral dining room, and there, to seriously tuck your napkin under your chin.

—Émile Erckmann and Alexandre Chatrian, ALSATIAN WRITING TEAM

Alsace Lorraine lies in the northeastern corner of France, next to Germany, with the French Ardennes to the west. Because of their mid-European location, both Alsace and Lorraine have had to endure repeated invasions, warfare, and changing nationalities.

Here the German influence is marked, as shown in place names (Turckheim, Kayserberg), wine grapes (Riesling), architecture (half timbered), and, most of all, the cooking of the region. Wine writer Hugh Johnson refers to the food as having "the amplitude of the Germans, the finesse of the French." Many major dishes are known by both French and German names. The French *saucisson de Strasbourg* (a fat sausage) is also seen as the German *Knackwurst*. The French *quiche Lorraine* is derived from the German *Kuchen* (cake). A meat-and-potato "baker's oven" casserole (*Baeckoffe*) and a sweet raisin bread (*Kugelhopf*) are frankly German dishes, but both are quite at home in Alsace. Like the Germans, Alsatians are fond of foods and beverages that have been fermented: beer, wine, cabbage, turnips, and sourdough bread.

I once spent an autumn weekend in Mulhouse near the Swiss border. After a long walk through the operetta-looking city, I told my hotel concierge, Mme Wir, how beautiful I found her town. Without missing a beat, she twinkled, *"Tout Alsace c'est beau!"* (All Alsace is beautiful!)

Atlantique-Bordeaux

PRÉ-SALÉ LAMBS GRAZING ON SALT-INFUSED GRASSES NEAR THE SHORE, WITH THE ATLANTIC IN THE DISTANCE.

The cooking of the ancient province of Poitou has a tranquility of the hearth that assures the gourmand reputation of a region.

—Curnonsky, ON THE NATURE OF POITEVIN CUISINE

The Atlantic Ocean runs along the western edge of France from Brittany in the north to Spain in the south. In between lies the Atlantic-Bordeaux region.

North of the city of Bordeaux, the fertile region of Charentes produces some of the finest butter in France, over fifty goat cheeses, first-rate fowl including Challans-raised ducks, and vegetables of distinction. The fish and shellfish are both abundant and of supreme quality. Oysters are farmed on the Ile-de-Ré near the port of La Rochelle, and mussels are raised on posts planted in the sand offshore at L'Aiguillon. Cognac, the brandy *sans pareil*, is distilled in a town of the same name on the Charentes River.

Bordeaux and its milieu is a distinguished and essential part of France, a kingdom where wine reigns. Here, wine lovers are very serious about their food. They demand the finest dishes to enjoy their premium wines fully. Beef from near Bazas, *pré-salé* lamb of Pauillac (with succulent meat resulting from a diet of coastal grazing), plentiful wild game, and wild mushrooms help meet that need. A lot of the cooking is *de luxe*, using truffles from neighboring Périgord and foie gras from nearby Gascony. Local cooks prefer shallots, which give the Bordelaise cuisine its accent, as garlic does in Provence.

Bordeaux is a particularly handsome, although somewhat somber, urban environment, a city of connoisseurs. Victor Hugo, discussing the beauty of its eighteenth-century architecture, observed, "Take Versailles, add Anvers, and you will have Bordeaux."

Auvergne

IN THIS TYPICAL AUVERGNE VILLAGE, STONE
BUILDINGS WITH HOLLOW-TILE ROOFS ARE
CLOSELY CLUSTERED. BUILDERS THROUGHOUT
FRANCE USE LOCAL MATERIALS TO CONSTRUCT
ROOFS—TERRA-COTTA TILE, SLATE, THATCH—
SO THAT ALL THE BUILDINGS BLEND IN WITH
THEIR SURROUNDINGS.

*Grandma's apron was filled up lettuce, cheese, onions, dried cod, salt
pork, Le Puy lentils, and six eggs wrapped up in newspapers.*

—Robert Sabatier, LES NOISETTES SAUVAGES,
ON GOING TO MARKET IN THE AUVERGNE WITH *GRAND-MÈRE*

Located in south-central France—Dordogne on its west and Burgundy to the east—the
Auvergne is a region isolated from much of the rest of France. High peaks from four-
thousand-year-old extinct volcanoes and deep valleys also seclude small communities from
one another. Except for the city of Clermont-Ferrand (setting for Marcel Ophuls's epic film,
The Sorrow and the Pity, that examines the France of World War II), this is a region of relatively
unknown towns and villages.

The cooking of the Auvergne is rural, untouristy, and rustic, or as one French writer
suggested, "*nourriture solide*." The cheeses are noteworthy—Cantal, Laguiole, Saint-Nectaire,
bleu d'Auvergne, bleu d'Ambert—and well worth seeking out. When the full-flavored Cantal is
whisked into garlicky potatoes to create *aligot*, it is a dream come true for garlic lovers and
mashed potato lovers. The reputation of green lentils grown near the town of Le Puy-de-Velay
is not exaggerated. The cooked lentils are flavorful, hold their shape, and retain their firm texture. Serious pursuers of the regional table should try the benchmark of Auvergnate cooking,
the *potée d'Auvergne* (known by locals as *glorieuse potée*) with aged hams, dried sausages, cabbage, and pot vegetables. A distinctive *digestif* is the fragrant lemon verbena-flavored liqueur
Verveine-de-Velay, also from Le Puy.

le pays Basque

A BASQUE FARMER NEAR THE VILLAGE OF
AÏNHOA IN THE FOOTHILLS OF THE PYRENEES.

The Basques are elves who dance on the mountains.

—Voltaire

The Basques are a people *isolé*. They have tucked themselves into a corner of southwestern
France as far away from the rest of the country as possible. The Atlantic Ocean lies to the west,
the Pyrenees and Spain (and Spanish Basque provinces) to the south. The mystery surrounding the origins of the Basques and their enigmatic language remains unsolved. The tongue the
Basques speak (living on either side of the French-Spanish border) is linguistically unrelated
to any known language in the world. Sad to say, but I've only seen tourists wearing rope-soled
espadrilles, although many Basques do wear berets.

The local people are striking, and their colorful, spicy cooking comes with echoes of
Spain, a blend of local ingredients from the sea and land, and many puzzling (often unpro-
nounceable) names. The region is small, but the cuisine is enjoyed throughout France. Once
in the Alps I found *poulet basquaise*, a Basque chicken dish, on a menu. Many Basque dishes
begin with a *pipérade*, a sautéed alliance of onions, sweet and hot peppers, and garlic, which is
often stirred into scrambled eggs and served with the local ham, *jambon de Bayonne*. The skin
of the well-known air-cured ham is aglow from the dried, ground *piment d'Espelette* rubbed
into its surface. The peppers, grown around the village of Espelette and available fresh and
dried, add verve to almost all Basque dishes.

Bourgogne

The charm, the delight of the land, made of hills and valleys so narrow they are ravines—the woods, the woods deep and overgrown, that roil and undulate . . . as far as one can see.

—Colette, ON HER NATIVE BURGUNDY

THE RED WINE MERCUREY, A BURGUNDY FROM
THE CÔTE CHALONNAISE, AGES IN WINE CASKS
IN A CAVE AT THE VINEYARDS.

Burgundy lies almost in the very center of France, physically and perhaps metaphorically as well. It is a region of superlatives and uncommon beauty. Because of its benign climate, most of the year the landscape is green and lush, whether pasturage for the white Charolais cattle, hilly forests, or acres of vineyards. The wines, primarily from the red Pinot Noir or white Chardonnay grapes, are believed by many to be unequaled. Fine wines are also made from the Aligoté grapes and from the Gamay cousins, which produce the Beaujolais wines.

The Burgundian cuisine is beautifully matched to its wines. The well-fed cattle produce quality beef and memorable cheeses. The region's colorful chickens, *poulets de Bresse*, are arguably the finest in France. Freshwater fish, wild game, and wild mushrooms are close at hand from the many ponds, lakes, rivers, and dense forests. With such considerable raw materials near the kitchen door, it is not surprising that many internationally acclaimed restaurants are concentrated in and around the city of Lyons, Burgundy's culinary paradise. It is here, wrote Curnonsky, the famed writer on food and wine, that "the rites of the good life have been elevated to the eminent dignity of a veritable religion."

Bretagne

Of lilies and sweet roses make a prize
For sisters Melanie and Marie
Who show us all by what they do
That the best cooking still lies
In making flavors taste fresh and true.

—Curnonsky, FROM A POETIC TRIBUTE TO TWO *RESTAURATRICES* OF RIEC-SUR-BELON

TRAPS TO SNARE PREMIUM BRETON LOBSTERS
ON THE DOCK AT THE FERRY AND FISHING PORT
OF ROSCOFF IN NORTHERN BRITTANY.

Brittany seems more an island than a peninsula. Thrust into the Atlantic and surrounded on three sides by the ocean, it is physically apart from the rest of France. It is also separated by the differences between the Celtic and Gallic cultures. Ancient pagan beliefs and early myths are apparent in the huge monoliths and vast alignments of stones that hold secrets we have yet to unravel. Brittany remains a region of religious fervor.

A Michelin guide observes that Breton cooking is distinguished more by "the quality of the materials used than by fine preparation." What is cooked in Brittany is what is harvested nearby—from the Atlantic waters or the inland farms. Freshness is the key. Seafood is eaten the same day it is caught, and vegetables (in the main, artichokes, onions, and cauliflower) are recently picked. Breton shellfish is unequaled. The lobsters, trapped in cold Atlantic waters, are considered the finest in France. The oysters are shipped off to Paris for distribution throughout that city, and onward to the rest of France and Europe.

The poor soil of Brittany has long plagued the region's people with economic hardships. Early attempts to grow wheat failed, and often-impoverished Bretons were too poor to afford bread. They could, however, raise buckwheat, which, while unsuccessful in bread baking, could be fashioned into crepes and *galettes* that were eaten as bread at meals.

THE GENTLY ROLLING LAND OF NORTHERN
FRANCE PROVIDES AGRICULTURAL AND VITI-
CULTURAL PLENTY.

I have seen at Sainte-Ménehould a beautiful thing. It is the kitchen of the hotel at Metz. It is a real kitchen. An immense room. One of the walls is filled with copper, the other with faiences. In the middle, facing the windows, the chimney, an enormous cavern in which a splendid fire fills. On the ceiling, a black web of magnificent, smoky beams from which hang all sorts of joyous things: baskets, lamps, a meat keeper, a large net or grating where a vast trapeze of bacon is stretched out. This kitchen is a world where the chimney is the sun.

—Victor Hugo, *VOYAGE AU RHIN*

This wide region sweeps from the North Sea to the Vosges Mountains of Lorraine, from Belgium south almost to Paris. Forests are found in the Ardennes area, but most of the region is flat or gently undulating. For centuries, because of its location and terrain, the north has been the crossroads for armies that have marched through or have stayed and fought. There are many battlefields, many graves.

Much of the land is fertile with large acreage used for growing sugar beets, Belgian endive, hops (there are many local breweries), and potatoes and other root vegetables. The naturally chalky soil nourishes the superb grapes used for the making of Champagne. This is the northernmost latitude in which any grapes are successfully grown.

The weather is always a little cool and misty, and the food reflects the need for warmth. It is simple, filling, and not particularly elegant. I can think of no greater culinary disparity in one region of France than the delicacy of a fine Champagne contrasted with the earthy *hochepot*, a dish with pig's ears and tails and everything in between.

Corse

PIGS ROAM FREELY ON THE ISLAND OF CORSICA.
RAISED AT LIBERTY TO GRAZE, THEY PROVIDE
THE MAKINGS FOR THE DEEPLY FLAVORED
LOCAL CHARCUTERIE.

The fire was quickly lit. Large slices of cut bread on little red earthenware plates, and there I was, around the kettle, plate stretched out, nostrils open. . . . Was it the countryside, the light, this horizon of sky and water? But I never have eaten better than this bouillabaisse of langoustines.

—Alphonse Daudet, *CONTES DU LUNDIS*

The original name of this astonishingly beautiful island is Korai, which comes from the Phoenician and means "covered with forests." The jagged coastline of the Mediterranean is not far from anywhere on Corsica; nor is the high, central mountain range that caused Montaigne to describe the island as "a mountain in the sea." Much of it seems untouched. One would hesitate to say that Corsica is backward, but in the sense that it has yet to be completely taken over by tourists, perhaps it is.

Corsica's native son, Napoléon Bonaparte, was a Frenchman solely due to a treaty, two years before his birth that forced Italy to cede Corsica to France after controlling the island for almost five centuries. Southern Corsica is only eight miles from the Italian island of Sardinia, and its architecture is Italianate, its dialects sound like Italian, and its place names are Italian.

Clearly, the origins of Corsican food are Italian and Mediterranean. The raw materials of good cooking are abundant: fruits and vegetables grown in a warm climate, prime seafood (particularly shellfish), pork from free-ranging pigs, chestnut forests, and wild game from the *maquis,* mountainous stretches of untamed shrubs and small trees. In addition to pasta, Corsican cooks like to use dried beans (white and red), fava beans, and chickpeas in their kitchens. They lavishly employ fresh herbs, which grow wild throughout the island, in all their cooking. Mint, which is not often found in Provençal and Italian cooking, is prevalent. Cheeses, especially *brocciu,* from both goat and sheep, are eaten fresh (and used in pastries) and preserved (salted, wrapped in leaves, and dried).

Dordogne

A GOOSE, THE ESTEEMED SOURCE OF BOTH FOIE GRAS AND *CONFIT D'OIE*, IN A BARNYARD OF THE DORDOGNE.

The ingredients of the good cooking are neither exotic nor rare here. Each farm possesses them. Foie gras? It is sufficient to gorge a goose. Truffles? It is a miracle of nature. Confit or the ballotine*? Doesn't the most modest farmer have a barnyard? Ham? All paysans raise a pig. In the Périgord, the meals of the country are often the* chef-d'oeuvre *of good taste.*

—André Maurois, *LA BELLE FRANCE,* ON PÉRIGORD CUISINE

The Dordogne, Bordeaux's next-door neighbor, is the modern region that was once the old provinces of Périgord and Quercy. Named for the river of the same name, this region has some of the country's most beautiful rivers, waterways that meander through deep gorges with hundreds of ancient castles overlooking the landscape.

A limited number of dishes have given the region its reputation as a gourmet center. Known as the major source for truffles and foie gras (the enlarged livers of fattened geese and ducks), the Dordogne produces these delicacies in a region-wide artisanal industry. This is not what the locals usually eat. Rather, this production is a way to earn a living. What the residents do eat, however, is equally delicious and is headed by succulent confits, goose or duck cooked and preserved in its own fat. In a nation of fine cooks, even those of the Dordogne stand out.

As is typically the case, the wines of the Dordogne are well suited to the local food. The "black" (actually a dark inky red) wine of Cahors nicely counters the richness of many dishes. The full-bodied Buzet is equally valued. Montbazillac, a Sauternes-like sweet wine from a town of the same name, is outstanding when served slightly chilled with the Dordogne's culinary jewel, foie gras.

Franche-Comté

COMTÉ CHEESE IN AN AGING CELLAR IN WHICH THE HUMIDITY IS CAREFULLY MONITORED.

Not one (region) offers for the table, provisions more varied.
—Lucien Tendret, *LA TABLE AU PAYS DE BRILLAT-SAVARIN*

Unusual wines, exceptional charcuterie, excellent cheeses, plentiful wild mushrooms, fresh mountain air—all of this is found in the least known of all French regions, Franche-Comté.

Geographically, the region, tucked between Burgundy and Switzerland, has two major landscapes. In the south, the Jura Mountains swing down from Alsace providing rushing streams that were at one time abundant with crayfish and frogs. This established a tradition for cooking those wild treasures. The forests are thought to be the most beautiful in all of France and yield many varieties of wild mushrooms, game, and nuts.

An immense wide plain across the north has been used for pasturage and vineyards. Franche-Comté, meaning "Free Country," is acclaimed for its distinguished cheeses produced by *fruitiers*, a French term derived from the notion that cheese is a "fruit" of the mountains, having come from cows who grazed on grasses there. The most celebrated are known as Comté (shortened from Gruyère de Comté), rich, aged at least four months; Morbier, with a thin layer of ash in its center; and Mont-d'Or (or Vacherin).

The regional wines are generally not exported, as they do not "travel well." They almost certainly taste better at home. The exception is the unusual Château-Chalon, a *vin jaune* (golden wine) unique in the wine world (page 187).

Ile-de-France

PARIS AND THE SEINE, THE RIVER THAT GAVE IT BIRTH, AT DUSK IN NOVEMBER, THE EIFFEL TOWER IN THE DISTANCE.

Morpheus has certainly never scattered his poppy seeds in La Halle. No silence, no rest, no let-up there. . . . The constant hubbub contrasts sharply with the sleep that envelops the rest of the city; at four o'clock in the morning, only thieves and poets are awake.
—Louis-Sébastien Mercier, *TABLEAU DE PARIS*, ON THE MARKET AT LES HALLES

Two distinct environments exist in the Ile-de-France: Paris itself, a sprawling urban core, and the countryside in which Paris is enclosed. Perfectly named, Paris and the Ile-de-France are indeed an *island* in the middle of the French republic. Point Zero, a marker imbedded in the sidewalk in front of the Notre Dame Cathedral, is the point from which all road distances in France are measured.

Paris itself is organized into twenty official neighborhoods (*arrondissements*), and these function as small villages might. Each has its own town hall and mayor, and its own outdoor *marché*, open daily or a few times a week. These satisfy French cooks who have traditionally shopped often—sometimes daily—for their produce, fish, meats, and cheeses. Les Halles, the venerable market in central Paris, home to the famed *soupe à l'oignon gratinée*, closed in 1969 and was relocated nine miles south of Paris at Rungis.

Beyond the Parisian outskirts, the Ile-de-France becomes more rural, with streams, wooded valleys. Wheat is an important crop in the area, and photographs of the cathedral at Chartres often show wheat fields in the foreground. Southeast of Paris, the famed Brie cheeses are made, each named for its particular locality.

In 1846, E. Briffault wrote in *Paris à table*: "When Paris sits down *à table*, the entire world stirs . . ."

Languedoc

NEARLY ONE-THIRD OF THE VINEYARDS OF FRANCE ARE FOUND IN LANGUEDOC, ON THE HILLS AND PLAINS OFF ITS MEDITERRANEAN COAST.

The vine, wine are grand mysteries. Alone in the plant kingdom, the vine intelligently delivers that which is the true flavor of the earth. What exactness in the translation! She feels, expressed by the grapes the secrets of the sun. . . .What journey without clouds, what late sweet rain decides that one year the wine will be greater than another? Human caring can be nearly nothing; there—all is celestial sorcery, the passage of the planets, the work of the sun.

—Colette, *PRISONS ET PARADIS*

The Languedoc is a huge domain stretched all across southern France, bordered by the Pyrenees to the south and the Mediterranean to the east. For centuries the home of ancient civilizations, the Languedoc has been invaded by Romans, Greeks, Iberians, and North Africans, all contributing culinary influences. The visual signs of these civilizations—Roman stone ruins, medieval walled towns, Spanish brick fortresses—give the region a cultural texture that is extraordinary.

Essentially two sections make up the Languedoc. The western part is land based, agricultural, and its heart is the handsome, very old city of Toulouse. Southeastern Languedoc near Spain, known as Roussillon, looks to the sea. So, too, do the immense vineyards that sweep right down to the Mediterranean. Local cooking, while using ingredients similar to Provence, has its own style, which is more Spanish or Catalan: highly flavored with olives, peppers, and anchovies.

Loire

BARREL STAVES, EVIDENCE OF THE COOPERS' ART (ESSENTIAL IN THE WINE-RICH LOIRE VALLEY), HANG AT THE ENTRANCE OF A CAVE DWELLING IN THE TUFA CLIFFS NEAR SAUMUR.

The pike of the Cher, the guinea hen, the white goat cheese rolled in a grape leaf, and what fruits, the pear and the peach . . .

—Maurice Genevoix, *TRENTE MILLES JOURS*, ON THE CUISINE OF ORLÉANS

The region of the Loire is a horizontal band of land in central France that follows the Loire River, the country's longest, as it makes its serpentine way west to empty into the Atlantic. Royalty who wanted to be reasonably close to Paris and *very* close to fine hunting grounds built the famed châteaus that are scattered along the river. Nearby, south of Orléans, the Sologne region offers ponds, streams, deep forests, and, to this day, exceptional game. In the valleys that border the Loire are unusual soft limestone caves, that have housed people, wines cellars, and now underground mushroom beds.

The rich and fertile Loire Valley is one extended garden, particularly around Tours. The French observe that the Touraine is the *jardin de la France* and add *à la tourangelle* to many fine vegetable dishes. The asparagus, in particular, is excellent. The gardens at the château of Villandry have been returned to their original sixteenth-century state with a *potager* (kitchen garden) bearing all the fruits and vegetables known at that time.

The major wines of the Loire are usually dry, fresh, clean, and light and are often combined into imaginative and diverse dishes using fish from the river. The Sauvignon Blanc grape produces Sancerre and Pouilly-Fumé; the Chenin Blanc grape makes a dry Vouvray and a sweet Coteaux du Layon. The Loire wines are ideal with salmon from the river, the famed *rillettes* (potted meat), the local goat cheeses, game pâtés, and the many wild mushrooms.

Normandie

BROWN-AND-WHITE "SPECTACLED" CATTLE OF
NORMANDY, WITH THE ENGLISH CHANNEL IN
THE DISTANCE.

*The table had been set up in the cart shed. On it were four sirloin roasts,
six chicken fricassées, a veal casserole, three legs of mutton, and, in the
center, a beautiful roast of suckling pig flanked by four large sausages
made of chitterlings and sorrel. At the corners stood decanters of
brandy. The cider was foaming up around the corks and every glass had
been filled to the brim with wine . . .*

—Gustave Flaubert, *MADAME BOVARY*,
ON THE NORMAN WEDDING BANQUET OF DR. BOVARY AND EMMA

The coastal and inland area in the northwest of France along the English Channel is the fertile, beautiful region of Normandy. Butter, cream, seafood, apples, cider, and Calvados are icons of this food lover's land.

Because grapevines need to struggle in difficult soil to produce the fullest-flavored fruits (hence the finest wines), no wines are made in Normandy. The soil is simply too rich. Apple trees, however, thrive, and cider the preferred beverage, is perfectly matched to the creamy, rich local foods. Calvados, a powerful oak-aged brandy distilled from cider, is treasured at home on Norman soil and away.

Cows thrive in Normandy as well. Uncompromisingly good butter and a wealth of cheeses are at the heart of Norman cuisine. Often, when *à la normande* is added onto the title of a recipe, the dish contains cream. The cheeses are *crème de la crème*.

The region's long coastline furnishes every imaginable kind of seafood. The docks of Dieppe, Fécamp, Honfleur, and Port-en-Basin glisten with displays of netted or line-caught fresh fish and shellfish. In local kitchens, cooks prepare dishes that marry their superior seafood with other products of the region: butter, cream, cider, and Calvados. Indeed, most of the good things to eat in Normandy come from the apple tree, the cow, or the nearby sea.

Provence

AN ASSORTMENT OF OLIVES AT THE MARKET IN
CARPENTRAS, AN ANCIENT TOWN IN A FERTILE
GARDEN AREA ABOUT FIFTEEN MILES NORTH-
WEST OF AVIGNON AND THE RHÔNE RIVER.

*The sausages of Arles, the tins of tuna and anchovies, the black olives
or the green picholine with green peppers, the almonds, the figs . . . all
these small, southern delicacies. . . .*

—Alphonse Daudet, *PREMIER VOYAGE, PREMIER MENSONGE*

South of the Alps, and hugging the Mediterranean from the Rhône River east to Italy, is the one region of France that everyone loves. It promises much: gentle mountains, aquamarine sea, fields of lavender, earthy-hued houses, ancient olive trees, Roman antiques, and the clearest sky in the country. And then there's the food.

The local vegetable dishes seem to be the most flavorful in all of France. Is it the olive oil? Is it their seasonal freshness? The renowned ratatouille is the harvest of a Provençal garden—eggplant, tomatoes, herbs, zucchini, garlic, and olive oil—simmered together. Bouillabaisse is the seafood counterpart, the supreme Provençal seafood dish known as *bouillon de soleil* (bouillon of the sun). Miraculous olive trees, clinging often to barren soil, figure in almost every dish. Garlic, "the truffle of Provence," is essential to all Provençal dishes: raw or cooked, pounded or pressed, whole (*en chemise*) or chopped, in salads and soups, meat stuffings, roasts, and gratins. It is fittingly known as *bulbe roi*.

Rhône-Alpes

[We] have not forgotten that good cooking is a proof of high civilization. . . . I have shown that the Vivarais, gripped between the Rhône and the mountains, has kept the art of good eating.

—Charles Forot, *ODEURS DE FORÊT ET FUMETS DE TABLE*

With Provence to the south, and the Rhône River on its west, the Rhône-Alpes region sweeps northward to Lake Geneva. It is separated from its close neighbors, Italy and Switzerland, by the Alps, giving the area some of the highest mountain peaks in Europe and deep, fertile valleys. There's a lot of room for cows to graze, and most of their rich milk is made into fine cheeses.

The cheeses—Abondance, Beaufort, Reblochon—for example, represent some of the best that France produces. Abondances, somewhat rare despite its name, is made from cows bearing the same name. Beaufort, known as the prince of the Gruyères, has a long and complicated fabrication prior to its required aging of one year. Reblochon has been made in the Alps since the Middle Ages. Alpine cream, layered with potatoes, also figures in the local *gratin à la dauphinoise*, which has emigrated from the Dauphiné region and been embraced by cooks worldwide.

The lakes of Annecy, Bourget, and Geneva in the Savoy yield freshwater fish, including *omble chevalier*, one of the finest in flavor and texture. When dozens of very small fish are tumbled in a deep fryer, the resulting *fritures* literally melt in the mouth. Special dishes in the region tend to borrow from neighboring Italy. Fat egg noodles (*fides*) are simmered in oniony broth and served sprinkled with cheese. Polenta, eaten widely in the region, is a tradition obviously shared with northern Italy.

DAIRY CATTLE AT PASTURE IN THE TARENTAISE REGION HIGH IN THE FRENCH ALPS.

Sud-ouest

In fact it was not long before it came to the boar's turn, for the king seemed to take pleasure in urging this on this famous guest. He did not pass any of the dishes to Porthos until he had tasted them himself, and he accordingly took some of the boar's head. Porthos showed that he could keep pace with his sovereign, and instead of eating half, as D'Artagnan had told him, he ate three-fourths of it. "It is impossible," said the king in an undertone, "that a gentleman who eats so good a supper every day and who has such beautiful teeth can be otherwise than the most praiseworthy man in my kingdom."

—Alexandre Dumas, *THE VICOMTE DE BRAGLELONNE*, ON THE APPETITE OF A GASCON

IF YOU CAN'T COME TO GASCONY, GASCONY CAN COME TO YOU.

This area, primarily the old provinces of Gascony and Béarn, is bordered by the Pyrenees to the south, the Atlantic to the west, and the Languedoc to the east. The gastronomic boundary between Gascony and its northern neighbor, the Dordogne, is elusive, as many of the foods and cooking concepts are alike.

Gascony is the country of the fowl: geese, ducks (which today largely supplant geese), turkeys, corn-fed chickens with pale yellow flesh, and farm-bred rabbits. Confit from goose and duck raised for their foie gras, as well as the *magret* (breast) from a duck specifically fattened for its liver, are important to local cooks.

The entire pig, a pillar of Gascon cooking, is used, however. The killing of the pig here, as in rural regions all over France, has traditionally been an event of importance and ceremony. Every French farm where the butchering took place was a repository of recipes for rustic soups made with the water in which the homemade sausages had been cooked. The famed dish from Béarn, *poule-au-pot*, is an entire meal: chicken with a rich stuffing, simmered with vegetables, frequently served with pasta. It is often named after *bon roi* Henri IV, who was born at Pau, capital of the Béarn region.

An elixir called Armagnac, the outstanding local amber brandy, is literally a heart-warming finale to a Gascon meal.

CHAPTER ONE

*The russet varnish of a basket of onions,
the bloody red of a pile of tomatoes, the
fading yellowness of a lot of cucumbers,
the dusky violet of a cluster of eggplant,
here and there, glowing . . .*
—Émile Zola, *LE VENTRE DE PARIS*

SOUPS *from*
THE FRENCH GARDEN: FRESH VEGETABLES

LEFT: AN EXPRESSION OF THE FRENCH
TRADITION OF GARDENING: IN THE FORMAL
GARDENS AT VILLANDRY, A SIXTEENTH-
CENTURY CHÂTEAU IN THE LOIRE VALLEY,
VEGETABLES ARE CULTIVATED ALONGSIDE
FLOWERING PERENNIALS, ROSES, AND SHRUBS.

FRANCE: A GARDEN CULTURE

I'll begin this chapter with a Voltaire *ending*: that of his story of *Candide*. After the calamities that he experienced, the irrepressible Candide has at last returned home; we leave him, hoeing his little plot of land at the conclusion of his tale. Candide's symbolic last words remind us: "tis well said, but we must cultivate our garden."

It must be in the French psyche. From my first visit to France to my most recent, I have found a national compulsion to grow things. Years ago one early September, as I journeyed through the French countryside toward Paris, my train sped past cottages and large country houses. Almost every home—no matter the size, had a well-kept garden. In every little patch of vegetation, there were rows of healthy leeks and thriving cabbages. In Paris I noticed a similar caring: windowsills in large city apartments either had pots of colorful blooms or window boxes. Only a few had been left unadorned. There are more kitchen gardens than flower gardens in France, and space is always found for the herbs that play such a vital part in French cuisine.

I have seen the French cultivate on every conceivable patch of earth, from a Basque plot on a slanty, narrow strip of land wedged between the base of the Pyrenees and a mountain stream to a few weather-beaten clay pots containing leeks, a straggly tarragon plant, and some healthy chives on the stoop of a good cook in Strasbourg to the "true" garden of France, the Loire Valley. There, lush, rich soils beside the meandering Loire River provide ample plots of ground, one after the other, that are leased to amateur gardeners who want to grow but don't have the space at their homes. Each plot has a unique, personalized tool shed belonging to the *cultivateur*. The most lavish vegetable garden in France is also in the Loire Valley, at the famed Villandry. Flowers, herbs, and vegetables grow together in a magnificent design; beauty and practicality become one and the same.

Why garden? Every gardener has his or her own response. Frugality. Freshness. Convenience. Tradition. Satisfaction. The French embrace all these reasons and more. Perhaps the most unusual testimony to French devotion to their horticulture is what I found in the Pas-de-Calais region's northwestern town of Arras in 1991: an extensive museum-quality exhibition, *Le grande exposition des fruits et legumes*. It had just opened, prior to a five-year tour to museums in northern France. It was not an agricultural show (as American county and state fairs), but rather a glorious presentation, overwhelming in scope and size, of paintings, historic documents, botanical illustrations, new species, and technological advances. Actual fresh vegetables and fruits (over thirty varieties of apples, for example) were also on display. An accompanying coffee-table volume was the official catalog of the exhibition.

One trip to France took me through Brittany and Normandy in early May when the countryside was unexpectedly flowering. From an ancient wisteria blooming right next to palm trees on the southern Brittany coast to the beauty of Monet's Giverny, I have found France to be a garden land. The hundreds of fresh vegetable soups are a reflection of that observation. For every *one* recipe that follows, there are countless variations.

RIGHT: A BASQUE GARDENER HAS TUCKED HIS VEGETABLE PATCH BETWEEN A MOUNTAIN STREAM AND AN ABRUPT MOUNTAIN SLOPE.

A BOUQUET FROM FRENCH GARDENS

There is no known substitute for the flavor imparted through the use of fresh-from-the-garden herbs during cooking. Understanding that, early French chefs selected a few green herbs suitable for the dish they were making, tied them together, and gave the little bundle a name. Fortunately for today's cooks, that bundle, a bouquet garni, has endured through the years and is now used in fine cooking, becoming a standard of excellence.

I cannot think of one national or ethnic cuisine that does not use special herbs and spices in its representative dishes. Many of the herbs are used fresh, and a lot of the spices are freshly ground. But only the French have ensured that each and every time they use a bouquet garni, a dish is ensured of an intrinsic freshness.

The traditional trio of fresh parsley, fresh thyme, and dried bay leaves imparts the fragrance of each of the herbs. These three essential elements are often tucked within a celery stalk or a leek green and tied with kitchen string. Depending on the ingredients in the dish, a bouquet garni may also include fresh tarragon, rosemary, marjoram, or fennel. Actually, any fresh herb the cook would like to include can become part of a special bouquet garni, and the bundle can be composed in any size needed. In every case it is removed from the dish with the tail of the string before serving.

The French word *bouquet* is apt in this use. It commonly means a little bundle of something sweet smelling. Here, however, bouquet has two meanings: it is the object, the bouquet of herbs that creates the aroma, and it is the aroma itself.

Garni translates as "accompanying" or "garnishing." For example, *choucroûte garni* is an Alsatian sauerkraut dish (*choucroûte*) that is accompanied with an assortment of meats and sausages. Hence, an accompaniment of a small bundle of herbs? The lovely and incomparable bouquet garni.

Ile-de-France

CREAM of SPRING PEA
POTAGE PURÉE SAINT-GERMAIN

MAKES **6** SERVINGS

2 OUNCES LEAN BACON (2 OR 3 SLICES), WELL CHILLED AND CUT INTO TINY DICE

½ CUP UNSALTED BUTTER

4 POUNDS FRESH TINY PEAS IN THE POD, SHELLED; 2 POUNDS SHELLED SMALL PEAS; OR 3 PACKAGES (10 OUNCES EACH) PETITE FROZEN PEAS, THAWED AND DRAINED

6 CUPS WATER

1 BOUQUET GARNI (6 FRESH PARSLEY STEMS, 2 BAY LEAVES, 2 FRESH THYME SPRIGS TIED IN 1 LARGE CELERY STALK)

1 TEASPOON SALT

6 FRESH CHERVIL SPRIGS

FRESHLY GROUND BLACK PEPPER

Forget about other pea soups you may have eaten. This graceful soup is quite unlike other versions. All the ingredients act solely to enhance the fresh flavor of the peas. There are no aromatics waiting in ambush, and the soup is not prepared with a chicken or veal broth, only clear water. What about the bacon? It is the absolute perfect touch—its subtle smokiness seems to make the peas even sweeter. Also, as you can imagine, the intensity of the soup's green color is as enticing as any hue could be.

Unless the fresh peas in the pod are very tiny and very fresh, you may be better off using petite frozen peas. Fresh peas in a pod that are large are not what this soup requires, as they may have become too starchy, thus losing their appeal.

Street vendors under Louis XIV called out: "Buy your green peas for Lent. Peas as sweet as any cream."

Put the bacon in a heavy 3-quart saucepan over very low heat. Sauté, stirring often, until the bacon is crisp, about 5 minutes. Using a slotted spoon, remove the bacon, drain on paper towels, and reserve. Pour off all the bacon fat and reserve for other cooking purposes.

Add 3 tablespoons of the butter and the peas to the saucepan and cook together over low heat, stirring often, for 2 to 3 minutes. Add the water, the bouquet garni, and the salt and bring to a boil over high heat. Reduce the heat to low and simmer until the peas are completely tender, about 15 minutes. (Frozen peas require much less cooking time.) Remove about ½ cup of the peas from the cooking liquid with a wire skimmer and reserve.

Remove the bouquet garni and discard. Drain the peas, reserving the cooking liquid. Working in batches, pass the peas through a food mill or purée in a food processor. Add the cooking liquid as needed to ease the puréeing. If you use a food processor, it will be necessary to strain the purée through a sieve after processing. Return the pea purée to the saucepan, adding cooking liquid as needed to achieve a good consistency. Reheat over low heat. Taste and add more salt if needed.

Melt the remaining 5 tablespoons butter in a small saucepan over medium heat. Cook the butter, stirring often, until lightly browned (*noisette*). Stir in the reserved peas and reheat gently.

Divide the buttered peas among 6 heated soup plates. Ladle in the pea soup and garnish each serving with an equal amount of the reserved bacon and a chervil sprig. Serve immediately, passing a pepper grinder at table.

CREAM of WATERCRESS

POTAGE ALÉNOIS

MAKES **6** SERVINGS

½ POUND WATERCRESS, STEMS REMOVED

¼ CUP UNSALTED BUTTER

3 SHALLOTS, FINELY MINCED

2 MEDIUM-SIZED WAXY POTATOES, PEELED AND FINELY CHOPPED

7 TO 8 CUPS WATER

1 TEASPOON SALT

1 CUP MILK

3 TABLESPOONS SOUR CREAM

¼ CUP FINELY CHOPPED FRESH CHERVIL OR PARSLEY

If you would like to serve this piquant soup chilled, use oil for sautéing the shallots and potatoes instead of butter. When watercress is not available at your market, small spinach leaves work equally well in the recipe but the flavor will be gentler. When you do buy watercress, use it shortly after purchase, as it tends to wilt and yellow quickly.

It is believed that the French word alénois is what happened to the word Orléanaise after many years of usage. (It is much the same as when some Americans say Frisco instead of San Francisco.) By extension, alénois has also taken to mean watercress or a dish prepared with watercress because of the high quality of the green that flourishes in the Orléans region near the Loire River.

Finely chop ½ cup of the watercress leaves and reserve. Coarsely chop the remaining leaves. Melt the butter in a heavy 4-quart soup pot over low heat. Add the shallots and the potatoes, and cook, stirring occasionally, until the shallots are softened, about 5 minutes. Add 7 cups of the water and the salt and bring to a boil over high heat. Reduce the heat to low and simmer, uncovered, for 15 minutes. Add the coarsely chopped watercress and cook until the watercress is wilted and the potatoes are tender, about 5 minutes longer.

Working with 2 or 3 ladlefuls at a time, purée the contents of the pot in a blender or food processor until velvety smooth, about 30 seconds per batch. Add the finely chopped watercress leaves and process until the light green soup is flecked with dark green.

Return the purée to the pot and place it over medium heat. Add the milk, then taste and add more salt if needed. Add additional water if necessary to achieve a good consistency. When the soup reaches a boil, pour immediately into a heated soup tureen and swirl in the sour cream. Sprinkle with the chervil or parsley and serve immediately.

FRESH WATERCRESS THRIVES IN THE SHALLOW
WATERS OF A STREAM IN NORTHERN FRANCE.

SORREL SOUPS *Soupe froide à l'oseille*, a chilled summer sorrel soup from Provence, is a close companion to *potage alénois*. It is constructed in almost precisely the same way as *alénois*, but the flavor is unusually suitable for warm weather. Unlike watercress, the minute sorrel hits the heat, it disappoints. The leaves change from a lively garden green to a grayed dark green. The important thing, however, is that the tart, bright flavor of sorrel remains.

Sorrel, with its long, oval green leaves, is relatively unfamiliar to American cooks, but its bright, citruslike flavor is a favorite among the French. Years ago, the delicious, beautiful, and celebrated salmon dish with a velvety sorrel sauce (created by French chefs Jean and Pierre Troisgros) introduced many outside of France to sorrel's wonderful flavor and its ease of cooking. It is a balancing accompaniment to rich seafood and meat dishes, as it keeps its tangy acidity after it has been cooked. Sorrel soups (or sorrel in soups) are prepared in nearly every region in France. I've discovered almost as many recipes for sorrel soups in French cookbooks as for any other soup ingredient (the possible exception being the ubiquitous onion). The elegant and sumptuous *crème Germiny* of classic French cooking is the polished offspring of the Provençal chilled sorrel soup.

2 TABLESPOONS UNSALTED BUTTER

1 MEDIUM-SIZED CELERY STALK, FINELY CHOPPED

1 MEDIUM-SIZED ONION, FINELY CHOPPED

½ TEASPOON CURRY POWDER (OPTIONAL)

4 CUPS FINELY CHOPPED YOUNG, SLENDER CARROTS

2 MEDIUM-SIZED WAXY POTATOES, PEELED AND DICED

1 TEASPOON SALT

6 TO 8 CUPS WATER

1 CUP MILK (SEE NOTE)

FRESHLY GROUND WHITE PEPPER

2 TABLESPOONS GRATED CARROT, AT ROOM TEMPERATURE (OPTIONAL)

6 TEASPOONS LOW-FAT SOUR CREAM OR CRÈME FRAÎCHE (OPTIONAL)

TINY POTATO *CROÛTONS* (RECIPE FOLLOWS)

Ile-de-France

CREAM of CARROT
POTAGE CRÉCY

MAKES 6 SERVINGS

There are two small villages that both claim the origin of the finest carrots in all of France, Crécy-en-Ponthieu to the north in Picard and Crécy-la-Chapelle near Paris. Potage Crécy takes its name from the carrot village or villages whose citizens are probably still debating the issue of origin. Not debatable is the excellence of the soup itself.

While the addition of the curry powder is not traditional in this particular soup, I like to add a little when cooking the celery-onion-carrot mixture. It adds a subtle distinction to the sweetness of carrots and onions that is almost imperceptible in the final soup.

Always buy young carrots with their dark green, feathery leaves still attached. If you happen to have older, larger carrots on hand, cut them into quarters lengthwise and cut out the center core, which is woody and tasteless. Many French recipes call for the rouge (red) of the carrot to be used, which means using only the exterior.

Melt the butter over low heat in a heavy 4-quart soup pot. Add the celery, onion, and the curry powder, if using, and cook, stirring often, until the vegetables are soft and lightly colored, about 10 minutes. Add the chopped carrots, potatoes, salt, and 6 cups of the water and bring to a boil. Reduce the heat to very low and simmer gently, uncovered, over very low heat until the carrots are very tender, 20 to 25 minutes.

Working with 2 or 3 ladlefuls at a time, purée the soup in a food processor or blender, processing each batch for at least 30 seconds and adding a little of the milk to each batch to achieve a creamy consistency.

Return the purée to the pot and place it over low heat. Bring the soup to a simmer and add more salt and the white pepper to taste. (If curry powder has been added, use caution with the white pepper.) Add more water if the soup needs a little thinning.

Ladle immediately into heated soup plates. If you'd like, float a spoonful of grated carrot (*râpée*) on each serving as a garnish. For a color contrast, form a swirl of sour cream on top prior to the garnish and accompany with the *croûtons*.

NOTE: Heavy cream may be used instead of milk in this recipe, creating a sumptuous soup. However, I usually have low-fat milk in the house, and it makes a wonderfully flavored *potage Crécy*.

CHILLED CREAM of CARROT   POTAGE CRÉCY GLACÉE

VARIATION: Prepare the recipe as directed, but do not reheat the puréed soup. Season as directed, transfer to a stainless-steel or glass container, cover with plastic, and refrigerate to chill thoroughly. Chill the soup plates in the freezer. Salt to taste and add lemon, if desired.

TINY
POTATO "CROÛTONS"
CROÛTONS de
POMMES de TERRE

2 LARGE RUSSET POTATOES, PEELED

1 TABLESPOON OLIVE OIL

1 TABLESPOON UNSALTED BUTTER

SALT

FRESHLY GROUND WHITE PEPPER

I discovered these hot "croûtons" in an old French cookbook, where they were included as an accompaniment to a hot version of potage Crécy. I think they are even better with a chilled soup, however.

Cut each potato into a rectangular block by trimming off the rounded edges. Carefully cut into ¼-inch-thick slices, then into ¼-inch-thick sticks, and then into ¼-inch dice. This takes a little time, not a lot, but the results will be worth it. Thoroughly dry the tiny potato cubes with paper towels.

Melt the oil and butter together in a large sauté pan over medium heat. Sauté the potatoes until golden, about 15 minutes. Toss gently with a metal spatula, or shake the pan so that the morsels color evenly. Remove from the heat and spread the potato dice on paper towels. Cover with additional paper towels and blot lightly to remove any excess cooking fat.

Sprinkle with salt and white pepper and serve at once. These *croûtons* may be sprinkled over the chilled soup or passed at table.

WHEN YOU'RE IN PARIS One of my favorite places to eat in Paris is near the Sorbonne on Rue des Écoles. Brasserie Balzar is an old-fashioned and distinguished restaurant and is the only place I know of in Paris where, when you order soup, the waiter (with a starched white apron so long it touches his toes) brings a tureen of steaming soup to your table. The surface still glistens with the dollop of butter that has been swirled in right before the tureen leaves the kitchen. Quite often the soup is *potage Crécy*.

¼ CUP UNSALTED BUTTER

½ SMALL HEAD Savoy CABBAGE (ABOUT ½ POUND), CORED AND CUT INTO SHORT, NARROW RIBBONS

3 SLENDER LEEKS, WHITE AND PALE GREEN PARTS ONLY, THINLY SLICED

2 CLOVES GARLIC, FINELY MINCED

3 QUARTS WATER

1 CUP CUT-UP GREEN BEANS (2-INCH LENGTHS)

1 TEASPOON SALT

2 YOUNG, SLENDER CARROTS, PEELED AND SLICED INTO ¼-INCH-THICK COINS

1 BOUQUET GARNI (6 FRESH PARSLEY STEMS, 2 BAY LEAVES, 2 FRESH THYME SPRIGS TIED IN 1 LEEK GREEN)

12 WALNUT-SIZED NEW POTATOES, UNPEELED

3 SMALL ZUCCHINI, TRIMMED AND THINLY SLICED

FRESHLY GROUND BLACK PEPPER

FINELY MINCED FRESH HERBS SUCH AS CHERVIL, SORREL, PARSLEY, OR CHIVES

Champagne–le Nord

MARKET GARDENERS' SOUP

SOUPE des HORTILLONS

MAKES **6** SERVINGS

The famed "floating" gardens of Amiens have inspired many soups, and the following is the definitive one in the genre of mixed-vegetable soups. The vegetables listed here are but a starting point. Stop by your greengrocer, select the freshest of your favorite vegetables and herbs, and cook them gently in clear, fresh water. Hortillonnages, the French word for the market gardens, particularly in Picardy, is a direct linguistic link to the Latin hortus, or "garden."

Melt the butter in a heavy 4-quart soup pot over medium heat. Add the cabbage, leeks, and garlic and cook, stirring often, until lightly colored, 10 to 12 minutes.

While the leeks and cabbage are cooking, prepare a large bowl of ice water. Bring 1 quart of the water to a boil in a large saucepan and add the green beans. Cook over high heat until tender, 4 to 5 minutes. Remove the beans with a slotted spoon and immediately immerse them in the ice water to retain their vivid green color. Drain and reserve.

Add the remaining 2 quarts water, the salt, carrots, bouquet garni, and potatoes to the soup pot. Bring to a boil, reduce the heat to low, and simmer, uncovered, until the vegetables are tender, about 10 minutes. Add the zucchini and reserved green beans and simmer for 1 minute.

Remove the bouquet garni and discard. Taste and add salt if needed and black pepper to taste. Stir in the minced herbs, ladle into heated soup plates, and serve at once.

IN LAND RECLAIMED BY DRAINING THE MARSHY REGIONS CREATED BY THE SOMME RIVER, THE MARKET GARDENERS OF AMIENS HAVE AN IDEAL SITE FOR GROWING THEIR VEGETABLES: EXCEPTIONALLY RICH SOIL AND AN EFFICIENT WAY—BY FLAT-BOTTOMED BOATS THAT SKIM ALONG THE WATERWAYS—TO TRANSPORT THE FRESH PRODUCE TO THEIR MARKET STALLS.

THE FLOATING GARDENS AT AMIENS

France, as I have said, is just one huge garden. There is one place, however, that is exactly that. In the ancient city of Amiens, I was able to visit the unique floating gardens, known as *les hortillonnages*. (The *hortillons* are the gardeners there.) Acres and acres of rich and fertile land are interlaced by waterways that were created by the runoff from the marshlands of the Somme River. Hundreds of individual cultivated plots may be visited by floating through the waterways in flat-bottomed boats or by walking leisurely along the intricate pattern of footpaths.

I chose a quiet autumn morning for my first waterside stroll, slowly absorbing the magic of my surroundings. I observed gardeners turn soil that was as soft and dark brown as cocoa and a housewife in her apron and a maroon cardigan, fishing quietly, distant in thought. The luxurious green of vegetables and the brilliance of flowers were everywhere on that October morning. I saw red cabbages as big as bushel baskets. An old Citroën that chugged out of the gardens on a narrow little road had cabbage leaves hanging out of its closed trunk, looking like a lady's slip showing. Certainly the most exhilarating sight was the slender spire of the Amiens cathedral rising at a distance from the midst of the rich vegetation. Both were perfect and beautiful, both were achievements of creative French men and women.

Languedoc

CATALAN HAM and GREEN BEAN KETTLE

OUILLADE de HARICOTS VERTS

MAKES **6** SERVINGS

1 TABLESPOON OLIVE OIL

1 MEDIUM-SIZED ONION, FINELY CHOPPED

8 TO 9 CUPS WATER

1 CLOVE GARLIC, MINCED

1 SLICE SMOKED HAM WITH A SMALL BONE, ABOUT ¼ POUND, MEAT FINELY DICED AND BONE RESERVED

6 NEW POTATOES, UNPEELED, QUARTERED

1 ONE-OUNCE PIECE SALT PORK (OPTIONAL)

1 POUND SLENDER GREEN BEANS, TRIMMED AND CUT INTO 1½-INCH LENGTHS

SALT

FRESHLY GROUND BLACK PEPPER

OLIVE OIL AND RED WINE VINEGAR

When I first began to prepare this Pyrenean dish, which also appears in Catalan cookbooks as ollada de montejas tendras, *I was tempted to cook the green beans separately, toss them in some ice water to set their fresh green color, and add them to the soup at the end of cooking. How lucky it was I decided to prepare the soup in the traditional rustic way, or I would never have discovered that the green beans become unusually good and full of deep country flavor when well cooked with the other ingredients. I have tried the soup both with and without the addition of a final dash of oil and vinegar, and it is tempting either way.*

Heat the 1 tablespoon olive oil in a heavy 4-quart soup pot over medium heat. Sauté the onion, stirring occasionally, until lightly colored, 10 to 12 minutes. Add 8 cups (2 quarts) of the water, the garlic, the ham and ham bone, the potatoes, and the salt pork, if using. Bring to a boil over high heat, reduce the heat to low, and simmer for 10 minutes. Add the green beans, cover, and cook until the beans are very tender, about 15 minutes.

Taste and add salt if needed and black pepper to taste. Remove and discard the ham bone and the salt pork, if used. If necessary, add as much of the remaining 1 cup water as needed to give the soup a good consistency. Ladle into warmed soup plates and accompany with cruets of olive oil and red wine vinegar. It is a Catalan tradition for the diners to drizzle a little oil and vinegar over their servings.

> **POTATOES** All potatoes used for soups in this book should be waxy, that is, smooth and pale colored. Do not use russet or any other baking potatoes, as they have a mealy character and will become mushy. Unpeeled new potatoes are always good to use in soups if the potatoes are to be cut into small pieces. The vitamin-rich skins contrast with the color of the potato and with the other ingredients as well.

8 PLUM TOMATOES, PEELED, SEEDED, AND CHOPPED

1 TABLESPOON RED WINE VINEGAR

4 TABLESPOONS FRUITY OLIVE OIL

2 MEDIUM-SIZED ONIONS, CHOPPED

4 CLOVES GARLIC, MINCED

2 MEDIUM-SIZED WAXY POTATOES, PEELED AND CUT INTO SMALL PIECES

RED PEPPER FLAKES

2 QUARTS WATER

1 ½ TEASPOONS SALT

FRESHLY GROUND BLACK PEPPER

1 SMALL EGGPLANT, PEELED, IF DESIRED, AND CUT INTO 1-INCH CHUNKS

FRESH THYME LEAVES

Languedoc

CATALAN ROASTED EGGPLANT and TOMATO SOUP

SOUPE d'AUBERGINES CATALANE

MAKES **6** SERVINGS

Catalan tomato soups are usually assertive and spicy, and this soup, with its garlic, vinegar, and red pepper flakes, is no exception. Often chunks of eggplant, sautéed in olive oil, are added at serving. To sauté the ever-absorbent eggplant to a golden turn, one usually needs to add more and more oil. Roasting the eggplant is not a Catalan tradition, but a good solution to the too-much-oil problem. Even less oil is needed at the beginning. And what of the roasted flavor? It's concentrated and heightened by the browning produced in the high heat of the oven. Another bonus: the chunks of eggplant come out of the oven meltingly tender but still holding their original shape. The eggplant may or may not be peeled. I think the skin on roasted eggplant tastes a little bitter, so I remove it, a personal choice.

Another option is to grill slices of eggplant, cut them into chunks, and add those to the soup.

The French aubergine *is derived from the Catalan* aubergínia, *which the Catalans, in turn, adopted from the Arabic. Hence, a little etymology relates the* histoire *of the arrival of eggplant into southern France.*

Combine the tomatoes and vinegar in a bowl, toss together, and reserve.

Heat 2 tablespoons of the olive oil in a heavy 3-quart saucepan over medium heat. Sauté the onions, stirring often, until lightly colored, about 10 minutes. Add the garlic, reduce the heat to low, and cook, stirring constantly, for 2 to 3 minutes. Do not let the garlic brown.

Add the potatoes, red pepper flakes to taste, water, and 1 teaspoon of the salt and bring to a boil over high heat. Reduce the heat to low and cook for 5 minutes. Add the tomatoes and continue cooking until the potatoes are completely tender, 10 to 15 minutes. Meanwhile, preheat the oven to 450°F.

Working with 1 or 2 ladlefuls at a time, purée the soup in a food mill or a food processor. Return the purée to the saucepan and taste, adding more salt if needed and black pepper to taste. Simmer over very low heat while eggplant is roasting.

Toss the eggplant with the remaining 2 tablespoons olive oil and ½ teaspoon salt and with black pepper to taste. Spread out the eggplant on a lightly greased baking sheet and brown in the oven for about 10 minutes. Watch closely and turn over any pieces that are getting too brown.

When eggplant is ready, ladle the soup into heated soup plates. Top with pieces of eggplant and sprinkle with fresh thyme leaves. Serve at once.

Provence

COUNTRY SORREL and POTATO SOUP

SOUPO d'EIGRETO ei TRUFO

MAKES 6 SERVINGS

6 TO 8 OUNCES SORREL LEAVES, PLUS SMALL SORREL LEAVES FOR GARNISH

2 TABLESPOONS FRUITY OLIVE OIL

1 LARGE ONION, FINELY CHOPPED

2 LARGE WAXY POTATOES, PEELED AND CUT INTO JULIENNE STRIPS 1 ½ INCHES LONG BY ¼ INCH WIDE BY ¼ INCH THICK

7 TO 8 CUPS WATER OR VEGETABLE BROTH

1 TEASPOON SALT

3 EGG YOLKS

½ CUP LOW-FAT SOUR CREAM

Eigreto *in Provençal dialect means "sorrel," and this sorrel soup is widely described by food writers of that region. It is a singularly tasty dish because its gentle tang, contributed both by tart sorrel and sour cream, is refreshing. At the same time, it seems rich to the palate, but it is decidedly not.*

Remove the stems from the larger sorrel leaves by either tearing them free or by folding each leaf in half lengthwise and, with a sharp knife, cutting away the stem. Stack several leaves at a time, roll up lengthwise, and cut crosswise into ribbons (*chiffonade*). Reserve a few tablespoons for garnish.

Heat the olive oil in a heavy, nonaluminum 4-quart soup pot over medium heat. Sauté the onion, stirring often, until lightly colored, 8 to 10 minutes.

Add the potatoes to the soup pot and, stirring continuously with a wooden spoon, allow them to color lightly, about 5 minutes. Add 7 cups of the water or broth and the salt and bring to a boil over high heat. Add the sorrel *chiffonade*, stir well, reduce the heat to low, and cook, uncovered, until the potatoes are tender, about 10 minutes.

Whisk together the egg yolks and sour cream in a small bowl until thoroughly combined. Whisk a ladle or two of the hot soup into the egg yolk mixture. Pour the tempered egg yolk mixture into the soup pot while stirring constantly. Cook over low heat, gently moving the pot back and forth on the burner and, at the same time, stirring constantly with a wooden spoon. Do not allow the soup to boil. It should thicken slowly.

Taste and add more salt if needed. Thin with as much of the remaining 1 cup water as needed to achieve a good soup consistency. Ladle into heated soup plates, garnish with the reserved *chiffonade* of sorrel and the small sorrel leaves, and serve at once.

RIGHT: POTATOES FOR SALE AT THE FRIDAY MORNING MARKET AT CARPENTRAS IN NORTHWESTERN PROVENCE.

Provence

CHILLED TOMATO and BASIL SOUP

SOUPE FROIDE aux TOMATES

MAKES 6 SERVINGS

1 TABLESPOON FRUITY OLIVE OIL

2 SLENDER LEEKS, WHITE AND PALE GREEN PARTS ONLY, THINLY SLICED

6 TO 7 CUPS WATER

1 CLOVE GARLIC, FINELY MINCED

7 TOMATOES, PEELED, SEEDED, AND COARSELY CHOPPED

1 BOUQUET GARNI (3 FRESH PARSLEY STEMS, 1 BAY LEAF, 1 FRESH THYME SPRIG TIED IN 1 CELERY STALK)

1 TEASPOON SALT

7 TABLESPOONS FINELY CHOPPED FRESH BASIL

FRESHLY GROUND BLACK PEPPER

$\frac{1}{2}$ TEASPOON SUGAR, IF NEEDED

6 WARM _CROÛTES_ (PAGE 79)

When summer's tomatoes are at their ripest and fresh basil abounds, it's time to create this refreshing soup, a welcome change from chilled gazpacho. Not distracted by cucumbers or peppers, it is distinctly and intensely tomato-y. Most soups benefit from textural contrasts, so be sure to include the garnish of chopped sweet summer tomatoes. I think warm toasty croûtes complement chilled soups as well. Both additions awaken the senses.

Heat the olive oil in a heavy, nonaluminum 4-quart soup pot over low heat. Cook the leeks, stirring often, until completely softened, 8 to 10 minutes. Add 6 cups of the water, the garlic, all but $\frac{1}{2}$ cup of the tomatoes, the bouquet garni, the salt, and 2 tablespoons of the basil. Bring to a boil over high heat, reduce the heat to low, and simmer, partially covered, until the leeks and the tomatoes are a harmonious mixture, about 20 minutes.

Remove the soup from the heat, discard the bouquet garni, and add 4 tablespoons of the basil. Working with 1 or 2 ladlefuls at a time, purée the soup in a blender, processing each batch for at least 30 seconds. Transfer the puréed soup to a glass or stainless-steel container, cover with plastic wrap, and refrigerate for at least 2 hours or as long as overnight. Chop the reserved tomato pieces quite finely. Refrigerate the tomato pieces, the remaining 1 tablespoon minced basil, and the remaining 1 cup of water separately. Place the soup plates in the freezer to chill.

Immediately before serving, taste for seasoning, adding salt if needed and black pepper to taste. Add more chilled water if the soup needs thinning to a good consistency. Add the sugar if it is needed to balance the acidity of the soup. Serve in the chilled soup plates. Sprinkle each serving with some tiny tomato pieces and minced basil and pass the warm _croûtes_.

FRESH BASIL (*BASILIC*), A WELCOME
ENHANCEMENT TO SUMMER COOKING AND
INDISPENSABLE IN PREPARING *PISTOU*,
AT A MARKET STALL IN PROVENCE.

REMEMBERING CORSICA It is believed that Napoléon, while exiled on
Elba, experienced a nostalgia and homesickness for his native Corsica, uttered, "With my
eyes closed, I can be in Corsica again, by remembering the herbal aromas that breathe
from the *maquis*." (The *maquis* are the bristly, fragrant shrubs that flourish all over Corsica.)

Corse

BOUQUET-of-HERBS SOUP

SUPPA d'ERBIGLIE

MAKES **6** SERVINGS

½ CUP DRIED RED BEANS

3 QUARTS PLUS 1 CUP WATER

2 TABLESPOONS OLIVE OIL

2 MEDIUM-SIZED ONIONS, FINELY CHOPPED

2 MEDIUM-SIZED WAXY POTATOES, PEELED AND DICED

2 CLOVES GARLIC, FINELY CHOPPED

1 TEASPOON SALT

4 PLUM TOMATOES, PEELED, SEEDED, AND DICED

1 LARGE BOUQUET ASSORTED FRESH HERBS (SEE NOTE)

FRESHLY GROUND BLACK PEPPER

If you can't gather fresh herbs from the fragrant Corsican hills, bring them in from your garden or the market. There should be at least three or four fresh herbs in your "bouquet" and mint is indispensable in this Corsican soup.

The tomatoes are added at two different times during the soup's preparation, to ensure a deep tomato flavor. The beans, potatoes, and aromatics benefit from simmering with tomatoes, and the completed soup is brightened by the last-minute addition of the uncooked fresh tomato morsels.

Rinse the beans, then place in a bowl and cover generously with cold water. Soak the beans overnight. The following day, drain, place in a heavy saucepan, and add 1 quart of the water. Bring to a boil and cook over high heat for 10 to 12 minutes. Reduce the heat to medium-low and cook for 30 minutes. Drain and reserve.

Heat 1 tablespoon of the olive oil in a heavy 4-quart soup pot over medium heat. Sauté the onions, stirring often, until they become golden, 10 to 12 minutes. Add 2 quarts of the water, the potatoes, the garlic, and the reserved red beans and bring to a boil over high heat. Reduce the heat to low, cover, and simmer, stirring occasionally, for 15 minutes. Add the salt and half of the tomatoes and cook until beans are tender, about 15 minutes longer.

Finely mince the herbs. Add the remaining tomatoes, black pepper to taste, and the herbs and cook for 1 minute. Stir in the remaining 1 tablespoon olive oil and adjust the seasoning, adding more salt if needed. If the soup is too thick, thin with as much of the remaining 1 cup water as needed to achieve a good consistency. Ladle into heated soup plates and serve immediately.

NOTE: You will need a generous ½ cup minced herbs to add to the soup. An example of a perfumed herb blend that will yield this amount is 2 small sorrel leaves, 5 fresh thyme sprigs, 5 fresh parsley sprigs, 5 fresh basil leaves, 5 fresh peppermint leaves, 5 fresh spearmint leaves, and 5 fresh sage leaves.

THE LEEK IS ESSENTIAL IN FRENCH COOKING. AT A MARKET IN BRITTANY, A VENDOR OFFERS STARTER PLANTS FOR HOME GARDENERS.

LEEKS Try to buy slender leeks (*poireaux*) when you will be using them as an ingredient to be sliced and cooked in a soup. When using whole leeks for flavoring, larger leeks are fine. Leeks are so much a part of French cooking that Nobel Prize winner Anatole France once observed, *Le poireau, c'est l'asperge du pauvre* (The leek is the poor man's asparagus).

ONIONS When a recipe in this book asks for chopped onion, I am referring to yellow onions and prefer to use medium-sized onions, as I feel they require less time to ready for the pot. It takes longer to remove the skins and trim small onions in preparation for chopping, while large onions have greater sections that take more time to chop. When whole onions are used for flavoring, sometimes studded with cloves, large ones are fine.

SCALLIONS In this book, the most common role for the green tops of scallions is as a garnish on the surface of soups, as they offer a whiff of aroma and a touch of refreshing color. They should be very finely chopped, and if the green stems are too fat, they should be sliced lengthwise before chopping.

Provence

VEGETABLE SOUP with FRESH BASIL

SOUPE au PISTOU

MAKES **6** SERVINGS

When planning a trip to southern France one autumn, I was intrigued to learn about Le Patio, a unique restaurant in Fontvieille, near the ancient city of Arles, that was formerly a sheep pen (bergerie) and had been transformed into a handsome dining room. I wrote to owner-chef Jean-Marc Chaminade to ask if he would prepare a regional soup. Chef Chaminade assembled a vivid soupe au pistou, *a dish that features fresh Provençal ingredients and mirrors the cuisine of neighboring Italy: beans and pasta are side by side in one dish. An echo of Genoa is heard in the last-minute addition of the heady* sauce au pistou, *the French version of Italian pesto. The chef also delighted me with his lamb chops, which he grilled in an immense walk-in fireplace in the dining room.*

½ CUP SHELLED FRESH WHITE SHELLING BEANS (ABOUT ½ POUND UNSHELLED), OR ⅓ CUP DRIED WHITE BEANS

3 TO 3½ QUARTS WATER

1 CUP CUT-UP GREEN BEANS (1-INCH LENGTHS)

3 TABLESPOONS FRUITY OLIVE OIL

1 MEDIUM-SIZED ONION, FINELY CHOPPED

2 MEDIUM-SIZED WAXY POTATOES, PEELED AND CUT INTO ¾-INCH DICE

1 CELERY STALK, FINELY CHOPPED

1 SMALL ZUCCHINI, TRIMMED AND CUT INTO ¼-INCH-THICK SLICES (½ CUP)

1 SLENDER LEEK, WHITE AND PALE GREEN PARTS ONLY, FINELY CHOPPED

3 ROUND TOMATOES OR 6 PLUM TOMATOES, PEELED, SEEDED, AND COARSELY CHOPPED

2 TEASPOONS SALT

½ CUP BROKEN THIN PASTA (2-INCH PIECES)

½ TEASPOON FRESHLY GROUND BLACK PEPPER

½ CUP GRATED PARMIGIANO-REGGIANO CHEESE (2 OUNCES)

For the *pistou:*

3 CLOVES GARLIC

4 CUPS FRESH BASIL LEAVES

¼ CUP OLIVE OIL

1 TABLESPOON BROTH FROM SOUP

If using fresh shelling beans, set aside. If using dried beans, rinse them, then place in a bowl and cover generously with cold water. Soak the beans overnight. The following day, drain, place in a heavy saucepan, and add 1 quart of the water. Bring to a boil and cook over high heat for 10 to 12 minutes. Reduce the heat to medium-low-and cook for 30 minutes. Drain and reserve.

Prepare a bowl of ice water. Bring a saucepan of water to a boil, add the green beans, and cook over high heat until barely tender, 3 to 4 minutes. Remove with a slotted spoon and immediately immerse the beans in the ice water to retain their vivid green color. Drain and reserve.

Heat the olive oil in a heavy 4-quart soup pot over medium heat. Sauté the onion, stirring occasionally, until lightly colored, 8 to 10 minutes. Add the fresh shelling beans or the reserved drained white beans, the potatoes, celery, and 2 quarts of the water. Bring to a boil, reduce the heat to low, cover partially, and simmer until the potatoes are barely tender, 10 to 15 minutes. Add the zucchini, the reserved green beans, the leek, the tomatoes, the salt, and the pasta. Cook, stirring occasionally, until the pasta is al dente and the white beans are tender, about 10 minutes. Taste and add more salt if needed and the black pepper. Thin the soup with the remaining ½ quart (2 cups) water as needed to achieve a good consistency.

While the soup is cooking, make the *pistou:* Place the garlic in a food processor and pulse at least 10 times to mince. Add the basil, 1 cup at a time, and pulse 10 to 12 times with each addition. When all of the basil has been added, purée for 20 seconds or so. With the motor running, add the olive oil and then add the 1 tablespoon hot broth. This makes ample *pistou* for this recipe with plenty left over for other dishes. Store in the refrigerator in a glass jar with a tight lid for up to a week.

Ladle the soup into heated soup plates, swirl in a spoonful of the *pistou,* sprinkle with a little grated cheese, and serve immediately. Pass additional *pistou* and cheese at table.

And, if you come, one summer's day,
to where I live, to the end of the garden
that I know, a garden dark in greenery
and without flowers, if you watched
*   from afar*
a gentle mountain turn blue,
where the pebbles, the butterflies and
*   the thistles*
become tinged with the same dusty
*   sky-blue mauve,*
you would not want to move
until the end of your life.
                —Colette, ON HER GARDEN

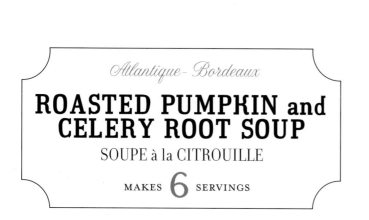

Atlantique- Bordeaux

ROASTED PUMPKIN and CELERY ROOT SOUP

SOUPE à la CITROUILLE

MAKES 6 SERVINGS

- 1 POUND PEELED PUMPKIN FLESH, CUT INTO 1-INCH CUBES (2 CUPS)
- 4 TABLESPOONS UNSALTED BUTTER
- 3 SLENDER LEEKS, WHITE AND PALE GREEN PARTS ONLY, THINLY SLICED
- 4 YOUNG, SLENDER CARROTS, PEELED AND DICED
- 1 CELERY ROOT, 5 TO 6 INCHES IN DIAMETER, PEELED AND CUT INTO 1/2-INCH DICE (ABOUT 1 CUP)
- 1 TABLESPOON SALT
- 8 TO 9 CUPS WATER
- 1/4 TEASPOON CAYENNE PEPPER, OR TO TASTE

FRESHLY GROUND BLACK PEPPER

An uncommon pairing of two dissimilar vegetables—pungent celery root and mellow pumpkin—creates a luscious, subtly flavored soup. Roasting the pumpkin concentrates its honeyness, deepens the soup's golden color, and produces a velvety texture.

The citrouille *(or* potiron*) of France is basically a pumpkin, as we know it, on the inside and an immense, ripply, vibrant red-orange pumpkin-shaped gourd on the outside. (I've read a French verse that observes: "potiron énorme, majesté difformé.") Since it is so huge, it is usually not sold whole like pumpkins in the States, but rather carved into irregular wedge-shaped chunks and sold in French markets by weight.*

Preheat the oven to 400°F. Lightly grease a baking sheet and spread out the pumpkin pieces on it. Roast in the oven until the pumpkin becomes very lightly colored and slightly shrunken, about 20 minutes. Remove from the oven and set aside.

Melt 2 tablespoons of the butter in a heavy 4-quart soup pot over medium heat. Cook the leeks, stirring often, until lightly colored, 8 to 10 minutes. Add the pumpkin, carrots, celery root, salt, and 8 cups (2 quarts) of the water and bring to a boil. Reduce the heat to medium, cover partially, and cook until the vegetables are tender, about 30 minutes.

Working with 2 or 3 ladlefuls at a time, purée the soup in a blender or food processor, processing each batch for at least 30 seconds. Return the purée to the soup pot, add the cayenne pepper, and season with black pepper to taste. If necessary, add as much of the remaining 1 cup water as needed to thin the soup to a good consistency.

Taste and add more salt if needed. Reheat the soup over medium heat, swirl in the remaining 2 tablespoons butter, and serve immediately in heated soup plates.

NOTE: Winter squash may be substituted for the pumpkin. Choose a butternut, cut it in half, and roast it before peeling, as it will be easier to peel once it is cooked. Acorn squash may also be used but is more difficult to peel.

RIGHT: PUMPKIN IN AN OCTOBER MARKET NEAR CAHORS, A TOWN IN SOUTHWESTERN DORDOGNE.

RADISH LEAF SOUP
POTAGE TOUT-VENANT

MAKES **6** SERVINGS

4 CUPS FIRMLY PACKED GREEN VEGETABLE TRIMMINGS

1 CUP ADDITIONAL FIRMLY PACKED PEELINGS FROM TURNIPS, CARROTS, OR OTHER ROOT VEGETABLES

8 TO 9 CUPS WATER

1 TEASPOON SALT

½ BUNCH SCALLIONS, TRIMMED AND CHOPPED

3 MEDIUM-SIZED WAXY POTATOES, PEELED AND DICED

1 EGG YOLK AND 1 TABLESPOON HEAVY CREAM, OR ¼ CUP LOW-FAT SOUR CREAM

FRESHLY GROUND BLACK PEPPER

FRESH LEMON JUICE

2 CUPS SMALL _CROÛTONS_ (PAGE 79)

A precise translation of tout-venant *is tricky. It's a French idiom that often refers to unsorted produce found at the market, such as a bushel of potatoes containing a variety of sizes—that is, "hit or miss" or "as is."*

Thrifty potage tout-venant *shares that catch-as-catch-can notion. It has traditionally been prepared in remote Alpine Savoy, where all scraps of vegetables, those that are usually discarded, were gleaned and used by gifted and practical cooks. Valuable vegetable peelings are included: leek scraps, lettuce trimmings, spinach stems, fresh pea pods, and, importantly, radish leaves. (The soup is closely related to the known* soupe de fanes de radis, *so I have given it the English name of Radish Leaf Soup.) More than frugality is involved here. Vegetable parts we often discard are rich in nutrients. Collect your vegetable odds and ends and freeze them. It takes little time to accumulate enough* soupçons *to make this healthful, frugal soup.*

A flavorful no-fat vegetable broth is made and then used to cook the potatoes. A purée completes the soup, colored a rich, princely green belying its spare origins. The final flavor of the soup varies according to the specific vegetable scraps included. For example, the more radish leaves, the more peppery the soup.

Put the vegetable trimmings and peelings, 8 cups (2 quarts) of the water, and the salt in heavy 4-quart pot. Bring to a boil over high heat, reduce the heat to low and cook, uncovered, until the vegetables trimmings are tender, at least 30 minutes.

Pour through a large sieve to drain, pressing firmly against the solids in the sieve to release as much flavor as possible. Discard the solids.

Return the broth to the soup pot. Taste and add more salt if needed. Add the scallions and potatoes, bring to a boil, reduce the heat to medium, and cook, uncovered, until the potatoes are tender enough to purée, about 15 minutes.

Working in small batches, purée the potatoes in a food mill, a blender, or a food processor. Be sure to use an ample amount of broth when processing each batch so that the potatoes do not become gluey. Return the puréed soup to the soup pot and place over medium heat to reheat.

To give the soup an appealing finish, whisk together the egg yolk and the cream in a small bowl until thoroughly mixed. Slowly whisk in a ladleful of the hot soup. Pour the mixture into the soup pot, whisking constantly, and heat thoroughly. Add as much of the remaining 1 cup water as needed to achieve a good soup consistency. Do not allow the soup to boil. Alternately, whisk the sour cream into the soup in the pot and thin with water as needed.

Taste a final time and add more salt if necessary and black pepper to taste. Add a squeeze of lemon juice to taste at this time. Ladle into heated soup plates and serve immediately. Pass a pepper mill and the small _croûtons_ at table.

Languedoc

GARLIC, TOMATO, and CABBAGE SOUP

MAYORQUINA

MAKES **6** SERVINGS

2 TABLESPOONS OLIVE OIL

6 CLOVES GARLIC, FINELY MINCED

1 MEDIUM-SIZED WHITE ONION, THINLY SLICED

6 PLUM TOMATOES, PEELED, SEEDED, AND CHOPPED

½ POUND SAVOY CABBAGE (ABOUT ¼ MEDIUM HEAD), CORED AND COARSELY CHOPPED

1 TEASPOON SALT

2 QUARTS WATER

FRESHLY GROUND BLACK PEPPER

¼ TEASPOON PAPRIKA

¼ CUP FINELY CHOPPED FRESH THYME OR PARSLEY

For most soups that contain cabbage, I prefer to use Savoy cabbage (chou de Milan) instead of white (or very pale green) cabbage. Its looser leaves cook more quickly, although in some long-simmering potées *this is not important. However, Savoy's dark green leaves always look prettier in any soup, and in* mayorquina *that green is vivid in contrast to the red tomato morsels.*

This old, robust soup from the southern French region of Roussillon reveals its Catalan origins in its traditional cooking vessel, an earthenware marmite *or* olla *(a Spanish clay cooking pot). If you don't have an* olla *in your cupboard, a large cast-iron Dutch oven would be almost as appealing.*

If possible, use a large (4-quart) earthenware casserole that can be placed over direct heat. Heat the olive oil in the casserole over medium heat. Sauté the garlic and onion until softened but not colored, 8 to 10 minutes. Add the tomatoes, cabbage, salt, and water and bring to a boil. Reduce the heat to low and simmer, uncovered, until the cabbage is tender, about 20 minutes.

Taste for seasoning, adding more salt if needed, black pepper to taste, and the paprika. Sprinkle with the thyme or parsley and serve immediately directly from the cooking vessel.

Auvergne

SMOKY CABBAGE SOUP

SOUPE aux CHOUX d'AUVERGNE

MAKES **6** SERVINGS

2 OUNCES LEAN SALT PORK

1 HAM BONE (OPTIONAL)

1 MEDIUM-SIZED ONION, FINELY CHOPPED

1 SLENDER LEEK, WHITE AND PALE GREEN PARTS ONLY, THINLY SLICED

½ HEAD SAVOY CABBAGE, CORED AND CUT INTO SHORT RIBBONS

2 YOUNG, SLENDER CARROTS, PEELED AND SLICED

1 TEASPOON SALT

8 TO 9 CUPS WATER

FRESHLY GROUND BLACK PEPPER

WHOLE-GRAIN MUSTARD

This is actually a somewhat light soup— not delicate, of course—but not as filling as you might imagine. In the Auvergne, the chunk of salt pork is still in the soup when it is served, but as it has yielded its flavor by the end of cooking, I have suggested you remove it at the same time as the ham bone.

A crock of whole-grain mustard is welcome at table for those who enjoy the nip of mustard with cabbage. Place a little mustard on the rim of the soup plate and then add to a spoonful of hot soup as desired. Crusty French bread also is a welcome accompaniment.

"My wife, with a little bacon, makes a cabbage soup that the king would eat."

—M. Marmont,
ONE TIME MARÉCHAL OF FRANCE

Place the salt pork, ham bone (if using), onion, leek, cabbage, carrots, salt, and 8 cups (2 quarts) of the water in a heavy 4-quart soup pot. Bring to a boil over high heat, reduce the heat to low, cover, and simmer until the vegetables are tender, about 30 minutes. Skim any foam that appears on the surface, replacing any liquid you have removed.

Taste and add more salt if needed and black pepper to taste. Remove the ham bone and salt pork. Add as much of the remaining 1 cup water as needed to achieve a good soup consistency. Ladle into heated soup plates and serve immediately. Pass the mustard at table.

CHOUX DE MILAN (SAVOY CABBAGES) AT THE
MARKET IN SOUILLAC, IN THE DORDOGNE.

AUVERGNE COOKING If any stretch of France conjures up regional cookery it is the Auvergne, located in the south-central part of the country known as the Massif Central. In the dense neighborhood of the Marais in Paris, there is a restaurant, Ambassade d'Auvergne, so convincingly Auvergnate that it is hard to imagine it lies within a great city. It is not the exposed brick, the heavy wooden beams, the no-nonsense chairs, or the aging hams that give this widely acclaimed eatery the feeling of the country. Rather, it is the modest simplicity of the menu, the quiet and unpretentious service.

One almost involuntarily says "cabbage" when one mentions the Auvergne. And cabbage it was the day I paid a visit to the restaurant. I had a fragrant steaming bowl of cabbage soup (*soupe aux choux*) cooked with care, the cabbage almost sweet. What surprised me was not how intensely flavored it was, but how very, very light. The broth was nearly clear, the strands of cabbage tenderly cooked, and the underlying *goût* of the smoked pork was robust but not overwhelming. A brace of breads arrived with the meal: a chewy, round country bread (*pain de campagne*) and the ever-present crunchy chunks of a long *baguette*. It was regional farm-kitchen cookery at its finest. To quote the Gault-Millau guide, "If you don't come from the Auvergne, a meal at the Ambassade will make you wish you did."

WALNUTS AND WALNUT OIL Harvesting walnuts and then shelling them is a major agricultural enterprise in France. Indeed, the walnut is so common in France that its name is just *noix* (nut), as if there were no others. The nuts are eaten raw, of course, but they also are pressed to produce a flavorful oil that continues to be in great demand, both at home and for export.

The French, as with people in all predominately Catholic cultures, observe the dietary restrictions of their church, including the prohibition of eating meat and animal products on specific days. Until recently, acceptance was generally never questioned. Dishes on nonmeat days were known as *maigre* (meager), and cooks, unable to use butter or fat, had to find a substitute cooking medium. The oil of preference, if olive oil was not readily available, was inevitably walnut oil.

In central France, I once poked around a hoary French walnut mill. Every surface in the small one-room stone building—floors, ceilings, window mullions, nooks, and crannies—was woolly with a thin film of walnut "dust." The mill itself was an immense concave container about waist high, with a spout for the oil to drain. The age-encrusted grindstone was motionless and silent for the moment, while an assortment of oddly sized buckets waited nearby to catch the flowing oil when crushing resumed. Corked bottles of walnut oil, displayed on an old table in the yard, were for sale, but the nutty aroma of roasted walnuts that saturated the air was not.

PEPPERCORNS AND PEPPER GRINDER Buy whole peppercorns (*poivre du moulin*) for grinding and use them. There is no substitute. Always add the ground pepper at the end of cooking a soup to achieve a full seasoning snap. The choice of pepper grinders is vast, but my favorite model is designed by Michael Graves and manufactured by Alessi, with a grinding mechanism by Peugeot. I usually don't find that designer kitchenware has the quality and engineering of this product. Owning *two* pepper grinders is ideal. Use one for grinding black peppercorns, and the other one for grinding white peppercorns into ivory or pale soups where dark specks would be unappealing.

For the walnut *croûtons*:

3 TABLESPOONS WALNUT OIL

1 TABLESPOON UNSALTED BUTTER

6 SLICES FRENCH BREAD, EACH 1 INCH THICK, CUT INTO 1-INCH CUBES

½ CUP COARSELY CHOPPED WALNUTS

For the soup:

¼ CUP WALNUT OIL

2 SMALL HEADS SAVOY CABBAGE, CORED AND THINLY SLICED

12 TO 15 TINY NEW POTATOES, UNPEELED, QUARTERED

2 TEASPOONS SALT

8 CUPS WATER

FRESHLY GROUND BLACK PEPPER

Bourgogne

CABBAGE SOUP with WALNUT OIL

SOUPE aux CHOUX à l'HUILE de NOIX de GANNAT

MAKES 6 SERVINGS

Gannat, the French village of the recipe title, lies within walnut forests in southern Bourbonnais, a close neighbor of Burgundy and Beaujolais. Near Gannat is well-known Vichy, source of the celebrated mineral water. It is also the birthplace of chef Louis Diat, who chilled a leek and potato soup (page 65), creating a dish he named vichyssoise in honor of his Bourbonnais home.

In the world of cabbage soups, this version is a departure for its use of walnut oil, creating an elusive fragrance and unique flavor. For that reason, the French do not add highly flavored aromatics, such as onions or garlic, to this soup, allowing the subtle delicacy of the walnut oil to emerge.

Buy your walnut oil from a merchant who has quick turnover of this item. If it sits too long on a shelf, it has a tendency to become rancid. At home, refrigerate your walnut oil (or any nut oil) to extend its life.

Some recipes for this soup include croûtons made by sautéing cubes of country bread in walnut oil. I have added a little butter to sweeten the walnut oil and some coarsely chopped walnuts. Their unexpected crunch and rich nuttiness add a delightful dimension to the croûtons.

To make the *croûtons*, preheat the oven to 200°F. Place 6 soup plates and a 9-by-13-inch baking pan in the oven. Heat the walnut oil and butter in a wide sauté pan over medium heat. Add the bread cubes and walnuts and cook, tossing and stirring, until the bread cubes are golden and the nuts are a golden brown. Drain briefly on paper towels, place in the heated baking pan, and reserve in the oven.

To make the soup, heat the walnut oil in a heavy 4-quart soup pot over low heat. Add the cabbage and cook, stirring often, until the cabbage is glazed with the walnut oil and softened, about 5 minutes. Add the potatoes, salt, and water and bring to a boil over high heat. Reduce the heat to low and simmer, uncovered, until the potatoes are tender, about 15 minutes.

Taste and add more salt if needed and black pepper to taste. Ladle into the heated soup plates and sprinkle with the warm walnut-scented *croûtons*. Serve at once.

Bretagne

CAULIFLOWER, ONION, and POTATO SOUP

POTAGE MALOUIN

MAKES **6** SERVINGS

1 CAULIFLOWER, LEAVES AND CORE REMOVED (ABOUT 1¼ POUNDS AFTER TRIMMING)

4 TABLESPOONS UNSALTED BUTTER

1 MEDIUM-SIZED ONION, THINLY SLICED

8 TO 9 CUPS WATER

1 TEASPOON SALT

1 CELERY STALK

3 MEDIUM-SIZED WAXY POTATOES, PEELED AND DICED

¼ TEASPOON FRESHLY GRATED NUTMEG

FRESHLY GROUND WHITE PEPPER

3 TABLESPOONS CRÈME FRAÎCHE OR LOW-FAT SOUR CREAM

¼ CUP FINELY MINCED FRESH CHIVES OR SCALLIONS

A wide sweep of land along the northern coast of Brittany is aflower with fields of vegetable treasures. This teeming truck-farm region is known in France as the "golden belt" (ceinture dorée). Three choice Breton vegetables, cauliflower, onions, and potatoes, are found in this soup, prepared in the style of Saint-Malo, an ancient walled city on this coast.

Those three vegetables are equally important in this, the ultimate cauliflower soup. Robust cauliflower flavor is mellowed by the potatoes and brightened by the onions and the tiny bite of celery. As you would expect, the soup is a delicate ivory color that looks best when sprinkled with fresh green chives or scallions at serving time.

Break and cut apart the cauliflower, freeing the small florets. Reserve 12 tiny florets for garnishing.

Melt 2 tablespoons of the butter in a heavy 4-quart soup pot over very low heat. Add the onion and cook, stirring often, until it has softened but not colored, about 5 minutes.

Add 8 cups (2 quarts) of the water, the salt, the whole celery stalk, the small cauliflower florets, and the potatoes and bring to a boil over high heat. Reduce the heat to medium, cover partially, and cook, stirring occasionally, until the cauliflower and potatoes are tender, about 15 minutes.

While the cauliflower and potatoes are cooking, prepare a bowl of ice water. Bring a small saucepan filled with water to a boil. Add the reserved tiny florets and cook until tender, 4 to 5 minutes. Remove the florets with a slotted spoon and immediately immerse them in the ice water to refresh them and to stop the cooking. Drain and set aside.

Remove the celery stalk and discard. Working with 2 or 3 ladlefuls at a time, purée the soup in a blender or food processor, processing each batch for at least 30 seconds. Return the puréed soup to the pot, and place over low heat. Add the nutmeg and white pepper to taste. Taste and add more salt if needed. Add as much of the remaining 1 cup water as needed to achieve a good consistency. Simmer for 2 minutes and swirl in the remaining 2 tablespoons butter.

Ladle into heated soup plates and garnish each serving with a spoonful of crème fraîche or sour cream, 2 very small florets, and a sprinkling of chives or scallions.

FLEMISH BEET and CELERY ROOT SOUP

POTAGE de BETTERAVES

MAKES 6 SERVINGS

4 SMALL BEETS (ABOUT 1 POUND), UNPEELED

6 SLICES FRENCH BREAD, EACH ¾ INCH THICK, CUT INTO ¾-INCH CUBES AND TOSSED IN OLIVE OIL

3 TABLESPOONS UNSALTED BUTTER

3 MEDIUM-SIZED ONIONS, FINELY CHOPPED

1 MEDIUM-SIZED CELERY ROOT, PEELED AND CUT INTO ½-INCH DICE

1 TEASPOON SALT

7 TO 8 CUPS WATER

½ TEASPOON FRESHLY GROUND BLACK PEPPER, OR TO TASTE

2 TABLESPOONS CHOPPED FRESH LOVAGE, PARSLEY, CHERVIL, CHIVES, OR SCALLION GREENS

RED WINE VINEGAR

Many cool-season root vegetables thrive in the north of France: potatoes, leeks, celery root, and, of course, beets. This soup is simple country fare, though, and quick to prepare when you need something to warm and nourish. It has an unusual glow, as the julienned beets retain their own jewel-like color, while the diced celery root cooks to a harmonious red-orange. The marvelous flavors are also in accord, as the pungent celery root, or celeriac, marries well with the mellow beets.

In France, beets are often sold in the markets already baked, wrapped in foil and ready to take home and eat. In this recipe, fresh beets are baked at home. Be sure to buy small beets, as the larger ones may be a little fibrous. Wash them carefully of their farm soil and do not trim. They may be baked as much as a day or two in advance.

Preheat the oven to 350°F. Wrap the beets in a single layer in a sheet of aluminum foil, sealing the edges tightly closed. Place in a baking pan and bake until tender, about 1 hour. During the last 10 minutes of baking, spread out the bread cubes on a baking sheet and toast in the oven to make *croûtons*. Remove the beets and *croûtons* from the oven. Unwrap the beets, allow to cool, peel, and cut into short sticks. Set the beets and *croûtons* aside.

Melt the butter in a heavy 4-quart soup pot over medium heat. Sauté the onions and celery root, stirring often, until golden, about 10 to 12 minutes. Add the salt, beets, and 7 cups of the water and bring to a boil over high heat. Reduce the heat to low and simmer, uncovered, until the celery root is tender, about 20 minutes.

Taste and add more salt if needed. Season generously with the pepper. Add as much of the remaining 1 cup water as needed to achieve a good consistency. Ladle into heated soup plates and sprinkle with the lovage or other fresh herb. Pass the *croûtons* and a cruet of good red wine vinegar at table.

> **LOVAGE** Lovage, which is similar to a wild celery, is a wonderful addition to any herb garden, and it literally grows like a weed. (It may also dominate its more delicate herbal neighbors, so keep it under control.) It is especially good in soups in which its celery taste plays an important role. Both the deep green stalks and the leaves of lovage add immeasurably to the flavor and appearance of any dish.

COOKED BEETS (*BETTERAVES ROUGES CUITES*) APPEAR IN MARKETS IN FRANCE, SAVING THE HOME COOK TIME IN THE KITCHEN.

GOOD HOUSEWIFE'S SOUP *Soupe bonne femme*—the "good housewife's soup" or the "good woman's soup"—is the name the French use for this simple leek and potato soup. I imagine *many* good housewives going to their kitchen gardens or to their root cellars. They wash the residue of farm soil from their leeks and potatoes and throw them into a pot of water. The leeks give fragrance and flavor, the potatoes add filling and substance, and the water, always a specific ingredient in France, cooks it all. The result is thrifty, easy, tasty, and satisfying. No wonder it has endured.

If milk or cream was available to the housewife at a reasonable cost, it was used instead of water and *potage bonne femme* was prepared. Once again the leeks and potatoes are essential, but the soup has taken on a richer flavor. When a curious cook investigated making *bonne femme* into a more refined soup, he or she put the entire soup through a sieve. That succulent purée blended with heavy cream became *crème bonne femme*. It's also known as *potage purée Parmentier*, to acknowledge the gentlemen who reportedly introduced the lowly potato to the French in the eighteenth century.

Ile-de-France

LEEK and POTATO SOUP
SOUPE BONNE FEMME

MAKES **6** SERVINGS

2 TABLESPOONS UNSALTED BUTTER

4 SLENDER LEEKS, WHITE AND PALE GREEN PARTS ONLY, THINLY SLICED

4 MEDIUM-SIZED WAXY POTATOES, PEELED AND DICED

8 TO 9 CUPS WATER

1 TEASPOON SALT

FRESHLY GROUND BLACK PEPPER

This soup is simplicity itself. At the outside, it takes maybe five minutes to toss together. Be sure to include a little of the pale green parts of the leeks. They are tasty and add some healthful fiber and a nice touch of color. This is not a soup with finesse, so freshly ground black pepper is expected.

An old Provençal proverb for gardeners: Plant leeks and cabbages between Saint Peter's and Saint Paul's Day. But they are fêted on the same day! So plant on June 29.

Melt the butter in a heavy 4-quart soup pot over very low heat. Sauté the leeks, stirring often, until golden, 8 to 10 minutes. Add the potatoes, 8 cups of the water, and the salt and bring to a boil over high heat. Reduce the heat to low and simmer, partially covered, until the potatoes are very tender, about 20 minutes.

When the potatoes are nearly falling apart, taste and add additional salt if needed and black pepper to taste. Crush the potatoes with a fork, if you like that texture. Add as much of the remaining 1 cup water as needed to achieve a good consistency. Then simmer briefly over medium heat to heat through.

Ladle into heated soup plates and serve immediately.

CREAM OF LEEK AND POTATO   POTAGE BONNE FEMME

VARIATION: Prepare the soup as directed, substituting milk for the water. Just before serving, whisk about ½ cup heavy cream into the soup.

CHAPTER TWO

*He had invented a recipe of lentils, cooked
in cider, served cold topped with olive oil
and saffron, served on grilled slices of
round bread used for pan bagnats.*
—Georges Pérec, *LA VIE MODE D'EMPLOI*

SOUPS *from*
THE HARVEST RESERVES:
DRIED BEANS AND GRAINS

LEFT: CHICKPEAS AND OTHER DRIED FOODS AT THE FRIDAY MORNING MARKET AT CARPENTRAS IN PROVENCE.

GATHERED FROM FERTILE FIELDS: A MOSAIC OF FORTIFYING STAPLES

The oldest of France's ancestral soups were more like today's porridges, prepared with some kind of grain or cereal. That heritage continues. Although eaten less and less today, there is a certain nostalgia for the cornmeal *gaudes*—a kind of "liquid" polenta—of the Franche-Comté.

Each small bean or lentil, or pea or grain of rice, its moisture gone in the drying process, is thirsty and ready to be plumped up by cooking in water and flavored by whatever ingredients are added. Since a liquid is essential to their use, a soup is a natural and inevitable way to prepare these dried reserves.

Volumes could be written on such French soups. The choices are immense: Dried beans are a kaleidoscope of colors and shapes and flavors and varieties. Lentils are coral, brown, green. There are chickpeas, split peas, and dried peas. Grains—rice, corn, wheat—and, by extension, grain products like breads and dumplings, expand the possibilities. Multiply all of these options by myriad flavoring-giving components and you literally have an *embarras de choix*.

The benefits of cooking dried beans are perhaps overlooked: they are packed with protein, rich in fiber, absorb a range of flavors, and are comfortingly filling. This last aspect has given dried beans a traditional role in rustic kitchens but has often prompted more sophisticated cooks to dismiss them. That is their loss. Two additional attributes add to the appeal of bean and lentil soups: they complement the richness of pig or goose, and they can extend the protein markedly in any dish that already contains meat.

LENTIL SOUP with BACON and GARLIC

SOUPE aux LENTILLES VERTES le PUY

MAKES **6** SERVINGS

¼ POUND LEAN BACON, FINELY DICED

1 MEDIUM-SIZED ONION, FINELY CHOPPED

2 CUPS DRIED LENTILS, PREFERABLY LE PUY LENTILS, WELL RINSED

2 QUARTS PLUS 1 CUP WATER

1 TEASPOON SALT

1 BOUQUET GARNI (4 FRESH PARSLEY STEMS, 2 FRESH THYME SPRIGS, 2 BAY LEAVES TIED IN 1 LARGE CELERY STALK)

2 CLOVES GARLIC, FINELY MINCED

3 MEDIUM-SIZED WAXY POTATOES, PEELED AND QUARTERED

FRESHLY GROUND BLACK PEPPER

¼ CUP FINELY MINCED FRESH PARSLEY

¼ CUP LOW-FAT SOUR CREAM

One of the specialties grown in the Auvergne region in central France are tiny, rounded deep green lentils known as lentilles vertes Le Puy. *They have a pronounced good flavor and retain their firmness and shape even when cooked until fully tender. The lentils are joined in this soup by smoked bacon, two cordial Auvergnate traditions. The alternatives to using smoked bacon are many, and you could choose your preference: sausage, ham, ham hock, or a combination. I think you need the smokiness, however, to add interest to the mellow lentil flavor.*

In the Haute-Loire département *of the Auvergne, one eats lentils on New Year's Day to be rich all year.*

Sauté the bacon in a heavy 4-quart soup pot over medium heat, stirring often, until crisp, about 10 minutes. Remove the bacon with a slotted spoon and drain on paper towels; reserve.

Discard all but 2 tablespoons of the bacon fat from the pot. Add the onion and sauté over low heat, stirring often, until lightly colored, about 8 minutes. Add the lentils and stir around in the bacon fat and onion until they are coated with the flavorful fat. Add the water, salt, bouquet garni, garlic, and potatoes and bring to a boil over high heat. Reduce the heat to low, cover, and simmer until the lentils and potatoes are tender, about 30 minutes.

Remove and discard the bouquet garni. Taste for seasoning and add more salt if needed and black pepper to taste. Quickly stir in the parsley. Ladle into heated soup plates and garnish each serving with a spoonful of sour cream and the reserved bacon pieces.

BACON With an eye toward health concerns, the recipes in this book that call for bacon (*lard fumé*) have been tested so that only the amount actually needed to give bacon's wonderful flavor is listed. Buy bacon that is *smoked*, not "smoke-flavored." It's important to read labels if you are unsure. As long as you are going to use bacon—even a small amount—by all means use the tastiest you can purchase.

¼ POUND LEAN BACON (ABOUT 5 SLICES)

1 MEDIUM-SIZED ONION, FINELY CHOPPED

1 YOUNG, SLENDER CARROT, PEELED AND CHOPPED

2 CLOVES GARLIC, FINELY MINCED

1 ROUNDED CUP GREEN SPLIT PEAS, WELL RINSED

2 TO 3 QUARTS WATER

1 TEASPOON SALT

½ SMALL HEAD LETTUCE, CORED AND CUT IN RIBBONS

1 MEDIUM-SIZED WAXY POTATO, PEELED AND DICED

1 BAY LEAF

2 FRESH THYME SPRIGS, OR ½ TEASPOON DRIED THYME

½-POUND PIECE SMOKED SAUSAGE

6 SLICES DARK RYE, EACH ½ INCH THICK, BUTTERED ON ONE SIDE

FRESHLY GROUND BLACK PEPPER

¼ CUP PLUM OR CHERRY EAU-DE-VIE

Alsace Lorraine

BACON and SPLIT PEA SOUP

SOUPE aux POIS CASSÉES et au LARD

MAKES **6** SERVINGS

One of the most commonly known French dishes is an open-faced bacon tart: the quiche Lorraine. In Lorraine, bacon is absolutely essential in local cooking. Not surprising are the many soups that include bacon (soupes au lard). Its popularity is also reflected in an old Lorraine saying: "A plate without bacon, it's a heart without joy!"

If you want to find a new level of enjoyment for this old workhorse soup, be sure to add the fruit-based eau-de-vie. The difference is so dramatic and the soup so remarkable that you'll be thinking of other dishes that could benefit from this culinary alchemy from Lorraine.

Mince 4 slices of the bacon to use as a garnish for the soup. Reserve 1 whole slice for flavoring the soup. Sauté the minced bacon in a heavy 4-quart soup pot over low heat, stirring often, until very crisp, 12 to 15 minutes. Remove the bacon pieces with a slotted spoon and drain on paper towels; reserve. Add the onion and carrot to the fat remaining in the pan and sauté over medium-low heat, stirring often, until lightly colored, 8 to 10 minutes. Add the garlic and stir into the other ingredients.

Add the split peas to the pot with 2 quarts of the water, the salt, lettuce, potato, bay leaf, and thyme. Bring to a boil over high heat, reduce the heat to low, and add the bacon slice and the sausage. Cover and simmer until all of the ingredients are well cooked, about 1½ hours.

Just before the soup is ready, preheat the oven to 400°F. Place the dark rye slices on a baking sheet and toast in the oven until crisp, 10 to 12 minutes. Set aside to use as *croûtes*.

Remove the bay leaf, thyme sprigs (if used), and bacon slice and discard. Remove the sausage, thinly slice, cover with aluminum foil, and reserve. Working with 1 or 2 ladlefuls at a time, purée the soup in a blender or food processor. Return the purée to the pot, reheat over medium heat, and add more salt if needed and black pepper to taste. Add enough of the remaining 1 quart water as needed to achieve a soup with the consistency of thick cream. Keep in mind that this soup somehow always continues to thicken.

Add the reserved sausage slices and the eau-de-vie and simmer for a few minutes until the soup is piping hot. Ladle into heated soup plates, sprinkle with the crisp bacon pieces, and serve immediately. Pass the *croûtes* at table.

dried beans

1 ROUNDED CUP DRIED WHITE BEANS, SUCH AS GREAT NORTHERN OR NAVY

3 ½ TO 4 QUARTS WATER

2 OUNCES SALT PORK, CUT INTO ¼-INCH DICE

1 YOUNG, SLENDER CARROT, PEELED AND CUT INTO THICK SLICES

1 CELERY STALK, SLICED

1 MEDIUM-SIZED ONION, CHOPPED

2 CLOVES GARLIC, FINELY MINCED

1 SLICE SMOKED HAM WITH A SMALL BONE, 3 TO 4 OUNCES, MEAT CUT INTO ½-INCH DICE AND BONE RESERVED

1 BOUQUET GARNI (6 FRESH PARSLEY STEMS, 2 BAY LEAVES, 2 FRESH THYME SPRIGS TIED IN 1 LARGE CELERY STALK)

¼ HEAD SAVOY CABBAGE, CORED AND COARSELY CHOPPED

1 MEDIUM-SIZED TURNIP OR 1 SMALL RUTABAGA, PEELED AND CUT INTO ½-INCH CUBES

1 MEDIUM-SIZED WAXY POTATO, CUT INTO 1-INCH CUBES

1 TEASPOON SALT

FRESHLY GROUND BLACK PEPPER

6 THICK SLICES RYE BREAD, CUT INTO ¾-INCH DICE, TOASTED

¼ CUP CHOPPED FRESH PARSLEY

Dordogne

PÉRIGORD HAM and BEAN SOUP

SOBRONADE

MAKES 10 TO 12 MAIN-COURSE SERVINGS

Eating a dish from Périgord is always festive. It is in the Dordogne, according to popular belief, that everyday cooking is as tempting as that of special occasions. This enduring soup illustrates that conviction. It is prepared with modest country ingredients, but would do honor to any celebration. In Périgord, the famed fattened geese and ducks provide their incomparable foie gras (and income for those who raise them). For family dining, however, it is the farm pig that continues to be the succulent standby, and it takes its place of honor in sobronade.

Rinse the beans, cover generously with cold water, and soak overnight. The next day, drain, place in a heavy saucepan, and add 2 quarts of the water. Bring to a boil and cook over high heat for 15 minutes. Reduce the heat to low and cook for 1 hour. Drain and reserve.

Sauté the salt pork gently in a heavy 4-quart soup pot over medium heat, stirring occasionally. When the pieces are golden and crisp, after 8 to 10 minutes, remove them with a slotted spoon, drain on paper toweling, and reserve.

Pour off all but 2 tablespoons of the fat from the pot. Add the carrot, celery, and onion to the fat and sauté over medium heat, stirring occasionally, until lightly colored, 10 to 12 minutes. Stir in the garlic and sauté for a few minutes, watching carefully. Add the ham and the ham bone, 1½ quarts of the water, the bouquet garni, reserved beans, cabbage, turnip or rutabaga, potato, and salt. Bring to a boil over high heat, reduce the heat to very low, and simmer, partially covered, until the beans are tender, about 30 minutes.

Taste, adding more salt if needed and a generous amount of black pepper. Thin with as much of the remaining ½ quart (2 cups) water as needed to achieve a good consistency. Simmer for a few minutes to blend the flavors.

Remove the ham bone and bouquet garni and discard. Ladle the soup into heated soup plates and garnish each serving with bits of salt pork, rye *croûtons*, and parsley.

½ CUP DRIED GREAT NORTHERN OR NAVY BEANS

3 ½ QUARTS WATER OR VEGETABLE BROTH

2 TABLESPOONS RENDERED DUCK FAT OR FINE-QUALITY LARD

3 MEDIUM-SIZED ONIONS, CHOPPED

2 OR 3 CLOVES GARLIC, FINELY MINCED

¼ TEASPOON RED PEPPER FLAKES

¼ TEASPOON *PIMENT D'ESPELETTE* (PAGE 120) OR CAYENNE PEPPER

1 SMALL HEAD SAVOY CABBAGE, CORED AND COARSELY CHOPPED

1 TEASPOON SALT

1 POUND PEELED PUMPKIN FLESH, CUT INTO 1-INCH CUBES (2 CUPS)

FRESHLY GROUND BLACK PEPPER (OPTIONAL)

le pays Basque

BEAN, PUMPKIN, and CABBAGE SOUP

SOUPE BISCAYENNE

MAKES **6** SERVINGS

The beautiful Bay of Biscay is the part of the Atlantic that lies off the Basque coast, and it has lent its name to this invitingly beautiful soup: deep orange pumpkin and dark green Savoy cabbage tumbled with plump white beans. This trio of vegetables is so vital to the cooking of the Basques that they call them les trois légumes rois *(three vegetable kings) and include them in most of their savory soups. Be sure to use duck fat or high-quality lard for this dish. It's indispensable if you want to build the full, deep flavor of the dish.*

Rinse the beans, then place in a bowl and cover generously with cold water. Soak the beans overnight. The following day, drain, place in a heavy saucepan, and add 1 quart of the water or broth. Bring to a boil and cook over high heat for 10 to 12 minutes. Reduce the heat to medium-low and cook for 45 minutes. Drain and reserve.

Melt the duck fat or lard in a heavy 4-quart soup pot over medium heat. Add the onions and cook, stirring often, until very lightly colored, about 8 minutes. Add the garlic, reduce the heat to low, and cook for an additional 2 to 3 minutes. Do not allow the garlic to brown.

Add 2 quarts of the water or broth, the reserved beans, red pepper flakes, *piment d'Espelette* or cayenne, and the cabbage and bring to a boil over high heat. Reduce the heat to medium and cook, uncovered, until the beans are almost tender, about 20 minutes.

Add the salt and pumpkin cubes and continue to cook until the pumpkin is tender, about 15 minutes. Taste and add more salt if needed and black pepper to taste, if desired. Serve immediately in heated soup plates.

Champagne-le Nord
PLOWMAN'S DRIED PEA SOUP
SOUPE au LABOUREUR
MAKES **6** SERVINGS

2 CUPS DRIED WHOLE PEAS

1 HAM HOCK, ABOUT 1 POUND

OLIVE OIL IF NEEDED

1 MEDIUM-SIZED ONION, FINELY DICED

2 SLENDER LEEKS, WHITE AND PALE GREEN PARTS ONLY, THINLY SLICED

4 YOUNG, SLENDER CARROTS, PEELED AND THINLY SLICED

2 TO 3 QUARTS WATER

1 ½ TEASPOONS SALT

½ TEASPOON FRESHLY GROUND BLACK PEPPER

WEDGES OF WHOLE-GRAIN COUNTRY BREAD

Using whole dried peas in a country-style soup is a good alternative to the more common split peas. Their lovely pale green is more appealing than the yellow-beige of split peas and is in harmony with the deep pink of the pork and the orange of the carrots. The dried peas are cooked until just tender, but not overcooked, so that they retain their shape. Since this is such a hearty dish (remember those laboureurs*), I urge you to buy or bake a round loaf of country bread with a crunchy crust. Cut the bread into thick wedges (*quignons*) like the French do and serve it at your table—or take the soup and the bread out to the fields as the French used to do.*

Soak the peas overnight in cold water to cover, or at least 2 hours in lukewarm water. Drain, rinse, and reserve.

Trim off little bits of fat from the ham hock and cook them in a heavy 4-quart soup pot over low heat, stirring often, until the fat is rendered, 15 to 20 minutes. You will need 2 tablespoons of fat. Discard the cracklings. Add olive oil, if needed, to make up the difference (see note).

Add the onion, leeks, and carrots to the pot with the rendered fat and sauté over medium heat, stirring often, until lightly golden, 8 to 10 minutes. Add 2 quarts of the water and the ham hock and bring to a boil. Reduce the heat to very low, cover partially, and simmer for 1 hour.

Add the reserved peas and continue to cook, stirring occasionally, until the peas are tender, about 40 minutes.

Remove the ham hock from the pot and place it on a carving board. Cut off the meat, dice it, and return it to the pot. Thin the soup with as much of the remaining 1 quart water as needed to achieve a good consistency. Taste for seasoning, carefully adding salt if needed (depending on saltiness of ham hock) and the black pepper. Reheat over medium heat. Ladle into heated soup bowls and serve. Pass a basket of the country bread at table.

NOTE: You may use all olive oil or good-quality lard in place of the rendered fat.

Corse

CHICKPEA SOUP with PROSCIUTTO

SOUPE de POIS CHICHES CORSE

MAKES **6** SERVINGS

2 CANS (15 OR 16 OUNCES EACH) CHICKPEAS

2 TABLESPOONS OLIVE OIL

2 CLOVES GARLIC, FINELY MINCED

1 SMALL ONION, FINELY CHOPPED

4 OR 5 FRESH SAGE LEAVES

1 BAY LEAF

2 SMALL FRESH ROSEMARY SPRIGS

2 TO 2 ½ QUARTS WATER

1 TEASPOON SALT

¼ POUND THINLY SLICED PROSCIUTTO, CUT INTO SHORT RIBBONS

FRESHLY GROUND BLACK PEPPER

6 THICK *CROÛTES* (PAGE 79)

3 PLUM TOMATOES, SEEDED AND CHOPPED

Vivid flavors are blended together in this chickpea soup. The fragrant herbs— rosemary, bay, and sage—are often found in French cooking, and the prosciutto is, of course, of Italian origin. (Superior Corsican prosciutto is produced on the island.) The chickpeas, garlic, and olive oil are traditional Mediterranean flavors. All these combine to create an unusual soup from the island of Corsica. In warm weather, this soup is served sprinkled with small chunks of vine-ripened plum tomato. Not only is the red color visually important, but also the fresh flavor of the tomato makes a sweet contrast to the herbal aromas and saltiness of the ham.

Empty the cans of chickpeas into a large sieve, rinse thoroughly, drain, and reserve.

Heat the olive oil in a heavy 4-quart soup pot over very low heat. Sauté the garlic and onion, stirring often, until lightly golden, 10 to 12 minutes. Add the chickpeas, herbs, and 2 quarts of the water, the salt, and the prosciutto. Bring to a boil over high heat, reduce the heat to low, and simmer until the onion is nearly melted, about 30 minutes.

Remove the herbs and discard. Taste, adding more salt if needed and black pepper to taste. Thin with as much of the remaining ½ quart (2 cups) water as needed to achieve a good soup consistency. Simmer for a few minutes to blend the flavors.

Place the *croûtes* in the bottom of heated soup plates and ladle the hot soup on top. Garnish with a sprinkling of tomato morsels and serve immediately.

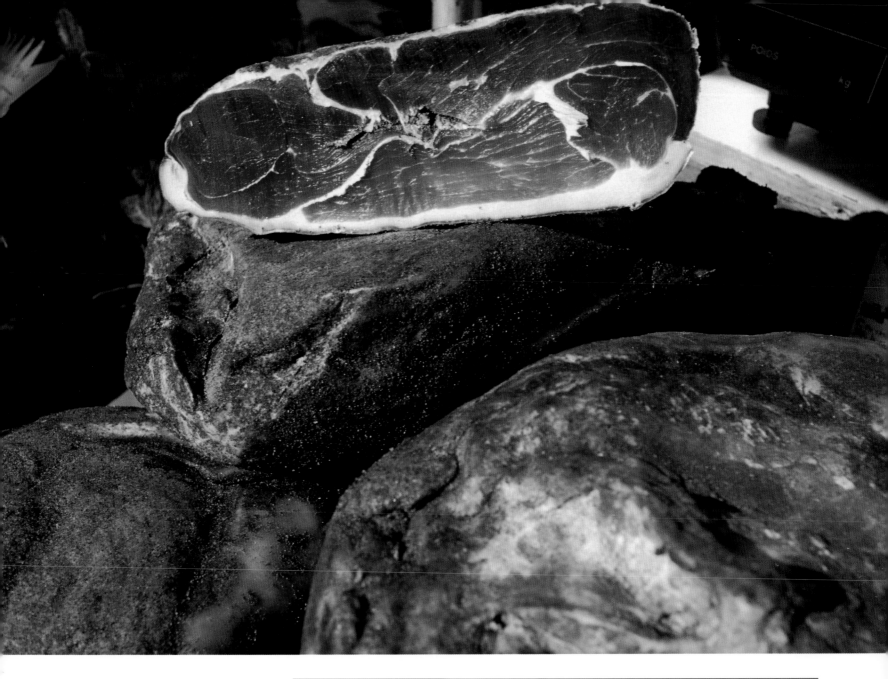

PROSCIUTTO AT MARKET ON THE PLACE
MARÉCHAL FOCH, AJACCIO, CORSICA.

CORSICA Of all the regions of France, none evokes more mystery than Corsica. Isolated in the Mediterranean, Corsica boasts a history that is as turbulent as we might expect of an island. It has long been coveted by traders and sailors for its strategic position on the Mediterranean trade routes. Its high granite peaks have made agriculture on the island laborious and difficult. With an abundance of local chestnut trees, the pigs of Corsica customarily find an ever-present supply of nourishment. They are raised at liberty for the most part and are free to forage for the nuts and to graze on native herbage. Consequently, Corsican pork is especially esteemed and enjoyed.

dried beans

½ CUP DRIED RED OR WHITE BEANS

2 ½ QUARTS WATER

2 TABLESPOONS SEASONED COOKING FAT (SEE NOTE) OR STRAINED
PAN DRIPPINGS FROM A ROAST

1 SMALL ONION, FINELY CHOPPED

2 YOUNG, SLENDER CARROTS, PEELED AND CUT INTO ½-INCH
DICE

1 MEDIUM-SIZED TURNIP, PEELED AND CUT INTO ½-INCH DICE

½ CELERY STALK, THINLY SLICED

1 BAY LEAF

¼ CUP LENTILS, RINSED

¼ CUP SPLIT PEAS, RINSED

1 TEASPOON SALT

FRESHLY GROUND BLACK PEPPER

Normandie

WINTER LENTIL, BEAN, and SPLIT PEA SOUP

POTAGE d'HIVER NORMANDE

MAKES **6** SERVINGS

This is a colorful and accurate rendition of a Norman country soup. It's essential to use the Norman animal fat mixture—so little is needed to add the authentic, characteristic flavor. If you don't have a small jar of graisse de Cherbourg (see note) in the fridge, you might think about making a batch. Another option is to save and strain some pan drippings from your next roast—beef, pork, chicken, or lamb—and use a little in this recipe.

Since this is a winter soup, only the standard root vegetables, carrots and turnips, are suggested. Obviously, include any other fresh vegetables you'd like, as they will work well with the three dried legumes. Note that there is no garnish for this simple soup, but should you have fresh herbs, it's always good to grace any dish with their aroma.

Rinse the beans, then place in a bowl and cover generously with cold water. Soak the beans overnight. The following day, drain, place in a heavy saucepan, and add 1 quart of the water. Bring to a boil and cook over high heat for 10 to 12 minutes. Reduce the heat to medium-low and cook for 45 minutes. Drain and reserve.

Heat the seasoned cooking fat in a heavy 4-quart soup pot over medium heat. Add the onion and cook, stirring often, until uniformly golden in color, 8 to 10 minutes. Add the carrots, turnip, celery, bay leaf, 1 quart of the water, the reserved beans, lentils, and split peas. Bring to a boil, reduce heat to low, and simmer, partially covered, until the beans are tender, about 20 minutes. (The turnips are well cooked before the rest of the vegetables and become translucent. But I like the flavor they add to the broth, so I add them when I add the rest of the vegetables.) Add the salt and simmer for an additional 5 minutes. Thin with as much of the remaining ½ quart (2 cups) water as needed to achieve a good consistency. Taste and add more salt if needed and black pepper to taste. Ladle the soup into heated soup plates and serve at once.

NOTE: Not content simply to use their abundant and delicious sweet butter, the frugal cooks of Normandy created another fat for cooking known as *graisse de Cherbourg* or *graisse normande* (Norman fat). Those who needed to use their cows' milk for making cheeses they could sell often made this *graisse*. The seasoned fat, a clarified blend of melted pork and beef fat, is given additional aroma by simmering it with fresh vegetables (onions, carrots, turnips) and herbs (parsley, thyme, rosemary). Like the goose or duck fat from a confit in southwestern France, even a small amount adds a unique flavor. It is even the basis for a special vegetable soup in western Normandy. This product is also commercially prepared and is sold in butcher's shops or *chez charcuterie*.

LEFT: OLD NORMAN FARMHOUSE AND SIDE
BUILDING, WITH STEEP THATCHED ROOF.

ADDING BREAD TO SOUPS

One of the most natural acts when dining informally is to spin a bit of bread around the bottom of a nearly empty bowl of soup. The French, understanding this age-old bread-and-soup connection, pair their fragrant loaves in countless ways to their repertoire of soups, adding texture, body, flavor, and often color in the match. Soup-soaked bread and bread-filled soup are homespun, thrifty, and appropriate partners.

PANADES: One extremely old soup idea is a *panade*, or bread soup. It is prepared by joining bread and liquid in an ovenproof pot and baking them together, to create a full-bodied soup. There is nothing as important when preparing nourishing and fortifying *panades*, as making sure the bread you begin with is appropriate. Have a good time at home and bake a husky loaf. If that is unrealistic, buy crusty, firm bread at your favorite bakery. Do not use commercially manufactured bread or the results may be dreadful. Also, before beginning a *panade*, the bread should be stale. The drier the bread, the more tasty soup it will soak up.

There are two ways of assembling a French *panade*. In one, slices or pieces of bread are immersed in the broth of a soup pot and simmered slowly until the bread dissolves. The soup is then whisked and the emulsified mixture of bread and broth becomes a purée, thickening the soup. (*Panades* have been used for many years to thicken sauces as well, especially prior to the development of roux-based sauces.)

A second and simpler *panade* method is ancient: slices of good bread are arranged in a seasoned broth and baked. I think the baked *panades* are even tastier when cooled and presented in individual earthenware crocks.

GRATINÉES: Many French soups are augmented by a cap of bread (and often cheese) before being placed in a hot oven or under a broiler to brown. A soup with a crusty, chewy exterior that yields to a succulent interior is known as *une gratinée*. The word *gratinée* is used internationally now, even finding its way to packaged grocery store items. The French verb *gratiner* means "to prepare a dish with bread crumbs." The French also speak of *le gratin*, Gallic slang that means "the upper crust" (of society).

DUMPLINGS: From Alsatian kitchens in northeast France to southwestern farmhouse stoves, French cooks enrich pots of soup by adding dumplings. They are based on a starchy solid (flour, cornmeal, bread cubes) enriched with a locally favorite fat (duck, goose, butter) and flavored with aromatics, and everything is bound together with eggs. Because of the eggs, dumplings should be cooked in a soup broth that barely simmers—a boiled dumpling is a tough dumpling. It is a good idea to put a lid on the soup pot so that the fragrant steam can be captured to help cook the dumplings. Leave plenty of growing room for the dumplings, too, as they will expand. Dumplings usually have finished cooking when they bob on the surface.

TREMPETTES: To bolster a soup, the French place a wedge or chunk of sturdy bread in the bottom of a bowl and ladle steaming soup over the top. In fact, most country soups are served in this manner. These pieces of bread that are meant to get a soaking are called *trempettes*, and the soup with the wedge of bread is a *trempée*. Freshly grated bread crumbs also find their way into French soups as a flavorful thickener. Of course, when all of these measures aren't quite enough, the French break off a crunchy piece of a baguette and eat bread at the side as well.

CROÛTONS AND CROÛTES: Diced nuggets of bread, toasted crisp and fragrant, accompany hot and cold soups, a practice that is no longer exclusively French, although the origin of *croûtons* (little crusts) surely is. Toasts of bread customarily sliced thin are *croûtes* (crusts).

The most important thing to remember when making a batch of crusty little cubes of bread (*croûtons*) or crisp, crusty slices of bread (*croûtes*) is not to be in a hurry. Your bread, which should have a good crust and firm crumb, must be absolutely stale. It takes time and some care to produce perfectly golden, uniformly cooked nuggets. Haste can result in burned *croûtes*.

The *croûtons* for serving with soup are not like those you want for salad. They have to be able to stand up to the heat and the wetness of the soup and stay reasonably crunchy as the soup is eaten—clear to the bottom of the bowl, if necessary. (Salad *croûtons* have a much easier time of it.) Therefore the bread should be stale and the *croûtons* crisp on all sides. The fat used for *croûtons* is generally butter or olive oil, while *croûtes* are sometimes browned in goose or duck fat, as well as butter or olive oil.

For *croûtons*, the easiest way to see to it that all sides brown evenly is to add 2 to 3 tablespoons of fat to a 10- to 12-inch sauté pan with sloping sides and to heat until hot but not smoking. Add 2 to 3 cups of stale cubes of bread of any size, from ¼-inch morsels of fine, firm white bread to ¾-inch chunks of coarse country bread, to the pan and toss and toss so that all the sides of the cubes are exposed to a little of the fat. Keep the pan moving or a metal spatula lifting the cubes up off the pan's surface. You can continue cooking the cubes over medium heat until they are the color you want, or you can put them on a baking sheet and finish their toasting in a 350°F oven. They need to be peeked at now and then until they are done (8 to 10 minutes), but they do not need the same constant care as they require on the stove top.

If you want your crusty *croûtons* to have a garlic scent, simply add 2 or 3 whole garlic cloves to the oil prior to the first browning step in the sauté. Let the garlic steep in the oil over very low heat for 5 minutes, stirring occasionally. Remove the garlic and raise the temperature of the oil before you add the bread.

For *croûtes*, the oven method is foolproof. Slice French bread into thin ovals (best for cream soups), and slice country, whole-grain, or rye bread into thicker slices or half slices (best for chunky, country-style soups). Spread each side of the bread with a *very* thin layer of fat. Place the slices in neat rows on a baking sheet and place in a 350° to 400°F oven. In 5 minutes, check the bottom of a bread slice (the bottom will brown more quickly than the top because of its contact with the hot metal baking sheet). As soon as the bottoms are golden brown (5 to 8 minutes), take the baking sheet out of the oven. Turn all of the bread slices over and return them to the oven. This time the browning takes less time, 3 to 5 minutes. Remove from the oven and cool the *croûtes* on a rack.

Store both the *croûtes* and the *croûtons* in a sealed canister. They will keep for several weeks.

For the dumplings:

2 EGGS

1 ½ CUPS ALL-PURPOSE FLOUR

1 TEASPOON SALT

½ TEASPOON FRESHLY GROUND BLACK PEPPER

¼ TEASPOON FRESHLY GRATED NUTMEG

For the broth:

2 QUARTS BEEF BROTH FROM POT-AU-FEU OR HOMEMADE BEEF BROTH

¼ CUP FINELY CHOPPED FRESH PARSLEY

1 CUP CRÈME FRAÎCHE

SALT

FRESHLY GROUND BLACK PEPPER

Alsace Lorraine

SMALL DUMPLINGS in BEEF BROTH

POTAGE aux FINES QUENELLES

MAKES **6** SERVINGS

When Alsatian cooks have made a pot-au-feu, this soup is often prepared for a light evening meal with the flavor-rich leftover broth. The recipe is also frequently seen, even in French cookbooks, by its German name, Riwelesupp, or by an appropriate union of the French and German (both culinary and linguistic), soupe aux riweles.

To make the dumplings, place the eggs in a food processor and process briefly to blend. Add the flour, salt, pepper, and nutmeg and pulse until the mixture becomes crumbly. Gently gather the dough into a ball. Pinch off small pieces of the dough and shape into thimble-sized ovals between your palms.

Bring the beef broth to a boil over high heat in a 4-quart soup pot. Reduce the heat to a gentle simmer, add the dumplings, cover, and cook for 10 minutes without lifting the lid. The dumplings are done when rise to the surface.

Add the parsley and crème fraîche to the soup pot and stir gently until thoroughly mixed. Simmer for a few minutes over low heat, then season the broth with salt and black pepper to taste. Ladle the dumplings and broth into heated soup plates and serve at once.

LEFT: THOSE SMALL FARMS THAT ARE LUCKY TO HAVE A FEW GOOD HENS FOR LAYING CAN READILY SELL THEIR SURPLUS TO FRENCH COOKS WHO INSIST ON "FARM-FRESH" EGGS.

Bretagne

ONION SOUP with BUCKWHEAT CREPES

SOUPE à l'OIGNON aux CRÊPES

MAKES **6** SERVINGS

¼ CUP LIGHTLY SALTED BUTTER

3 MEDIUM-SIZED ONIONS, THINLY SLICED

2 TABLESPOONS ALL-PURPOSE FLOUR

2 QUARTS WATER OR VEGETABLE BROTH

1 TEASPOON SALT

FRESHLY GROUND BLACK PEPPER

4 TO 6 BUCKWHEAT CREPES (RECIPE FOLLOWS)

¼ CUP FINELY CHOPPED SCALLION GREENS

I like this old idea of putting crepe ribbons in an onion soup. In Breton homes, crepes made without sugar often replace bread at table. As French cooking evolved, classical chefs picked up on the idea and the elegant consommé Celestine, a faultless clear chicken broth with slender ribbons of delicately herbed crepes, was created.

Melt the butter in a heavy 4-quart soup pot over low heat. Add the onions and cook, stirring often, until soft and golden, 10 to 12 minutes. Add flour and cook an additional 2 minutes, stirring often. Pour the water or broth over the onions and add the salt. Cover partially and simmer until the onions become meltingly tender, 20 to 30 minutes. Taste and add more salt if needed and black pepper to taste.

Cut each crepe in half and then cut crosswise into short ribbons ¼ inch wide. Ladle the soup into heated soup plates, add the crepe ribbons, and sprinkle with the scallions. Serve immediately.

THE ONIONS OF ROSCOFF One of the many places in France known for the quality of its fresh vegetables is Brittany, and the northern coast, particularly near the town of Roscoff, is legendary for exceptionally fine onions. Not only have these onions been shipped all over France, but they also are known across the English Channel. Accounts exist from the past that describe English housewives waiting impatiently for the arrival of the "Johnny Roscoffs," or Breton onion vendors, who crossed the channel in their small boats brimming with onions. Relying on the lusty typical cries (*les criées*) of a French vegetable hawker, the Bretons handily sold their pungent products on the streets of London.

BUCKWHEAT CREPES
CREPES au SARRASIN
MAKES 12 TO 15 CREPES

2 TABLESPOONS LIGHTLY SALTED BUTTER, MELTED

1 CUP BUCKWHEAT FLOUR

2 EGGS

¼ TEASPOON SALT

1 CUP MILK

¼ CUP WATER

2 TO 3 TABLESPOONS UNSALTED BUTTER, MELTED, MIXED WITH
1 TABLESPOON OIL FOR COOKING CREPES

To make the batter in a blender, combine all the ingredients in the blender container and mix at high speed for 10 seconds or so. Turn off the motor, clean the sides of the container with a rubber spatula, and then replace the lid. Blend for another 30 to 40 seconds. Pour the batter into a storage container and refrigerate for at least 1 hour before using. Add additional milk or water if necessary to thin. It should have the consistency of heavy cream. To make the batter by hand, combine the butter, flour, and eggs in a mixing bowl and whisk until thoroughly mixed. Whisking continuously, add the salt and ½ cup of the milk to the batter to make a smooth paste. Add the remaining milk and the water as needed to make a thinner batter if desired.

Heat a 6- or 7-inch crepe pan over high heat until a drop of water sizzles instantly when flicked into the pan. Brush with a small amount of the butter-oil mixture. Pour in about 2 tablespoons of the crepe batter and swirl the batter to cover the bottom evenly. Any batter that does not stick to the bottom should be poured back into the batter container. The crepes should be extremely thin—no thicker than 1/16 inch.

Cook the crepe until the edges become golden brown (generally 30 to 40 seconds) and can be loosened with a metal spatula. Flip the crepe over with the spatula and cook the other side even more briefly, about 20 seconds. Transfer to a plate. Repeat with the remaining batter, brushing the pan with more of the butter-oil mixture and adjusting the heat as necessary. Separate the crepes with a piece of parchment or waxed paper as they are stacked on the plate. Wrap the crepes, plate and all, with plastic wrap and refrigerate. Bring to room temperature before separating and using the crepes.

SUBSTANTIAL COUNTRY BREAD IS OFTEN SOLD
BY WEIGHT OR BY THE SLICE, RATHER THAN BY
THE LOAF.

TREMPETTES Folkloric descriptions stand in place of precise recipes for the following three soups that give us a glimpse of the France of another time, of a time when an abundance of local wine and plenty of leftover bread were always at hand. The most well known of these traditional soups is *bijane*, from the western part of the Loire Valley. The other two, from central France as well, are known as *trempées*, from the French verb *tremper*, "to soak."

BIJANE D'ANJOU, from Anjou in the Loire: "The *bijane* is a small collation made especially in the afternoon, around four o'clock, in the hot summer. It is composed of crumbled bread in red country wine, the wine being sweetened with sugar and very chilled."

TREMPÉE AU VIN NIVERNAIS, from the ancient province of Nivernais in Burgundy: "Crumble dried bread in a sandstone bowl and moisten half with cold water, half with red wine, equally cold. Sugar according to your taste."

TREMPÉE AU VIN ORLÉANAIS, from Orléans in the Loire: "Crumble some very dry bread in a faience bowl. Moisten with some cold water. Sugar according to your taste. Pour, at the moment of service, a good bottle of red wine, raised from the cellar. Stir and eat with a spoon."

Bourgogne

LYONNAISE RICE and ONION SOUP

SOUPE au RIZ à la LYONNAISE

MAKES 6 SERVINGS

2 TABLESPOONS LARD

1 MEDIUM-SIZED ONION, FINELY MINCED

3 TABLESPOONS WATER

2 QUARTS CHICKEN BROTH

1 TEASPOON SALT

6 TABLESPOONS ARBORIO RICE, RINSED

FRESHLY GROUND BLACK PEPPER

FINELY MINCED SCALLION GREENS (OPTIONAL)

Hands down, this is my favorite rice soup. With the grains of rice so plump, it's like a liquid risotto, a light dish but also satisfyingly filling at the same time. Its restorative flavor depends on three important elements: that an authentic lard be used fearlessly (so little adds so much goût), that the onions be very slowly cooked until golden, and that a homemade chicken broth or a low-sodium canned broth that has been rescued (page 214) be used.

Originally the Lyonnaise prepared this soup with barding fat or unsmoked bacon that was cut into nuggets to melt with the onions. It is easier today to use good-quality lard.

Melt the lard in a heavy 4-quart soup pot over low heat. Add the onion and water, cover, and cook, stirring as needed to prevent scorching, until the onion is golden but not brown, about 20 minutes. Keep a little cup of water by the soup pot and add a spoonful now and then, as water helps in this slow-cooking process.

Once the onion is golden, add the broth and salt. Cover partially and cook over low heat, stirring occasionally, 15 to 20 minutes. Remove the cover, add the rice, and continue to cook, uncovered, over low heat for 15 minutes. Bite into a few rice grains to test their firmness. The rice should hold its shape but should also be succulently tender. Continue to cook until that point is reached.

Taste and add more salt if needed and black pepper to taste. Ladle the soup into heated soup plates and serve immediately, very hot. If you have them, sprinkle with minced scallions.

Franche-Comté

PURÉED ROOT VEGETABLE SOUP with BACON-and-ONION TOASTS

POTAGE aux RAVES et CROÛTES COMTOISE

MAKES 6 SERVINGS

2 SLENDER LEEKS, WHITE AND PALE GREEN PARTS ONLY, THINLY SLICED

2 MEDIUM-SIZED WAXY POTATOES, PEELED AND SLICED

2 YOUNG, SLENDER CARROTS, PEELED AND SLICED

1 RUTABAGA, PEELED AND CUT INTO 1-INCH PIECES

1 PARSNIP, PEELED AND SLICED

1 TURNIP, PEELED AND SLICED

1 SMALL TO MEDIUM-SIZED CELERY ROOT, PEELED AND CUT INTO 1-INCH PIECES

1 RED ONION, SLICED

1 TEASPOON SALT

6 FRESH PARSLEY SPRIGS

6 TO 7 CUPS WATER

FRESHLY GROUND BLACK PEPPER

BACON-AND-ONION TOASTS (RECIPE FOLLOWS)

As one of the simplest soups in this book to prepare, this soup has the added bonus of being the one with the fewest calories. All the ingredients are cooked to tenderness and puréed. While it may be more customary to brown the aromatics in fat, I have not done that with this dish. Given the wealth of full-of-flavor vegetables, this soup has more than ample intensity. And since it is fat free, the accompanying croûtes *can be enjoyed nearly guilt free.*

Put the leeks, potatoes, carrots, rutabaga, parsnip, turnip, celery root, onion, salt, 4 sprigs of the parsley, and 6 cups of the water in a heavy 4-quart soup pot. Bring to a boil, reduce the heat to low, and simmer, uncovered until the vegetables are tender, about 20 minutes. All the vegetables should be tender when a knife easily slides through a carrot slice. While the soup cooks, remove the leaves from the remaining 2 parsley sprigs and finely mince them. Set aside.

Working with 1 or 2 ladlefuls at a time, purée the soup in a blender, processing each batch until it is creamy. Return the purée to the pot and place over medium-low heat to reheat. Thin with enough of the remaining 1 cup water to achieve a good consistency.

Taste and add more salt if needed and black pepper to taste. Ladle into heated soup plates, sprinkle each serving with the reserved parsley, and accompany with the *croûtes*.

BACON-and-ONION TOASTS
CROÛTES COMTOISE
MAKES 6 SERVINGS

These great croûtes *(toasts) can take even the most banal soup (canned, for example) and make it an event. The aroma alone from the oven sets the tone that something special is about to be served.*

1 POUND (ABOUT 22 SLICES) LEAN BACON, CUT CROSSWISE INTO ¼-INCH-WIDE RIBBONS

1 MEDIUM-SIZED ONION

2 TABLESPOONS ALL-PURPOSE FLOUR

¼ CUP MILK

3 TO 4 OUNCES COMTÉ, OR OTHER GRUYÈRE-STYLE CHEESE, THINLY SHAVED OR GRATED

SALT

FRESHLY GROUND BLACK PEPPER

FRESHLY GRATED NUTMEG

6 THIN SLICES COARSE COUNTRY BREAD

2 TABLESPOONS UNSALTED BUTTER, MELTED AND LIGHTLY BROWNED

Put the bacon in a heavy 2-quart saucepan and cover with cold water. Slowly bring to a simmer over low heat to remove the excess salt. Drain off the water and lay the bacon on paper towels to dry. Chop the onion and bacon together into small pieces.

Add the bacon-onion mixture to the same saucepan. Cook over low heat, stirring often, until the onion is tender but has no color, about 15 minutes. If necessary, add a little water to avoid browning the onion. Preheat the oven to 450°F.

Pour off any excess bacon fat. Sprinkle the flour over the bacon-onion mixture and combine well. Add the milk and cook over medium heat, stirring often, until the flour is well cooked and the mixture has becomes a thick spread, about 10 minutes. Stir in the cheese and taste for seasoning, adding salt and black pepper and a little freshly grated nutmeg to taste.

Divide the bacon-onion mixture into 6 equal portions and spread a portion on each slice of bread. Drizzle each with a little browned butter and place on a baking sheet. Brown in the oven for 2 to 3 minutes. Serve the toasts very hot with the puréed root vegetable soup or your favorite soup from the Franche-Comté.

BAY-SCENTED CHICKPEA FLOUR SOUP (*SOUPE AU BÂTON*)

This simple, bland soup has an affecting story to tell. In the past, during the lean winter
months in the hill villages of Provence, fresh vegetables were difficult to find and meat
impossible. Provençale cooks took readily available dried chickpeas, ground them, and
made a flavorful flour, which they used for thickening broth. They included garlic, of
course, for aroma, and for flavor they stirred the mixture with a branch—*bâton*—from the
bay tree (*laurier*). (Occasionally, I have seen recipes for this soup that call it *fournado*, in
the Provençal dialect.)

The procedure was simple: cook together water, olive oil, bay leaves, plenty of garlic,
chickpea flour, salt, and black pepper and stir vigorously with a branch of bay. According
to old cookbooks, the soup is done when the *bâton* "stands straight." The resulting soup is
pale yellow, creamy, and appealing. The nutty flavor of chickpea flour is good to know
about, and another tasty and traditional Provençal dish, *panisses*, uses it as well. It begins
in much the same way as the soup, but the mixture is cooked until quite thick, then allowed
to cool, and cut into little cakes in various shapes, and the cakes are fried.

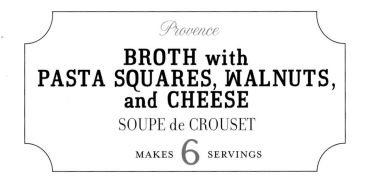

Provence

BROTH with PASTA SQUARES, WALNUTS, and CHEESE

SOUPE de CROUSET

MAKES **6** SERVINGS

1 POUND FRESH PASTA SHEETS

2 QUARTS CHICKEN BROTH

  SALT

  FRESHLY GROUND BLACK PEPPER

1 CUP CHOPPED WALNUTS

¼ CUP GRATED GRUYÈRE CHEESE

¼ CUP GRATED PARMESAN CHEESE

I was delighted when I discovered the recipe for this soup in an old Provençal cookbook I found in a cluttered, dusty, Gauloise-smoke-filled used bookstore in Montpellier. I think it is a real winner. According to the text, it is traditionally served on Christmas Eve in the Var, a region of northern Provence and the Dauphiné (land of walnut trees). It is named for the square shape of the pasta, known as croix *in French or* crous *in Provençal dialect. The pasta was traditionally rolled out on the lid of a kneading trough used for bread baking. That pasta-making procedure is essentially the only work in putting this dish together. If you buy prepared pasta, or even wonton wrappers as a substitute, the soup is prepared in seconds. You'll be happy I found the recipe, too.*

Preheat the over to 400°F. Prepare the fresh pasta according to your favorite recipe or purchase it. Cut into 1½-inch squares. Bring a large pot of salted water to boil.

Meanwhile, pour the chicken broth into a large saucepan and bring to a simmer over medium-high heat. Pre-cook the pasta in boiling water until al dente and drain. Quickly add the pasta sqares to the chicken broth and simmer for 1 or 2 minutes to heat through and for the flavors to blend. Add salt and black pepper to taste.

Divide the broth and pasta among 6 ovenproof soup bowls placed on a large baking sheet. Sprinkle them evenly with the walnuts and then top with the grated cheeses. Place in the oven and allow the cheese to brown, 7 to 10 minutes. Remove with care from the oven and serve immediately.

CHAPTER THREE

Fish, my handsome friend . . .
You will be in my skillet; and whatever you
shall say,
Tonight you shall fry.

—Jean de la Fontaine,
LE PETIT POISSON ET LE PÊCHEUR

SOUPS *from*
THE COASTAL WATERS: FISH AND SHELLFISH

LEFT: FISHING AND PLEASURE BOATS ARE SEEN
IN THE TIDY HARBOR AT SAINT-JEAN-DE-LUZ.

A BOUNDLESS COASTLINE

The soups of the French seacoasts are uncommonly varied, changing their basic concepts as the conditions change. The cold waters of the English Channel and the sun-warmed Mediterranean each yield specific, distinctive catches, from Dover sole to scarlet *rascasse*. Geographical specialties come into play as regional soils cause local agriculture to offer different ingredients, from butter and cider in Normandy to orange peel and olive oil in Provence. Finally, cultural contrasts between the regions reveal ancestral eating preferences, from the sardine soups of Brittany to the salt cod soups of the Basques.

The amount of seafood in the waters around France is so enormous, and the variety so great, that fish and shellfish have long been a French dietary mainstay. Widely available, when weather permitted putting out to sea, seafood long ago became the basis for satisfying, nutritious, and thrifty soups. All-in-one main courses, high in protein and lower in calories, these soups were often prepared economically with fish too bony to be eaten with knife and fork.

It takes little cooking time to make a first-rate seafood soup. Combining an assortment of fish, cut into even-sized pieces with a few aromatic vegetables and an ample amount of liquid, is about as difficult as the preparation gets.

THE NECKLACE OF GEMS The eloquence of the French language is demonstrated in the "necklace" of gems—the names of the beautiful coasts—that encircles France: in the north in the Calais region, the *Côte d'Opal* (Opal Coast); along the English Channel's chalky cliffs, the *Côte d'Albastre* (Alabaster Coast); reaching fine white sand beaches of the Normandy, the *Côte Fleurie* (Floral Coast); nearing Brittany, the *Côte Nacre* (Mother of Pearl Coast); along the abundant hills and valleys of northern Brittany, the *Côte d'Emeraude* (Emerald Coast); farther along the Breton peninsula, the gray and rose granite cliffs of the *Côte Granit*; along the Atlantic Coast near the Charentes region, with many marshy areas, the *Côte de Jade*; reaching the Languedoc on the western Mediterranean, the *Côte Vermeille*; and finally, the beautiful coastal region across southern France, the jewel of them all, the *Côte d'Azur* (Blue Coast).

4 TO 5 POUNDS BLUE CRABS OR DUNGENESS CRABS, OR 1 POUND
CRABMEAT

1 ½ POUNDS (1 QUART) MUSSELS

4 SHALLOTS, FINELY CHOPPED

3 ½ CUPS DRY WHITE TABLE WINE, PREFERABLY MUSCADET

4 ½ CUPS WATER

3 TABLESPOONS UNSALTED BUTTER

3 SLENDER LEEKS, WHITE PART AND PALE GREEN PARTS ONLY,
THINLY SLICED

2 YOUNG, SLENDER CARROTS, PEELED AND SLICED

1 TEASPOON SEA SALT

¼ TEASPOON SAFFRON THREADS, STEEPED IN ¼ CUP HOT WATER

1 BOUQUET GARNI (6 FRESH PARSLEY STEMS, 2 BAY LEAVES,
2 FRESH SPRIGS THYME TIED IN 1 LARGE CELERY STALK)

1 ½ POUNDS SEA ROBIN, CLEANED AND CUT INTO SLICES
(SEE NOTE)

FRESHLY GROUND BLACK PEPPER

¼ CUP FINELY MINCED FRESH PARSLEY

¼ POUND GRUYÈRE CHEESE

Champagne–le Nord

CALAIS CRAB and SEAFOOD SOUP
COURQUIGNOISE

MAKES **6** MAIN-COURSE SERVINGS

What makes courquignoise *so special
(as if juicy crabmeat, tender mussels, and
fresh seafood weren't enough) is the nutty,
buttery, freshly grated Gruyère added
at the moment the soup is served. One old
French recipe suggests that the cheese be
sprinkled with* abondament, *which does
not translate as taking leave of the senses,
but rather, it means with "abundance,"
lavishly. Simply put, add plenty.*

*Remember to remove the Gruyère
cheese from the refrigerator and let it come
to room temperature while you prepare the
soup. Grate it immediately before serving
(a rotary grater works best), so that the
cheese is tender, fragrant, and supple
when served.*

Scrub whole crabs thoroughly under cold running water and reserve. If using crabmeat,
reserve.

Preheat the oven to 250°F. Place a roasting pan, a platter, and 6 soup plates in the oven
to preheat.

Clean the mussels according to the directions on page 97. Put the mussels, 1 chopped
shallot, and ½ cup each of the wine and water in a wide stainless-steel or enameled skillet
and place over high heat. Cover and cook, shaking the skillet to distribute the mussels so
they will open evenly, until all the mussels have opened, 5 to 7 minutes. Remove from the
heat and discard any mussels that have not opened. Shell the mussels, put them in the
heated roasting pan, cover with aluminum foil to keep warm, and reserve in oven. Strain
the mussel poaching liquid through a sieve lined with a double layer of damp cheesecloth
and reserve to use in the final soup assembly.

Melt the butter in a heavy 4-quart soup pot over low heat. Add the remaining 3 shallots
and the leeks, cover, and cook for 10 minutes, stirring from time to time. The vegetables
must soften but not take on any color. Add the remaining 3 cups wine, the remaining
4 cups water, the carrots, sea salt, saffron and water, and the bouquet garni. Bring to a boil
over high heat, reduce the heat to low, cover, and simmer for 5 minutes.

If using whole crabs, add them to the soup pot, cover, and simmer until the crabs are pink or red and completely cooked throughout, not more than 10 minutes. Lift out the crabs and let cool until they can be handled, then remove the claws and legs and the meat from the bodies (see page 96 for directions). Add the crabmeat and crab legs and claws to the roasting pan, re-cover with foil, and return to the oven to keep warm.

Add the reserved mussel cooking liquid to the soup pot and stir well to combine. Add the fish slices, cover, and poach over very low heat at a simmer until the fish is opaque throughout, 8 to 10 minutes.

Carefully remove the fish from the pot with a slotted spoon and place in the center of the heated platter. Add the crabmeat to the fish and surround with the mussels and crab legs and claws. Pour a ladleful of the soup broth over the hot seafood platter and cover with foil to keep hot.

Remove the bouquet garni and discard, and then strain the broth through a fine-mesh sieve. Return the broth to the soup pot, taste and add salt if needed, black pepper to taste, and the parsley. Simmer over low heat while you grate the cheese. (You should have about 1 cup cheese.)

Ladle the broth into the heated soup plates. Sprinkle with plenty of Gruyère cheese and serve the seafood platter along with the broth. Don't forget to provide nutcrackers or special shellfish pincers for your guests.

NOTE: The authentic recipes for this soup call for sea robins (*grondins*), also known as gurnards, which are unavailable in most of the United States. Substitute mullet or cod, but remember that the fish play a supporting role here: the crabs are the stars of *courquignoise*. Available all year, the hard-shelled blue crab on the Atlantic coast and the Dungeness on the Pacific coast are true American counterparts of the common European crab (*tourteau*) used by the French on the English Channel. Figure on about ¾ pound of whole crab per person. Crab shells deepen the flavor and color of the soup immeasurably, so try to prepare *courquignoise* with whole crabs. In a pinch, however, dressed or picked crabmeat may be substituted.

CRABS AT A SHELLFISH STALL ON THE DOCK AT BOULOGNE-SUR-MER, THE LARGEST FISHING PORT IN FRANCE.

CRACKING AND CLEANING CRABS

In the recipes in this book, all the crabs are cooked before their meat is extracted. The crabs you buy should be very much alive when you add them to the pot. Cook them according to the directions in individual recipes. There is scrumptious meat in the body, the claws, and the legs. To retrieve these treasures takes a little time, but it is not difficult. In some recipes, however, the meat is not extracted by the cook; rather, it is done at table.

Once the crab is cooked, twist the claws and legs to break them free from the crab body. With a nutcracker, break through the shell of the legs and carefully pick out the meat with a shellfish pick. Crack, but do not crush, the harder shells of the claw. Again, pick out the meat.

On the underside of the crab body is a tail flap. Twist to remove this and discard. Remove the interior body from the hard top shell, and find and discard the little twin gills that sit on each side of the body. Carefully remove the meat from the body by sorting through and picking it out, discarding any connective membranes.

Save all the crab shells. Put them into a heavy-duty clear plastic bag and smash into small pieces. Freeze for another recipe.

This whole procedure is much simpler than it sounds. It almost takes longer to read these directions than to gather the gems of crabmeat.

FARM-RAISED OYSTERS AND MUSSELS ARE AVAILABLE AT THIS SMALL SHOP NEAR SÈTE ON THE MEDITERRANEAN COAST.

CLEANING MUSSELS Today, most of the mussels that we buy are harvested from safe, controlled breeding grounds, so we do not have to worry about those taken from polluted waters. These blue-black bivalves must be alive when you begin to cook them, however. If a shell is opened slightly, tap on it and it should close. If it does not, discard the mussel.

Scrub mussels under cold running water, either using a brush or briskly scraping one shell against another. The beard of a mussel is its lifeline. One end is attached deep within its shell, the other is fastened to underwater surfaces. When mussels are harvested, beards are ripped free with an occasional fragment still clinging to the mussel. Only pull these inner beards free reasonably close to cooking time, so the mussels will remain alive. If the mussels are large, you can remove the rubbery dark ring around the mussel meat before serving.

There are two schools of thought about soaking mussels before cooking. Some people believe they emit sand if they are soaked in salted water for a few hours and, by adding flour or cornmeal to the soaking water, the mussels fatten at the same time.

Others believe that, along with the sand, some fresh sea flavor is lost during soaking. I choose a middle method. I clean the mussels thoroughly and leave them in a large bowl of cool water while assembling everything else needed for the dish. I steam open the mussels in the recipe's liquid and aromatics. I then remove the mussels and *slowly* and carefully pour the broth through a sieve lined with dampened cheesecloth. Most of the remaining sand stays at the bottom of the soup pot, while tiny grit will be caught in the dampened layers of the cheesecloth. Highly absorbent paper towels or coffee filters can be used in place of the cheesecloth.

3 CUPS DRY WHITE TABLE WINE

3 CUPS WATER

2 SHALLOTS, MINCED

1 1/2 POUNDS ASSORTED FIRM-FLESHED FISH SUCH AS SEA BASS
FILLETS, HALIBUT FILLETS, COD STEAKS OR FILLETS, OR
SNAPPER FILLETS, BONES AND SKIN REMOVED

1 TEASPOON SEA SALT

1 1/2 TEASPOONS FRESHLY GROUND BLACK PEPPER

1 POUND (ABOUT 3 CUPS) MUSSELS

2 MEDIUM-SIZED ONIONS, FINELY MINCED

1 MEDIUM-SIZED LEEK, WHITE AND PALE GREEN PARTS ONLY,
VERY THINLY SLICED

1 YOUNG, SLENDER CARROT, PEELED AND SHREDDED OR VERY
FINELY MINCED

3 CLOVES GARLIC, MINCED

2 BAY LEAVES

1 FRESH THYME SPRIG, OR 1/2 TEASPOON DRIED THYME

2 POUNDS TINY NEW POTATOES, UNPEELED, HALVED AND EACH
HALF CUT INTO THIN WEDGES

1/2 CUP MINCED FRESH PARSLEY

2 EGG YOLKS

1/2 CUP MILK

Champagne - le Nord

NORTHERN CHANNEL CHOWDER
CAUDIÈRE BERCKOISE

MAKES **6** MAIN-COURSE SERVINGS

The little coastal town of Berck-sur-Mer, which faces the winds off the English Channel, is the home of this soup. About fifty miles from England, its chilly beaches look over the channel as it narrows into the Straits of Dover.

The proportions of potatoes, onions, and fresh seafood in this recipe are ideal, creating a chowder that is creamy but not too rich, savory, and satisfying. The important technique is to cook the mussels and seafood until just barely tender and then carefully and quickly remove them from the pot. The sweet juices perfume the rest of the soup as it finishes cooking. Tiny new potatoes, tender and tasty, soak up the flavors of the seafood and the aromatic onions and garlic.

French recipes for this soup call for conger eel along with the other seafood, but I have never been able to track down a source in the United States. If you discover a supply, by all means use it. I usually use three kinds of fish, halibut, cod, and snapper (sometimes called rockfish), which are rather lean, mild in flavor, and are easily cut into chunks. The sea bass is lean as well, but a little denser. You could substitute haddock, pollock, lingcod, or grouper for any of these choices.

Make a simple court bouillon for the initial poaching of the fish: Combine 2 cups of the white wine, 2 cups of the water, and the minced shallots in a wide stainless-steel or enameled skillet. Place over high heat until the liquid reaches a boil. Reduce the heat to low and simmer for 5 minutes.

Rinse the fish thoroughly. Cut into 3- to 4-inch pieces. Arrange the pieces of fish in a single layer in the court bouillon. Do not crowd the fish; the size of your skillet may require cooking the fish in batches. Cover and poach the fish on one side for 1 to 2 minutes. Carefully turn over each piece with a small spatula and repeat the process on the second side. The fish pieces should be firm, opaque, milky white, and slightly undercooked at this point. They will finish cooking during final assembly of the chowder.

Remove the skillet from the heat. Gently lift the fish from poaching liquid with a skimmer, allowing each piece to drain briefly. Reserve the court bouillon. Place the fish pieces on a large platter and let cool. When they are cool enough to handle, gently pull out any errant bones. Cut the fish into 1-inch cubes, then sprinkle with 1/2 teaspoon of the sea salt and 1/2 teaspoon of the black pepper, seasoning on all sides. Reserve the fish. Strain the court bouillon through a sieve into a large measuring pitcher and reserve.

Clean the mussels according to the directions on page 97. Put the mussels and the remaining 1 cup each wine and water in the fish-poaching skillet and place over high heat. Cover and cook, shaking the pan often to distribute the mussels so they will open evenly, until the mussels have opened, 5 to 7 minutes. Remove from the heat and discard any mussels that have not opened. Reserve 6 mussels in the shell for garnish. Shell the remaining mussels. Slowly pour the mussel-cooking liquid through a sieve lined with a double layer of dampened cheesecloth into the measuring pitcher. Add cold water as needed to total 6 cups.

Cover the bottom of a heavy 4-quart soup pot with a layer made up of the onions, leek, carrot, garlic, bay leaves, and thyme. Cover with the potato wedges. Sprinkle with the remaining ½ teaspoon sea salt and ¼ cup of the parsley. Pour the reserved 6 cups liquid into the pot and place over high heat. Bring to a boil, cover partially, reduce the heat to low, and simmer until the potatoes are cooked, 10 to 12 minutes; do not allow them to overcook.

In a small bowl, thoroughly whisk together the egg yolks and milk. Add a ladleful of the hot soup broth, stirring constantly. Pour the egg-milk mixture into the soup pot while stirring constantly but gently. Reheat over low heat but do not boil. Remove the bay leaves and the thyme sprigs and discard. Add the reserved mussels and the fish to the soup pot and barely simmer for 1 to 2 minutes to heat to the center of the tender seafood. Do not overcook.

Taste for seasoning, adding more salt if needed and the remaining 1 teaspoon black pepper. Plenty of black pepper is one of the secrets of this soup's success. Sprinkle with the remaining ¼ cup of parsley. Serve in heated soup plates, garnished with the reserved mussels in the shell.

NOTE: Don't worry if all the bones are not removed from your fish piece before poaching in the court bouillon. If there are a few strays, they add a bit of flavor to the finished soup and are easy to pluck out as you cut the fish into easy-to-eat cubes.

THE NEWFOUNDLAND CONNECTION Some people think that the linguistic and culinary connection between American and French chowder began in the 1100s on the cod banks of Newfoundland, when Breton and Basque fishermen swept the Atlantic searching for more plentiful fishing grounds. Even the progression of the name—cauldron (pot), *caudière, chaudière, chaudrée,* chowder—shows the American link to French chowder, which was named after the pot in which it was cooked.

In those days, when the fishermen would bring in their haul, the entire village would gather to make and share one large community pot of chowder. Each fisherman contributed some of his catch, along with aromatics, potatoes, and either wine or cider. This must have spread (as good cooking usually does) from France to Newfoundland and down the Atlantic coast to Nova Scotia, New Brunswick, and New England. Essentially, the same recipe also radiated both north and south along the French coast, each region adjusting mostly the name and the variety of fish. *Caudière berckoise* is one of many versions.

Normandie

NORMAN SHELLFISH MARMITE

MARMITE DIEPPOISE

6 MAIN-COURSE SERVINGS   8 LUNCHEON SERVINGS   12 FIRST-COURSE SERVINGS

This is one of the finest seafood soups, not only of France but also of any cuisine. The light whiff of curry and the hint of tomato offset its richness, and the tiny dash of cayenne gives it a gentle—but real—warmth. Marmite dieppoise is beautiful as well, a delicate pale straw color flecked with bits of pink and red.

A lavish seafood soup, this marmite needs all the diversity of flavors from the shellfish and fin fish. Depending on seafood costs at your fish market, you can juggle the amounts according to your budget. Do try to include a little of each of the varieties listed, however. If you cannot locate crayfish, additional shrimp can be used.

1 ½ POUNDS (1 QUART) MUSSELS

6 CUPS WATER (OR SUBSTITUTE AN AMOUNT OF SHRIMP BROTH; SEE NOTE)

3 CUPS DRY WHITE TABLE WINE

1 SHALLOT, FINELY MINCED

3 TABLESPOONS UNSALTED BUTTER

2 MEDIUM-SIZED ONIONS, FINELY CHOPPED

1 SLENDER LEEK, WHITE AND PALE GREEN PARTS ONLY, FINELY CHOPPED

1 TABLESPOON ALL-PURPOSE FLOUR

1 TEASPOON CURRY POWDER

3 RIPE TOMATOES, PEELED, SEEDED, AND FINELY CHOPPED

1 TEASPOON SEA SALT

24 MEDIUM-SIZED SHRIMP, PEELED AND DEVEINED

6 SOLE FILLETS, ABOUT 2 OUNCES EACH

6 TURBOT FILLETS, ABOUT 3 OUNCES EACH (ADDITIONAL SOLE MAY BE SUBSTITUTED)

12 CRAYFISH (SEE OPPOSITE)

6 SEA SCALLOPS

2 PINCHES OF GROUND FENNEL, OR ½ TEASPOON FENNEL SEEDS GROUND IN A MORTAR

⅛ TEASPOON CAYENNE PEPPER, OR TO TASTE

½ CUP HEAVY CREAM

FRESHLY GROUND BLACK PEPPER

Clean the mussels according to the directions on page 97. Put the mussels, 1 cup of the water, 1 cup of the wine, and the shallot in a wide stainless-steel or enameled skillet over high heat. Cover and cook, shaking the pan often to distribute the mussels evenly, until the mussels have opened, 5 to 7 minutes. Remove from the heat and discard any mussels that have not opened. Remove the top shell from each mussel and discard. Place the mussels on their half shells on a heated platter and cover with foil to keep warm. Carefully, watching for any fugitive sand, pour the mussel-cooking liquid through a sieve lined with a double layer of dampened cheesecloth placed over a small bowl; reserve.

Melt the butter in a heavy 4-quart soup pot over low heat. Sauté the onions and leek, stirring occasionally, until they are softened but not colored, about 5 minutes. Add the flour and the curry powder and cook for 3 to 4 minutes more, stirring often.

Add the tomatoes, sea salt, the remaining 5 cups water, and the remaining 2 cups white wine to the pot and bring to a boil. Add the shrimp and boil for 1 minute. Remove the shrimp with a slotted spoon, place on the heated platter with the mussels, and keep warm. Reduce the heat so the liquid is at a gentle simmer and carefully add the fish pieces, crayfish, and scallops. Cook for 2 to 3 minutes, remove the fish and shellfish from the liquid with a slotted spoon, place on the platter, re-cover, and keep warm.

Add the fennel, cayenne, cream, and reserved mussel-cooking liquid to the soup pot and whisk thoroughly into the liquid. Simmer over very low heat for 7 to 10 minutes to blend the flavors completely. Taste for seasoning, adding more salt if needed and black pepper to taste. Add the reserved fish pieces and the scallops to the pot and heat together with the soup, stirring very slowly and carefully with a rubber spatula.

Ladle the hot soup into a heated soup tureen or heated soup plates and garnish with the mussels, shrimp, and crayfish. Serve at once.

NOTE: Consider making a simple broth from shrimp shells to flavor the final dish. After peeling the shrimp, put the shells into enough cold water to cover, add a few aromatic vegetables (carrot, leek, celery), and simmer for 15 minutes or so. Strain and use this broth in place of some of the water listed in the ingredients list. Or, freeze the shrimp shells for later use in twin sealable plastic bags, one inside the other.

CLEANING CRAYFISH Crayfish should be either very alive or frozen. Today most crayfish is farm raised and cleaned or purged before they are brought to market. This is the case whether they are alive or have been frozen. If you are lucky enough to catch wild crayfish, they need to be cleaned of their intestinal tract. To do this, hold each crayfish with one hand (preferably gloved or protected by a towel) with the tail exposed. The tail has five little flanges. Pull out the center one and the intestinal matter will follow.

Rinse live crayfish in plenty of water and cook according to the directions in individual recipes. To retrieve the sweet tail meat, gently pull the cooked crayfish head away from the tail. The tail meat can be pulled out in one piece if you can loosen its tip at the end of the tail. The tail shell is semihard but it can be peeled away. If you are not serving whole crayfish, save all the shells and put them in a heavy-duty clear plastic bag. Crush the shells with a rolling pin, then double seal in another plastic bag and freeze to use as a base for broth.

12 OYSTERS

1 CUP MUSCADET OR OTHER DRY WHITE WINE

¼ CUP UNSALTED BUTTER

12 FRESH WHITE MUSHROOMS (ABOUT ¼ POUND), TRIMMED AND SLICED

2 YOUNG, SLENDER CARROTS, PEELED AND CUT INTO PAPER-THIN SLICES

2 SLENDER LEEKS, WHITE AND PALE GREEN PARTS ONLY, THINLY SLICED

1 BOTTLE (750 ML) DRY CIDER (SEE NOTE)

1 BOUQUET GARNI (6 FRESH PARSLEY STEMS, 2 BAY LEAVES, 2 FRESH THYME SPRIGS TIED IN A BUNDLE)

1 TEASPOON SEA SALT

3 POUNDS SOLE OR FLOUNDER FILLETS

12 MEDIUM-SIZED SHRIMP, PEELED AND DEVEINED

1 CUP HEAVY CREAM

1 CUP LOW-FAT SOUR CREAM

FRESHLY GROUND WHITE PEPPER

1 TABLESPOON CALVADOS OR FINE BRANDY

¼ CUP FINELY MINCED FRESH CHERVIL OR PARSLEY

CROÛTONS (PAGE 79)

Normandie

SOLE, SHRIMP, and CIDER SOUP

MATELOTE NORMANDE

MAKES **6** MAIN-COURSE SERVINGS

The classic and elegant sole à la Normande, *allegedly created by chefs in Paris, maybe have drawn inspiration from this traditional Norman* matelote. This matelote *has the same choice ingredients (sole, shrimp, cream) and delicate flavors, but it is a simpler, more informal dish. Serve the soup in wide-rimmed, shallow soup plates to show off the choice seafood.*

In poaching fish, it takes about five minutes to cook a boneless piece of fish ½ inch thick. In seafood soups, I think it is often better to undercook the fragile seafood slightly. By the time the dish is served, the internal temperature of the fish will be perfect.

Preheat the oven to 250°F. Put a roasting pan and 6 soup plates in the oven to preheat.

Open the oysters according to the directions on page 109, carefully reserving their liquor. Put the oyster liquor and white wine in a shallow nonaluminum pan, add the oysters, and cook gently over very low heat until their edges begin to curl, about 1 minute. Remove the oysters with a slotted spoon, place in the heated roasting pan, cover with aluminum foil, and return to the oven to keep warm. Strain and reserve the cooking liquid.

Melt the butter in a heavy 4-quart soup pot over medium-low heat. Sauté the mushrooms, carrots, and leeks, stirring often, until they become lightly colored, about 8 minutes. Add the cider, bouquet garni, and sea salt and bring to a boil over high heat. Reduce the heat to medium-low, cover partially, and simmer for 10 minutes to create a full-flavored broth.

Depending on the size of the pot, it may be necessary to poach the seafood in batches. Place as many of the sole pieces and shrimp as will fit in a single layer in the soup pot and poach over low heat until nearly done, about 2 minutes. They should be firm to the touch. With a perforated spatula, carefully remove the sole and shrimp, add to the roasting pan with the oysters, re-cover with foil, and reserve in the oven. Repeat with the remaining sole and shrimp, remembering that thin fillets need much less cooking time. Re-cover all the seafood and reserve in the oven.

Add the reserved oyster-poaching liquid to the pot and bring to a boil over high heat. Reduce the heat to medium and cook until reduced by one-half. Remove the bouquet garni and discard. Add the heavy cream and whisk in the sour cream. Simmer for 3 to 4 minutes.

Taste and add more salt if needed and white pepper to taste. Stir in the Calvados or brandy; gently add the fish pieces, shrimp, and oysters and heat for 1 minute. Carefully ladle into heated soup plates, sprinkle with the chervil or parsley, and accompany with the *croûtons*.

NOTE: When a French recipe calls for cider (*cidre*), it is referring to the fermented, mildly alcoholic beverage that most Americans call "hard" cider. It is tart and refreshing and does not have the flavor of apples as such. Four kinds of cider are produced in French apple-growing regions, each a balanced blend of tart and sweet apples (much as a vintner carefully blends his grapes for a perfectly flavored wine). Calvados, of course, is the eau-de-vie that is distilled from hard cider in its own specific district in Normandy.

To prepare this Norman soup, try to find the appropriate cider at your wine retailer. There are a number of domestic and imported ciders, and they are food-friendly, thirst-quenching, and unusual additions to your wine cellar.

MUSCADET AND SHELLFISH The tradition of drinking reasonably priced Muscadet with shellfish evolved because it is *not* a complex, layers-of-flavor wine. The precise, delicate flavor of shellfish is enhanced, not altered, by this trim, springlike beverage.

All Muscadet is produced in an area curved around Nantes, a city on the western Loire River near the Atlantic coast. The original name of this wine's grape was Melon de Bourgogne, which became Muscadet over the years. The majority of Muscadet stays home in France as *vin ordinaire*, often an unbottled and inexpensive table wine. We may find in the United States, however, a bottle of a higher grade, Muscadet des Côteaux de la Loire. The quality to look for is Muscadet de Sèvre-et-Maine and the designation *sur lie*. This delicious wine is not bottled until it has rested over the winter on the sediment resulting from the wine-making process. Nestled on its own grape solids, Muscadet *sur lie* emerges crisp and fresh.

POACHED OYSTERS in POTATO-LEEK CREAM

SOUPE LOCMARIAQUER

MAKES **6** SERVINGS

2 DOZEN MEDIUM-SIZED OYSTERS (SEE NOTE)

4 TABLESPOONS UNSALTED BUTTER

¼ POUND BACON, CUT INTO 1-INCH PIECES

2 MEDIUM-SIZED LEEKS, WHITE PARTS ONLY, THINLY SLICED

½ POUND WAXY POTATOES, PEELED AND THINLY SLICED (2 SMALL TO MEDIUM POTATOES)

1 QUART MILK

6 FRESH PARSLEY STEMS

½ BAY LEAF

1 LARGE FRESH THYME SPRIG

1 LARGE ROSEMARY SPRIG

1 TEASPOON SEA SALT

⅛ TEASPOON CAYENNE PEPPER

PINCH OF FRESHLY GRATED NUTMEG

12 OVAL *CROÛTES* (PAGE 79)

¼ CUP FINELY MINCED FRESH CHIVES

FRESHLY GROUND BLACK PEPPER

If you long for melt-in-the-mouth, barely cooked oysters and the creamy richness of leeks and potatoes cooked and puréed together and perfumed with fresh herbs, this satiny soup is for you. The herbs suggested here serve as only a beginning. Although I had some concern about using robust rosemary with delicate seafood, the parsley-thyme-rosemary marriage of three resulted in a subtly scented soup. When you are buying herbs, look for both what is freshest and what you like the most.

I wish that everyone reading these words could spend a tranquil moment in tiny Locmariaquer. I originally visited the town because I read Eleanor Clark's The Oysters of Locmariaquer *and loved it. It is a rich and complex tapestry that describes oyster culture, interweaving it with Celtic myths, scenes of Breton life, and French philosophy. M. Cabelguen, patron of Hôtel L'Escale at Locmariaquer, has shared this soup recipe, discovered in an old cookbook that belonged to his grandmother.*

Open the oysters according to the directions on page 109, carefully reserving their liquor.

Melt 1 tablespoon of the butter in a heavy 4-quart soup pot or Dutch oven over medium heat. Add the bacon and sauté until crisp, 4 to 5 minutes. Using a slotted spoon, transfer to paper towels to drain. Reserve.

Pour off all but 3 tablespoons of the fat from the pot. Add the leeks and sauté over medium-low heat until completely softened, about 5 minutes. Do not allow them to color.

Add the potatoes, milk, parsley, bay leaf, thyme, rosemary, and sea salt to the leeks and bring to a boil over high heat. Cover, reduce the heat to low, and simmer very gently until the potatoes are tender, 12 to 15 minutes. Remove the herb sprigs and bay leaf and discard.

Working with 1 or 2 ladlefuls at a time, purée the contents in a blender or food processor until the mixture is satinlike, 30 to 40 seconds per batch. Return the purée to the pot and reheat slowly.

Add the cayenne, nutmeg, and reserved oyster liquor to the soup. Simmer over low heat for 5 minutes to blend the flavors. (The soup may be prepared to this point and refrigerated for up to 3 days before continuing.)

Poach the oysters in the simmering soup over very low heat until they are barely cooked, 10 to 15 seconds. Taste for seasoning, adding more salt if needed. Swirl in the remaining 3 tablespoons butter.

Place two *croûtes* in each of 6 heated soup plates and ladle in the soup. Sprinkle with the reserved bacon pieces and the chives. Pass the pepper grinder at table.

NOTE: If you prefer to use preshucked oysters for this soup, buy the smallest and freshest ones you can find. Make sure to ask your fishmonger to save all the liquid after opening the oysters and to deliver it in the same container. The liquid surrounding the oysters should be clear, not at all cloudy.

Nés avec de l'eau de mer autour de coeur. *(Born with seawater around their heart.)*

—OLD BRETON SAYING

BRETON SHELLFISH Any shellfish, bivalve (mussel, oyster, or clam), or crustacean (lobster, crab, shrimp, or langoustine) from Breton waters is particularly prized all over France. Menus in Paris restaurants often boast of haute cuisine dishes of Breton lobster, but most of the seafood cooking of Brittany is fairly unsophisticated. The simplicity of dishes such as shrimp poached in cider, scallops simmered in Muscadet, grilled lobster, or a hearty chowder illustrates how good unadorned seacoast cooking can be when the essential fish and shellfish are at their very freshest.

Bretagne

BRETON FISHERMAN'S SOUP

COTRIADE

MAKES **6** TO **8** SERVINGS

3 POUNDS OF AT LEAST THREE KINDS OF LEAN FISH SUCH AS COD, SNAPPER, TURBOT, SOLE, OR HALIBUT, CLEANED

1 POUND OILY FISH SUCH AS MACKEREL OR BLUEFISH, CLEANED

2 OUNCES UNSMOKED BACON, SALT PORK, OR PANCETTA, FINELY DICED

8 SMALL WAXY POTATOES (ABOUT 1 ½ POUNDS), PEELED, HALVED, AND CUT INTO ¼-INCH-THICK SLICES

3 MEDIUM-SIZED ONIONS, FINELY CHOPPED

2 QUARTS WATER

1 TEASPOON SEA SALT

1 BOUQUET GARNI (6 FRESH PARSLEY STEMS, 2 BAY LEAVES, 2 FRESH THYME SPRIGS TIED IN 1 LARGE CELERY STALK)

¼ CUP FINELY MINCED FRESH PARSLEY

FRESHLY GROUND BLACK PEPPER

6 TO 8 THICK SLICES COARSE COUNTRY BREAD FOR SERVING

For the vinaigrette:

2 SHALLOTS, FINELY CHOPPED

½ TEASPOON SEA SALT

FRESHLY GROUND BLACK PEPPER

¼ CUP CIDER VINEGAR OR WHITE WINE VINEGAR

½ CUP OLIVE OIL

2 TABLESPOONS FINELY MINCED FRESH TARRAGON OR PARSLEY

Cotriade differs somewhat from most seafood main-course soups because of the way it is eaten. The chunks of hot fish and tender potatoes may be offered first, accompanied with a dipping sauce of peppy vinaigrette. After that, the intense, oniony broth is served, scalding hot with coarse country bread and lightly salted Breton butter.

The use of bacon in this soup is a vestige of an old tradition in Brittany. Seafood soups were characteristically flavored by cooking the ingredients in pork fat. Because nearby seas could be dangerous, or even deadly, for weeks on end, the availability of fresh fish, a valuable protein, was at hazard. Raising hogs in coastal Brittany provided a backup food supply for those times when the Atlantic did not permit fishermen to put out to sea. Even though it is not authentic, you can use an oil or some butter if you prefer. The taste of the pork fat will be subtly different and probably a little richer, however.

Cut all the fish into 1- to 2-inch pieces. Fish bones may be removed, but it is neither traditional nor necessary. Set the fish aside.

Sauté the bacon, salt pork, or pancetta in a 10-quart soup pot over medium heat, stirring often, until golden, 5 to 7 minutes. Add the potatoes and cook over medium-high heat, turning over the slices often, until both sides are golden, 8 to 10 minutes. Remove the bacon and the potatoes with a slotted spoon, drain on paper towels, and reserve.

Add the onions to the fat remaining in the soup pot and sauté over low heat, stirring often, until lightly colored, 5 to 8 minutes. Scrape the bottom of the pot often to prevent scorching.

Add the reserved bacon and potatoes, the water, sea salt, and bouquet garni and bring to a boil over high heat. Reduce the heat to low, cover partially, and simmer until the potatoes begin to soften, about 10 minutes. The liquid should remain at a constant, gentle simmer. Add the fish, cooking the fish with bones for 10 minutes and the boneless fish for 5 minutes. Any fragile fish, such as sole or turbot, should cook for only 2 to 3 minutes.

AN OILY FISH SUCH AS MACKEREL (*MAQUEREAU*), WITH ITS DISTINCTIVE BLACK STRIPE, IS ESSENTIAL FOR AN AUTHENTIC BRETON *COTRIADE*.

Meanwhile, make the vinaigrette: Combine the shallots, sea salt, black pepper to taste, and vinegar in a small bowl. Whisk in the oil and herb.

With a slotted spoon, carefully remove the potatoes and fish pieces from the pot and divide among 6 heated soup plates. Spoon a little hot cooking broth over the seafood and sprinkle with the parsley.

Strain the remaining cooking broth and reheat over low heat. Taste and add more sea salt if needed and black pepper to taste. Keep the broth hot over very low heat.

Serve the seafood and potatoes as a first course accompanied by the vinaigrette as a dip. Follow by serving the hot broth in heated cups and pass the bread at table. The presentation of *cotriade* also may be reversed: cover the plates of hot fish and potatoes with foil and reserve in a warm oven while serving the broth.

Atlantique-Bordeaux

OYSTER and CREAM SOUP with PINEAU des CHARENTES

Les TROIS GLORIEUSES des CHARENTES

MAKES 6 TO 8 SERVINGS

30 TO 36 SMALL OYSTERS

4 TABLESPOONS UNSALTED BUTTER

1 MEDIUM-SIZED ONION, FINELY CHOPPED

2 TABLESPOONS ALL-PURPOSE FLOUR

5 CUPS HALF-AND-HALF OR HEAVY CREAM

1 TEASPOON SEA SALT

½ CUP PINEAU DES CHARENTES

FRESHLY GROUND BLACK PEPPER

PAPRIKA

CROÛTONS (PAGE 79)

Simple to prepare, this exceptional soup has a depth of flavor that is surprising. There are only a few ingredients—the clear, marine flavor of the oysters, enhanced by a little onion, cracked pepper—but the intriguing Pineau des Charentes takes this dish out of the ordinary.

In J.-E. Progneaux's book on the cuisine of the Charentes region, he defines les trois glorieuses des Charentes (the three glories of Charentes), but he surprises us. I believe he actually lists four: succulent Marennes oysters, Pineau des Charentes, local sweet butter, and Cognac. Three of the four glorieuses are found in my version of the soup.

Open the oysters according to the directions opposite, carefully reserving their liquor. Strain the liquor through a fine-mesh sieve to eliminate any shell fragments.

Place the shucked oysters and their liquor in a large sauté pan and gently heat until their edges begin to curl, 15 to 20 seconds. (It is better if the oysters are quite undercooked, but that decision is up to the cook. They should never, never be overcooked, however.) With a slotted spoon, remove the oysters and reserve them. Reserve the liquor separately.

Melt 2 tablespoons of the butter in a 4-quart soup pot over low heat. Sauté the onion until very soft but not colored, about 5 minutes. Add the flour and stir with a wooden spoon for 2 or 3 minutes. Add the half-and-half or cream, oyster liquor, and sea salt and mix thoroughly using a wire whisk. Simmer over very low heat, until slightly thickened, 10 to 15 minutes. Watch closely to keep the soup from boiling over. Scrape the sides of the saucepan frequently with a rubber spatula, then whisk well. When the mixture has thickened, add the Pineau des Charentes and a generous amount of black pepper. (One French recipe suggests _avec résolution_).

Add the reserved oysters, stir in the remaining 2 tablespoons butter, and taste and add more salt if needed. Allow to heat thoroughly, but do not boil. Ladle into heated soup plates, sprinkle with the paprika, and top with the _croûtons_. Serve at once.

OYSTERS IN THE OYSTER-FARMING BEDS ON THE ILE-DE-RÉ OFF THE ATLANTIC COAST AT LA ROCHELLE.

CLEANING AND SHUCKING OYSTERS
Since oysters, like all shellfish, are highly perishable, test each one, if you can, before buying. The shell of an oyster should be tightly closed; if not, tap on the shell, and it should snap shut.

Oysters shouldn't be washed, but if they are covered with seaweed or muddy, quickly rinse them under cold running water. Refrigerating oysters for a couple of hours before opening them can make them a little more cooperative.

Use an oyster knife with a strong, stiff blade with a pointed tip and a sturdy, round hand guard to protect from mishaps. Also protect your oyster-holding hand by wearing a thick glove or by wrapping your hand in a kitchen towel. With the flatter shell on top, insert the point of your knife into the dimple in the shell where the hinge is. Once the knife is firmly in place, twist it a quarter-turn and pry apart the twin shells.

Using the knife, cut through the muscle that attaches the oyster to its top shell. Be careful not to spill any of the oyster juices that now lie in the bottom rounded shell as you carefully cut the oyster away.

Atlantique-Bordeaux

SEAFOOD SOUP with RED WINE

SOUPE de MOULES ROCHELAISE

MAKES **6** MAIN-COURSE SERVINGS

The particular beauty of this soup, a rusty, winy red, with pink shrimp and black mussel shells, can only hint at how delicious it is. All the components—the red wine, of course, the aromatics, the tomatoes, the shellfish, the saffron—lend their specific qualities to a soup that is complexly flavored.

The French are adept at pairing fish and red wine, and many regional freshwater fish matelotes are prepared with the local red wines. The red wine in this soup is from the Ile-de-Ré, off the coast of La Rochelle in the Charentes region, and the fish are from the Atlantic Ocean. Since Tannat, the Ile de Ré red wine, is not exported, you can instead use a full-bodied red in the style of the southern Rhône reds. It should have plenty of tannin, such as a wine from Syrah grapes.

2 POUNDS (ABOUT 1 1/2 QUARTS) MUSSELS

2 CUPS COLD WATER

1/2 CUP UNSALTED BUTTER

2 MEDIUM-SIZED ONIONS, FINELY CHOPPED

2 CLOVES GARLIC, CRUSHED

12 MEDIUM-SIZED SHRIMP, PEELED AND DEVEINED

1 POUND PLUM TOMATOES, PEELED, SEEDED, CHOPPED

3/4 POUND SEA BASS OR HADDOCK FILLETS, CUT INTO 6 EQUAL PIECES

3/4 POUND RED MULLET, GROUPER, OR OCEAN PERCH FILLETS, CUT INTO 6 EQUAL PIECES

1 BOTTLE (750 ML) FULL-BODIED RED WINE (SEE RECIPE INTRODUCTION)

4 CUPS HOT WATER

1/2 TEASPOON SAFFRON THREADS, STEEPED IN 1/2 CUP HOT WATER

2 YOUNG, SLENDER CARROTS, PEELED AND THINLY SLICED

1 TEASPOON SEA SALT

1 BOUQUET GARNI (6 FRESH PARSLEY STEMS, 2 BAY LEAVES, 2 FRESH THYME SPRIGS TIED IN 1 LEEK GREEN)

FRESHLY GROUND BLACK PEPPER

1/4 CUP FINELY MINCED FRESH PARSLEY

CROÛTES (PAGE 79)

Preheat the oven to 250°F. Place a large bowl and 6 soup plates in the oven to preheat.

Clean the mussels according to the directions on page 97. Put the mussels and the 2 cups cold water in a wide stainless-steel or enameled skillet and place over high heat. Cover and cook, shaking the pan often to distribute the mussels evenly, until the mussels have opened, 5 to 7 minutes. Remove from the heat and discard any mussels that have not opened. Reserve 6 whole mussels for garnish. Shell the remaining mussels, put them in the heated bowl, cover with aluminum foil, and reserve in the warm oven. Slowly pour the mussel liquid through a sieve lined with a double layer of dampened cheesecloth and reserve.

Melt the butter in a heavy 4-quart soup pot over medium-low heat. Sauté the onions, stirring often, until golden, 8 to 10 minutes. Add the garlic and cook for 1 to 2 minutes, stirring often. Add the shrimp and cook, stirring constantly, until they turn pink, 2 to 3 minutes. Using a slotted spoon, remove the shrimp from the soup pot and combine with the mussels in the heated bowl, re-cover, and return to the warm oven. Precooking the shrimp is not traditional in this French soup, but I prefer the shrimp flesh to remain pink.

Add the tomatoes to the soup pot and cook for 2 to 3 minutes. Carefully place the fish pieces on top of the onions, garlic, and tomatoes. Cook for 2 to 3 minutes. Add the red wine, hot water, saffron and water, carrots, sea salt, and bouquet garni. Bring to a boil over high heat, reduce the heat to medium-low, and simmer for 5 minutes. The fish should be cooked at this point. With a slotted spoon, remove the fish pieces and divide evenly among the heated soup plates; cover with foil to keep warm. Add the reserved mussel-cooking liquid to the soup pot and stir to blend well.

Working with 1 or 2 ladlefuls at a time, purée the remaining liquid and the vegetables in a blender or food processor, processing each batch for at least 30 seconds until very smooth. Return the purée to the pot and simmer over medium-low heat for 2 to 3 minutes. Taste and add more salt if needed and black pepper to taste. Add the reserved shrimp and mussels to the soup pot and simmer over very low heat for about 1 minute to heat the shellfish thoroughly. Do not allow the soup to reach a boil.

Ladle the hot soup and shellfish over the fish in the soup plates. Garnish each with parsley and a whole mussel. Serve the *croûtes* at the side.

LES MOULES DU BOUCHOT The story goes that in the year 1235, a boat carrying a load of sheep and belonging to an Irishman, Captain Patrick Walton, sank off the French Atlantic coast. To be sure he had a source of food, the marooned skipper stuck some posts (*bouchots*) in the sand offshore and contrived a ropelike snare to capture sea birds for his supper. After some amount of time, Walton had a delectable surprise. Hanging below water level from his bird-catching snares were clusters of mussels, ready for eating.

Mussels will attach themselves to any number of marine objects, including the hulls of oceangoing ships. Walton's unexpected cultivation of French mussels was just the beginning. An entire industry—raising *moules du bouchot*—grew up on these shores allegedly due to a sheep boat that never made it to a harbor.

SEA SALT OF GUÉRANDE (*SEL DE GUÉRANDE*)
PRODUCED FROM SALTWATER EVAPORATION BEDS.

SEA SALT   I like to use coarse sea salt even though sometimes it is hard to find. Pure sea salt ensures that the flavor of your cooking will be appropriately enhanced and the dish seasoned with subtlety. Also, sprinkling coarse sea salt with your fingertips gives you an immediate tactile recognition of the amount you are using.

In a country that chooses to define and limit sources for wine, chickens, cheeses, butter, and almost everything select that is enjoyed *à table*, it is no surprise that its salt would be no different.

The salt from Guérande on the Atlantic coast is produced by evaporation of seawater in shallow beds. Moving the saltwater into rectangular ponds that are less and less deep helps the natural elements of the sun and breezes in their work. Once no water remains, the salt is harvested, raked by *paludiers* (salt-marsh workers) into huge mounds. The top layer of white salt is known as the *fleur*, and its crystals are delicate and subtle.

Languedoc

CATALAN SAFFRON FISH and POTATO SOUP

BOUILLINADA

MAKES **6** MAIN-COURSE SERVINGS

1 EEL, ABOUT 1 POUND, CLEANED AND SKINNED (SEE NOTE ON PAGE 177)

6 OUNCES HAKE, WHITING, OR HADDOCK FILLET

6 OUNCES COD FILLET

6 OUNCES MONKFISH FILLET, ALL MEMBRANES REMOVED

3 TABLESPOONS PORK FAT, GOOD-QUALITY LARD, OR OLIVE OIL

3 CLOVES GARLIC, FINELY MINCED

6 TABLESPOONS CHOPPED FRESH PARSLEY

1 TEASPOON SEA SALT

CAYENNE PEPPER

2 MEDIUM-SIZED WAXY POTATOES, PEELED AND CUT INTO PAPER-THIN SLICES

1 RED BELL PEPPER, SEEDED AND FINELY MINCED

2 TABLESPOONS ALL-PURPOSE FLOUR

½ TEASPOON SAFFRON THREADS, STEEPED IN ½ CUP HOT WATER

2 QUARTS WATER

1 TABLESPOON OLIVE OIL

Once on the crowded sidewalks of Perpignan in southeastern France, I saw a sandwich board outside a small café announcing that bouillinada *was on the noon menu. I went in and ordered the unusual Catalan seafood soup. After lunch, I asked the waiter about the ingredients in the* bouillinada, *and I was taken by surprise when he told me it contained primarily eel. It was utterly delectable.*

The soup is extremely easy to prepare. Once all the ingredients are ready, layered in the pot, and the heat turned on, there is nothing left to do but to wait. The bouillinada *really cooks itself—and emerges beautifully colored and perfumed from the pot. I cannot stress enough to use the lavish amounts of parsley. The herb is one of the keys to the success of the soup.*

It is traditional to prepare this dish with pork that is slightly rancid, which guarantees a flavor characteristic of the southeastern Ariége region. (This is obviously optional.) It is also customary to cook this soup in a glazed clay casserole that can be used both on the top of the stove and in the oven. Enameled cast iron also works for this dish.

Cut all the fish into 1-inch pieces and reserve.

Cut the pork fat into very tiny dice and place it in the bottom of a flameproof 6-quart casserole of glazed earthenware or enameled cast iron. If using lard, melt it slowly in the bottom of the casserole and then remove from the heat. If using olive oil, coat the bottom of the casserole with it. Sprinkle the chopped garlic and half of the parsley over the pork fat or other fat. Dust with the sea salt and cayenne to taste. Top with a layer of potatoes and bell pepper followed by a layer of the fish pieces. Sprinkle with a little of the flour and some of the remaining parsley. Repeat the layering of the potatoes, bell pepper, fish, flour, and parsley until the casserole is full. Try to arrange at least three complete layers of the ingredients.

Add the saffron and water and the 2 quarts water to the casserole, immersing the layers completely. Cover either with a lid or with aluminum foil, place the casserole over medium-high heat, and bring just to a boil. At this moment, uncover and sprinkle the 1 tablespoon olive oil over the surface. Reduce the heat to very low, re-cover, and simmer until the fish is cooked and firm to the touch, about 15 minutes. Serve this full-meal soup very hot directly from casserole.

le pays Basque

FISH and SHELLFISH STEW

TTORO

MAKES **6** TO **8** MAIN-COURSE SERVINGS

The Basques have a gift for brilliantly colored, deeply flavored dishes. Peppery ttoro, *the most celebrated Basque soup, started out as a fisherman's broth of cod bones and a few vegetables poured over the bread. Today's soup is quite different from that rough original. The mild, sweet flavor of cod and the meaty tenderness of monkfish pair perfectly with the spiciness of the bell peppers and the kick of the hotter red pepper flakes. As in most of such wonderful old dishes that have evolved over time, the flavors are carefully in balance, no one component overpowering any other.*

For the fish broth:

2 POUNDS HEADS AND FRAMES FROM OF SEVERAL KINDS OF FISH

1 MEDIUM-SIZED ONION, FINELY CHOPPED

4 SLENDER LEEKS, WHITE AND PALE GREEN PARTS ONLY, FINELY CHOPPED

1 BOUQUET GARNI (6 FRESH PARSLEY STEMS, 2 BAY LEAVES, 2 FRESH THYME SPRIGS TIED IN 1 LARGE CELERY STALK)

2 CUPS JURAÇON OR DRY CÔTE-DU-RHÔNE WHITE WINE

2 QUARTS WATER

For the stew:

1¼ POUNDS COD FILLETS

1¼ POUNDS MONKFISH FILLETS

1½ POUNDS (ABOUT 1 QUART) MUSSELS

8 TABLESPOONS FRUITY OLIVE OIL

1 MEDIUM-SIZED ONION, FINELY CHOPPED

2 CLOVES GARLIC, FINELY MINCED

7 PLUM TOMATOES, PEELED, SEEDED, AND FINELY CHOPPED

1 EACH RED AND GREEN BELL PEPPER, SEEDED, AND FINELY CHOPPED

1 CUP DRY WHITE TABLE WINE

⅛ TEASPOON RED PEPPER FLAKES, IF NOT USING *PIMENT D'ESPELETTE*

1 TEASPOON SEA SALT

PIMENT D'ESPELETTE (PAGE 120) OR CAYENNE PEPPER

1 CUP WATER

12 LARGE SHRIMP, PEELED AND DEVEINED

CROÛTONS (PAGE 79)

To make the broth, carefully rinse the fish frames and heads under cold running water, rinsing away any traces of blood or viscera that would add bitterness to the broth. Put the fish frames and heads, onion, leeks, bouquet garni, white wine, and water in a 4-quart soup pot. Bring to a boil, reduce the heat to low, and simmer gently, uncovered, for 20 to 25 minutes. With a skimmer or tongs, remove the larger pieces of fish bones and heads and vegetables and discard. Pour the liquid through a sieve lined with a double layer of dampened cheesecloth into a measuring pitcher. Add enough tap water to total 8 cups; reserve. Wash and dry the soup pot.

Cut the cod fillets into 1½-by-¾-inch pieces and reserve. Trim away any membrane on the monkfish, then cut the fish into ¾-inch cubes and reserve. The denser monkfish, taking a little longer to cook, is cut into the smaller pieces, as both fish will be added to the pot at the same time. Clean the mussels according to the directions on page 97 and reserve.

Heat 2 tablespoons of the olive oil in the soup pot over medium-low heat. Add the onion and sauté, stirring frequently, until completely softened and lightly colored, about 8 minutes. Add the garlic, 6 of the chopped tomatoes, the bell peppers, the white wine, and the pepper flakes, if you are adding cayenne later. Bring to a boil, reduce the heat to very low, partially cover, and simmer, stirring occasionally, until the mixture becomes a thick tomato sauce, 10 to 12 minutes. Add the 8 cups reserved fish broth and season with the sea salt and the *piment d'Espelette* or cayenne to taste. Cover partially and reserve over low heat at a bare simmer.

Put the cleaned mussels in a wide stainless-steel or enameled skillet with the 1 cup water and ¼ cup of the tomato mixture and place over high heat. Cover and cook, shaking the pan often to distribute the mussels evenly, until the mussels have opened, about 5 minutes. Remove from the heat and discard any mussels that have not opened. Remove the top shell from each mussel and discard. Slowly pour the mussel-cooking liquid through a sieve lined with a double layer of dampened cheesecloth and add to soup pot. Set the mussels in their half shells aside.

Dry the cod and monkfish pieces with paper towels. Heat the remaining 6 tablespoons olive oil in a heavy, wide skillet over medium-high heat. Sauté the fish pieces, turning once, until lightly colored, less than 30 seconds on each side. Add the fish pieces to the soup pot. Bring the soup to a boil, reduce the heat to medium-low, and simmer, stirring very gently, for 5 to 6 minutes. The fish pieces should be nearly cooked. Add the shrimp and cook until they turn pink, about 1 minute. Add the reserved mussels and simmer only until they are heated thoroughly.

With a slotted spoon, remove the mussels and shrimp and divide among 6 heated soup plates. Gently add the fish pieces, again dividing evenly. Taste the broth, adding more salt if needed and additional *piment d'Espelette* or cayenne, if you want a spicier dish. Ladle the remaining broth into the soup plates and garnish with the remaining chopped tomato. Serve immediately and pass the *croutons* at table.

le pays Basque

SOUP of GRILLED TUNA with CHILE

MARMITAKO

MAKES **6** TO **8** GENEROUS MAIN-COURSE SERVINGS

Tuna taken from the nearby Atlantic and peppers harvested close at hand are in dispensable to Basque cooks, and marmitako incorporates both. Put aside misgivings about using premium tuna in a soup as you won't regret the results. Instead, regard this as the thriftiest and tastiest way to serve tuna as a main dish. You only need 1 ½ pounds to treat six to eight guests. The soup's other virtues? It goes together quickly, it's vivid to look at—colorful as the Basque flag—and best of all, the flavors are wonderful.

The Basque grill tuna studded with slivers of garlic much as we would a piece of beef, or braise it (thon basquaise) with peppers, tomatoes, garlic, and onions. Marmitako is a variation of the latter, but I have added grilling tuna to the preparation. Although it is nontraditional, I like the subtle smoky taste in the finished dish.

Marmitako is traditionally made with red tuna, but if the catch happens to be white (germon) use it, as the Basque would. At your fish market, you may find bluefin tuna, yellowfin tuna, or even bonito, all of which will give a true flavor to this Basque dish.

1 ½ POUNDS TUNA FILLET, SKINNED AND CUT AGAINST THE GRAIN INTO ¾-INCH-THICK SLICES

4 TABLESPOONS FRUITY OLIVE OIL

2 LARGE RED BELL PEPPERS

2 LARGE GREEN BELL PEPPERS

2 MEDIUM-SIZED RED ONIONS, FINELY CHOPPED

1 SMALL JALAPEÑO CHILE, SEEDED AND FINELY CHOPPED

4 CLOVES GARLIC, FINELY CHOPPED

1 CELERY STALK

1 CARROT, PEELED

2 BAY LEAVES

½ TEASPOON CAYENNE PEPPER, OR TO TASTE

2 TEASPOONS SEA SALT

2 CUPS DRY WHITE TABLE WINE

2 QUARTS WATER

1 ½ POUNDS TINY NEW POTATOES, UNPEELED, QUARTERED

6 PLUM TOMATOES, PEELED, SEEDED, AND CHOPPED (ABOUT 2 CUPS)

3 TABLESPOONS FRESH LEMON JUICE, STRAINED

FRESHLY GROUND BLACK PEPPER

CROÛTES (PAGE 79)

Prepare a hot fire in a charcoal grill, or preheat a gas grill. Quickly wipe the grill with a cloth or paper towel to remove any persisting blackened material. Carefully dry the tuna slices with paper towels and brush with a very thin film of the olive oil. Working in batches if necessary, arrange the tuna slices on the grill. To create cross-hatching marks, grill on the first side for 30 seconds, then rotate 90 degrees and grill for another 30 seconds. Turn over each slice and repeat as with the first side. Remove from the grill and reserve until cool enough to handle, then cut the tuna into ¾-inch cubes and reserve.

Trim and seed the red and green bell peppers and cut them into narrow, short ribbons about 1 inch long by ¼ inch wide.

Heat the remaining olive oil (about 3 tablespoons) in a heavy 4-quart soup pot over medium heat. Sauté the onions, chile, and bell peppers, shaking the pot and stirring the contents, until the onions are lightly colored, about 5 minutes. Add the garlic, celery, carrot, bay leaves, cayenne, sea salt, wine, and water and bring to a boil. Reduce the heat to low, cover partially, and simmer for 10 minutes to develop a flavorful broth.

Add the potatoes and simmer until the potatoes are tender, 10 to 12 minutes. Do not overcook. Add the reserved tuna and the tomatoes and simmer briefly until the tuna is firm and tender, 2 to 3 minutes. Remove from the heat and allow to rest, covered, for 5 minutes.

Remove the carrot, celery, and bay leaves and discard. Add the lemon juice. Taste and add salt if needed and black pepper to taste. Ladle into heated soup plates and accompany with the *croûtes*.

THE ESSENTIAL LEMON Lemon juice is a great flavor enhancer. We all know the effect of fresh lemon juice on *sole meunière* or on a freshly shucked oyster. But it is not just seafood that benefits. The Florentines, for instance, finish a perfectly grilled steak with a few squeezes of lemon and garnish with the wedges. One of the world's favorite soups is the Greek *avgolemono* (egg and lemon) in which savory chicken broth, rice, and eggs are brightened by zesty lemon juice.

The flavor of seafood soups can be enhanced by a last-minute addition of lemon juice *à table*, and these soups are often more radiant when garnished with carefully seeded wedges or slices of lemons.

1 POUND SALT COD, PREFERABLY BONELESS

8 CUPS WATER

¼ TEASPOON *PIMENT D'ESPELETTE* (PAGE 120) OR CAYENNE PEPPER

SALT, IF NEEDED

FRESHLY GROUND BLACK PEPPER

For the toasts:

¼ CUP OLIVE OIL, OR AS NEEDED

3 CLOVES GARLIC, FINELY MINCED

1 SMALL FRESH CHILE, TRIMMED, SEEDED, AND FINELY CHOPPED

6 THICK SLICES STALE FRENCH BREAD, EACH ABOUT ¾ INCH THICK

PIMENT D'ESPELETTE OR CAYENNE PEPPER

le pays Basque

SALT COD SOUP with CHILE TOASTS

ZURRAKUTUNA

MAKES 4 TO 6 SERVINGS

Salt cod, after washing and soaking, yields a firm, delicately flavored fish. It is moist and sweet, abandoning any saltiness in its lavish water baths. I limited the intensity of hot chiles, but if you like your cooking to have fireworks, add more chiles to the cooking broth.

There's an unusual technique in Basque zurrakutuna. The toasts that accompany the soup are enkindled by being sautéed in the oil, garlic, and chiles that are part of the completed soup.

Soak the salt cod overnight in plenty of cold water, changing the water several times if possible. Before preparing the soup, put the bowl holding the salt cod under the faucet and allow cold water to run gently over it for 5 minutes. Drain.

Put the fish in a heavy 4-quart soup pot. Add 6 cups of the water and bring just to a boil. Remove the pot from the heat immediately, as the cod should never cook at a high temperature. Allow the cod to remain in its own broth for 1 hour.

Meanwhile, prepare the toasts: Heat the ¼ cup olive oil in a sauté pan over very low heat. Add the garlic and chile and cook, stirring constantly, until the garlic is faintly colored, 2 to 3 minutes. With a slotted spoon, remove the garlic and chile from the oil and reserve. In this same oil, sauté the bread slices, adding a little olive oil if necessary to prevent scorching, until both sides of each slice are golden brown. Remove the bread and drain on paper towels. Dust one side of each slice lightly with *piment d'Espelette* or cayenne.

To finish the soup, remove the salt cod from its broth with a slotted spoon and reserve. Add the remaining 2 cups water, the reserved garlic and chile, and the *piment d'Espelette* or cayenne to the soup pot with the cooking broth. Bring to a boil over high heat, reduce the heat to low, and simmer for 15 minutes.

Discard any skin or bones from the cod, then crumble or flake the fish and add it to the soup. Simmer over low heat, stirring gently with a wooden spoon, until the cod flakes and the soup broth is fully flavored, about 15 minutes.

The soup will probably not need salt (taste nonetheless), but add black pepper to taste at this time. Ladle the soup into heated soup plates and garnish with the toasts.

SALT COD (*MORUE*) AT MARKET IN BOULOGNE-SUR-MER.

SALT COD The tradition that Basque salt cod soup represents is as old as it is universal. Because of the widespread availability of cod, fishermen have been catching it for centuries. To ensure a food supply when fresh fish was not available, salting cod became an immense industry. Currently, with refrigeration and consumers' demand for fresh fish, salt cod is not as necessary or as prevalent. However, many cultures, the French included, have a nostalgia and taste for the commodity, and it is still produced.

AT THE ENTRANCE TO MANY BASQUE VILLAGES, THE COMMUNITY'S NAME IS DISPLAYED ON A SIGN IN BOTH FRENCH AND BASQUE. ESPELETTE IS RENOWNED FOR ITS DISTINCTIVE PEPPER, *PIMENT D'ESPELETTE*.

PIMENT D'ESPELETTE The Basque chile pepper, known as the *piment d'Espelette*, grows around Espelette, a small Basque village less than twenty miles from the Atlantic. The peppers are eye-catching as they dry, collected into swags hanging from whitewashed, red-tile-roofed Basque houses against a backdrop of the Pyrenees. They give a comfortable if vigorous heat. These exact chiles are unavailable in the United States, but red pepper flakes in combination with a small amount of cayenne pepper can be substituted (also see Sources). Because the amount of hotness in a particular dish is largely a matter of taste, feel free to use your own favorite chiles. Remember that Basque seasoning is bold, but not incendiary.

Ingredients

2 POUNDS MONKFISH FILLETS

¼ CUP FRUITY OLIVE OIL

3 SLENDER LEEKS, WHITE AND PALE GREEN PARTS ONLY, CUT INTO LARGE PIECES

2 MEDIUM-SIZED ONIONS, EACH CUT IN HALF AND EACH HALF STUCK WITH 1 WHOLE CLOVE

1 BOUQUET GARNI (6 FRESH PARSLEY STEMS, 2 BAY LEAVES, 2 FRESH THYME SPRIGS TIED IN 1 LARGE CELERY STALK)

1 FRESH TARRAGON SPRIG (OPTIONAL)

1 SMALL FENNEL BRANCH, OR ½ TEASPOON DRIED FENNEL SEED

15 WHOLE ALLSPICE

1 TEASPOON SEA SALT

2½ QUARTS WATER

GARLIC MAYONNAISE (RECIPE FOLLOWS)

FRESHLY GROUND WHITE PEPPER

¼ CUP CHOPPED FRESH CHIVES

¼ CUP CHOPPED FRESH PARSLEY

CROÛTONS (PAGE 79)

Languedoc

MONKFISH SOUP with GARLIC CREAM

BOURRIDE de BAUDROIE SÈTOISE

MAKES **6** MAIN-COURSE SERVINGS

There are at least two major versions of bourride, *one from Languedoc and one from Provence. They are similar, sharing the powerfully flavored and emulsifying* aioli *as well as the use of the freshest fish possible. Provençal* bourride *is made with a mixture of seafood, while the cooks of Languedoc prepare their* bourrides *with monkfish alone and pound the liver of freshly caught fish into the mayonnaise.*

The spice trade, flourishing in the ports of the Mediterranean ports since the thirteenth century, probably accounts for the unexpected use of whole allspice in the Languedoc version of bourride. *Montpellier, an ancient city of Languedoc, its name meaning "mountain of spice," reflects the influence of spice markets in local history and its cooking.*

Although a thin, tough membrane that must be removed surrounds the monkfish, the firm flesh and lack of bones makes the fish reasonably easy for cooks to prepare. The flavor is mild and often echoes other ingredients with which it is cooked. (That is also why it is sometimes called "poor man's lobster"—dipped in butter, some claim its flavor is similar to that of the shellfish.) Another monkfish plus: it is extremely low in calories.

Trim away all of the thin membrane from the monkfish, cut into 1½-inch squares, and reserve. Preheat the oven to 250°F and place a tureen in the oven to preheat.

Heat the olive oil in a heavy 4-quart soup pot over medium heat. Add the leeks and onions and cook, stirring often, until the vegetables are lightly colored, about 8 minutes. Add the bouquet garni, tarragon (if using), fennel, whole allspice, sea salt, and water and bring to a boil over high heat. Reduce the heat to low, cover partially, and simmer for 15 minutes to produce a flavorful broth.

Add the monkfish pieces, cover partially, and poach them over very low heat for 5 to 6 minutes. They should be tender but firm. Remove the monkfish with a skimmer, arrange in the heated tureen, cover lightly with a lid or aluminum foil, and keep warm in the oven.

Strain the cooking liquid through a fine-mesh sieve into a large bowl. Place 1 cup of the mayonnaise in the soup pot. Very slowly, add 8 cups of the strained hot broth while whisking continuously. Place the soup pot over low heat and heat thoroughly, stirring often, and guarding that the soup does not boil. Taste and add more salt if needed and white pepper to taste.

Remove the tureen of fish from the oven and pour in the hot thickened broth. Sprinkle with the chives and parsley and serve with the *croûtons*. Pass the remaining mayonnaise at table.

(RECIPE CONTINUES)

For the mortar method:

8 CLOVES GARLIC, CRUSHED

½ TEASPOON SEA SALT

3 EGG YOLKS, AT ROOM TEMPERATURE

1 ¾ CUPS EXTRA-VIRGIN OLIVE OIL, AT ROOM TEMPERATURE

JUICE OF 2 MEDIUM-SIZED LEMONS, STRAINED AND AT ROOM TEMPERATURE

⅛ TEASPOON FRESHLY GROUND WHITE PEPPER

For the machine method:

6 CLOVES GARLIC

3 EGG YOLKS, AT ROOM TEMPERATURE

1 ¾ CUPS EXTRA-VIRGIN OLIVE OIL

3 TABLESPOONS FRESH LEMON JUICE, STRAINED AND AT ROOM TEMPERATURE

SALT

FRESHLY GROUND WHITE PEPPER

GARLIC MAYONNAISE
AÏOLI

ABOUT 1 ¾ CUPS

It concentrates in its essence the heat, the force, the joy of the Provençal sun.

—Frédéric Mistral,
PROVENÇAL POET, ON AÏOLI

To make in a mortar: Combine the crushed garlic and sea salt in a mortar and mash with a pestle until the mixture becomes paste-like. The salt acts as an abrasive and assists in breaking down the garlic pieces. Add the egg yolks and continue to pound the mixture until it has become a paste. Beginning with a drop at a time, add the oil, working the pestle constantly. Continue to add oil slowly until the mixture becomes a thick sauce. Gradually stir in the lemon juice and white pepper. Taste and add salt if needed.

To make in a blender or food processor: Pulse the garlic until finely minced. Add the egg yolks one at a time, processing until a thick paste forms. With the motor running, slowly add the oil in a very fine, steady stream until a thick emulsion forms. Once the mixture is emulsified, the balance of the oil can be added a little faster. Gradually add the lemon juice, processing until the mixture becomes a golden, satiny mayonnaise. Transfer to a bowl, taste and add salt and white pepper, stirring them in with a little whisk or a fork.

RIGHT: BY CLINGING TO ROPES HUNG FROM WOODEN FRAMES, MUSSELS GROW TO MATURITY UNDERWATER IN A QUIET INLET OFF THE COAST OF LANGUEDOC.

MIXED SEAFOOD STEW

BOUILLABAISSE à la MARSEILLE

MAKES **8** MAIN-COURSE SERVINGS

Marseilles is home to bouillabaisse, and there is not a more famed seafood dish in the world. It embodies all the choice ingredients that may be found in the vigorous, spontaneous cooking of this region. Garlic, olive oil, fennel, saffron, a whiff of Pernod, the scent of orange, ripe tomatoes—all of these release their perfume. The flavors mirror both eastern Mediterranean and African cuisines. The port of Marseilles often seems to be more international than French.

What is included in a real bouillabaisse is a subject of continual debate. Food writer Waverley Root once described two sides of one fierce argument by writing that "a man who would put lobster in bouillabaisse would poison wells . . . a man who would leave it out would starve his children."

This is essentially a dish of more humble origins, so this recipe contains no costly shellfish. As always the case in a mixed seafood soup, the greater the variety of fish used, the better the soup.

Serve this to at least eight guests—more fish varieties, no leftovers. Bouillabaisse is for those cooks who enjoy bold flavors, high color, and the satisfaction of making a dish with a legendary history.

2 POUNDS ASSORTED FULL-FLAVORED FISH FILLETS SUCH AS SEA BASS, GROUPER, AND ROCKFISH

2 POUNDS ASSORTED DELICATE FISH FILLETS SUCH AS FLOUNDER AND POLLOCK

2 POUNDS FISH FRAMES AND HEADS

4 QUARTS WATER

2 MEDIUM-SIZED ONIONS, CHOPPED

2 SLENDER LEEKS, WHITE AND PALE GREEN PARTS ONLY, SLICED

4 TO 6 PLUM TOMATOES, PEELED, SEEDED, AND CHOPPED

4 CLOVES GARLIC, FINELY CHOPPED

1 LARGE BOUQUET GARNI (6 FRESH PARSLEY STEMS, 2 BAY LEAVES, 2 FRESH THYME SPRIGS TIED IN 1 LARGE CELERY STALK)

1 1/2 TEASPOONS FENNEL SEEDS

3 PIECES OVEN-DRIED ORANGE PEEL, EACH ABOUT 1 BY 2 INCHES (SEE NOTE)

1/2 TEASPOON SAFFRON THREADS, STEEPED IN 1/2 CUP HOT WATER

1 TEASPOON SEA SALT

2 TEASPOONS PERNOD (OPTIONAL)

FRESHLY GROUND BLACK PEPPER

30 *CROÛTES* (PAGE 79)

2 CUPS SPICED MAYONNAISE (RECIPE FOLLOWS)

Prepare the fish fillets by cutting into 1½- to 2-inch pieces and reserve. Carefully rinse the fish frames and heads under cold running water, rinsing away any traces of blood or viscera that would add bitterness to the broth.

Put the fish frames and heads, water, and onions in a heavy 10-quart soup pot and bring to a boil over high heat. Reduce the heat to medium and simmer for 20 minutes. Remove and discard any large pieces of bone. Pour the broth through a fine-mesh sieve into a clean vessel. (It is not necessary to use cheesecloth for this straining.)

Rinse out the pot and return the broth to the pot. Add the leeks, tomatoes, garlic, bouquet garni, fennel seeds, orange peel, saffron and water, and sea salt. Bring to a boil over high heat, reduce the heat to medium, cover partially, and simmer for 30 minutes. Preheat the oven to 250°F and put a large platter and 8 soup plates in the oven to preheat.

When the soup has simmered for 30 minutes, remove the bouquet garni and orange peel and discard. Lower pieces of the firmer fish into the broth and cook for 1 to 2 minutes. Add the more delicate fish and cook for 1 to 2 minutes. Remove the fish with a skimmer and arrange on the heated platter. Spoon some of the broth over the seafood, cover with aluminum foil, and return to the oven to keep warm.

If you like the taste of Pernod, and feel the soup would benefit from additional anise flavoring, add it at this time. Taste and add salt if needed and black pepper to taste. Ladle the hot broth into the heated soup plates and accompany with the *croûtes* and mayonnaise. Serve the platter of seafood after the broth.

NOTE: When you prepare the orange peel for Mediterranean recipes, remove the entire peel from an orange, cut it into pieces, and dry all the pieces, rather than just the single piece you need for the bouillabaisse. To dry the pieces, place them in a pie pan or on a baking sheet in a preheated 350°F oven until they feel dry to the touch and are lightly browned around the edges. This should take about 10 minutes. When cool, place in a sealable plastic bag in the freezer.

Having dried orange peel tucked away in your freezer is like having a secret ingredient on hand for adding subtlety and mystery to a number of dishes. For example, I like to cook lamb shanks with garlic, onions, rosemary, and dried orange peel in a slow cooker. Dried orange peel is also a fragrant surprise when making chicken broth for preparing Chinese food, and I like to add it to curried sauces, too. The ideas will begin to flow once you have a stash of the peel. You will find that the elusive sensation of the dried peel is much more compelling than the flavor of fresh orange in many dishes.

(RECIPE CONTINUES)

SPICED MAYONNAISE
SAUCE ROUILLE

ABOUT 1 CUP

This sauce is essential to bouillabaisse, but it may enhance many other dishes as well. A small spoonful goes a long way on lightly poached fish, chilled shrimp, grilled chicken breast, or even stirred into pasta salad.

8 CLOVES GARLIC

½ TEASPOON SALT

4 EGG YOLKS, AT ROOM TEMPERATURE

1 CUP OLIVE OIL, AT ROOM TEMPERATURE

1 TEASPOON CAYENNE PEPPER

1 TEASPOON HUNGARIAN PAPRIKA

1 TABLESPOON TOMATO PASTE (OPTIONAL)

Combine the garlic and salt in a mortar and mash with a pestle until the garlic is thoroughly crushed, or mince finely on a cutting board with a sharp knife.

Dampen a small tea towel and fold it into a square to make a nonskid base for the mixing bowl. Put the egg yolks in the bowl and add the mashed garlic. Whisk until the ingredients have become one thick paste. Very carefully add the olive oil, a drop at a time, while continuously whisking. When the yolks have absorbed all the olive oil, whisk in the cayenne and paprika. You can thin the mixture a little bit by adding a spoonful or two of bouillabaisse broth. If you want a little more color (or the flavor of tomato), add tomato paste and mix well.

AN OFFSHORE BOUILLABAISSE Because the waters around Corsica are so rich with shellfish, Corsican cooks have freely added langoustines and lobsters to *aziminu*, their version of Mediterranean bouillabaisse. Shellfish make an intense broth and a sumptuous soup. In *aziminu*, because the fresh seafood is first bathed in a saffron-laden marinade that intensifies the ultimate flavor, the Corsicans speak of their lavish *aziminu* as a golden soup (*soupe d'or*).

TOP RIGHT: SHRIMP (*CREVETTES*) COME TO MARKET WITH TAILS AND HEADS INTACT.

BOTTOM RIGHT: IN FRANCE, FISHMONGERS AND FRENCH COOKS ALIKE PREFER SCALLOPS (*COQUILLES SAINT-JACQUES*) WITH THEIR SHELLS AND CORALS INTACT.

PURÉED FISH SOUP
SOUPE de POISSONS à la PROVENÇALE

MAKES **6** GENEROUS SERVINGS

Although the basic flavors in this soup are Provençal, bistros and cafés all over France list it on their menus. French chefs like to prepare it and diners love to eat it. The finest soupes de poissons are velvety (carefully cooked fish, properly puréed) and satiny (inclusion of puréed scallops, for instance), with an intense seafood flavor.

The French accurately call this radiant, blush-colored seafood dish, "soup of fish" (soupe de poissons), not soup with fish (soupe aux poissons). The semantic difference may seem subtle, but it indicates how vital the large quantities and varieties of fish are to the success of the soup.

2 QUARTS FISH BROTH (PAGE 212)

2 POUNDS OCEAN PERCH OR ROCKFISH FILLETS

1 POUND WHITING FILLETS

3 TABLESPOONS FRUITY OLIVE OIL

4 MEDIUM-SIZED ONIONS, CHOPPED

2 SLENDER LEEKS, WHITE AND PALE GREEN PARTS ONLY, THINLY SLICED

4 CLOVES GARLIC, FINELY MINCED

4 TOMATOES, PEELED, SEEDED, AND CHOPPED

1 TEASPOON SEA SALT

1 BOUQUET GARNI (6 FRESH PARSLEY STEMS, 2 BAY LEAVES, 2 FRESH THYME SPRIGS TIED IN 1 LARGE CELERY STALK)

PINCH OF CAYENNE PEPPER

¼ TEASPOON SAFFRON THREADS, STEEPED IN ¼ CUP HOT WATER

½ TEASPOON FRESHLY GROUND BLACK PEPPER

CROÛTES (PAGE 79)

GRATED GRUYÈRE CHEESE FOR SERVING

1½ CUPS SPICED MAYONNAISE (PAGE 126)

Make the fish broth as directed, then strain and reserve.

Wipe the fish with a damp cloth and cut into uniform-sized pieces. Reserve.

Heat the olive oil in a heavy 4-quart soup pot over medium heat. Sauté the onions and leeks, stirring often, until they are a light golden color, about 8 minutes. Add the garlic, tomatoes, and sea salt and continue to cook, stirring often, for 5 minutes. Add the bouquet garni, fish broth, and pieces of fish and bring to a boil over high heat. Reduce the heat to very low, cover partially, and simmer until all of the ingredients appear inseparable, about 30 minutes.

Remove any fat from the surface of the soup with a ladle. Remove and discard the bouquet garni. Working with 1 or 2 ladlefuls at a time, purée the soup in a blender or food processor, processing each batch for at least 30 to 40 seconds until smooth. Push the puréed soup through a coarse sieve and return to the soup pot. Bring to a boil again and add the cayenne and the saffron and water. Taste and add more salt if needed and the black pepper.

Ladle into heated soup plates and serve immediately. Place the *croûtes*, the cheese, and the mayonnaise on a platter and take to the table to accompany the soup.

NOTE: To prepare this soup in the authentic manner of Provence, you need a variety of small, whole ocean fish that are generally rather bony. Remove the heads, clean them carefully, and add them to the soup pot with the other ingredients. After cooking, because of the tiny fish bones, you cannot purée the soup in a food processor. Instead, you must push the well-cooked solids through a *tamis* sieve (a flat screen mounted over a wooden ring). The bones stay on one side of the screen while the fish flesh, tomato pulp, onions, and garlic emerge out the other side. Many food writers believe that *soupe de poissons* should only be created in this way.

AT THE WATER'S EDGE I enjoyed an optimistic suggestion by Corsican food writer Marie Ceccaldi that fish dishes should be prepared only at the water's edge, so that the fish never touches ice. Today this seems impossible to imagine, but it is good to know that there were—or might be—such places in the world. Careful cooks make sure their fishmongers place an insulating barrier between the fish and the ice, as direct contact can damage the flesh of fresh seafood.

CHAPTER FOUR

Our meals are charming, although modest,
Thanks to the deep talent that makes use of the rest
Of the roast from yesterday or today's pot-au-feu,
In hash or in a stew.

—Paul Verlaine, *CHANSONS POUR ELLE*

SOUPS *from*
THE FARMHOUSE KITCHENS: MEAT AND POULTRY

LEFT: THE WIFE OF A GASCON FARMER BEGINS
HER MORNING CHORES.

FARMHOUSE KETTLES

Traditional French soups prepared with ingredients from the barnyard, pasture, or henhouse fall into three essential and obvious groups based on the principal ingredient: the *potée* is made from pork, the *pot-au-feu* is made from beef, and the *poule-au-pot* is made from a chicken. These three designations are not rigidly adhered to, however, as cooks always mix and match a wide range of components. Farmhouse soups are consistent in one frugal aspect, however, that of being prepared with the least expensive pieces of meat.

Food historian Stephen Mennell, in his *All Manners of Food*, uses the term "the domination of the cauldron." That seems appropriate in this context because of the way the French have identified their three major meat soups; they all contain the French word *pot*, meaning "kettle" or "pot."

The word *potée* itself is the earthenware pot or kettle in which the soup is traditionally cooked. I imagine that in English it might best be translated as "potted." The French say, "A beautiful pig, it is sunshine in the house," and the foundation of their *potées* is the meat of "a beautiful pig." There's usually no indication of what else any given *potée* may contain, except a regional adjective, such as *alsacienne*, may be added, thus identifying the other ingredients.

Usually cabbage is included in a *potée*, which is a vegetable that seems appropriately teamed with pork. What else can we look for? The *potée* from Alsace, for example, is made with smoked bacon, fresh pork, vegetables, and beans (page 134). In Lorraine, cooks also insist on bacon in their *potée*, plus smoked pork shoulder and ham rind. Local sausages are added in Franche-Comté. The Champagne region adds chicken to ham and sausage in *potée champenois* (page 139), and a fairly upscale *potée* with rabbit, sausage, and beef ribs from the Anjou region is a French national treasure (page 152).

I love a version from Brittany, *potée d'Elven*, which features pork plus beef and lamb, all the meats attached to the bone. It makes a succulent broth, but it is the beets in the dish that deliver the *coup de maître*. No matter how I worked with the recipe, however, I could not make a plausible reader-friendly recipe for this book.

It is understood that the *pot-au-feu* is a beef dish, even though the name only tells us that a pot is, indeed, on the fire (page 144). Traditionally, prime beef that could be grilled or roasted was seldom included in a soup, not only because of economics but also because those cuts of meat are not the best for making a soup. I once saw an American recipe for a "steak soup." What would a French farmwife say? "It is *heresie!*"

The *poule-au-pot* leaves no question that a chicken is in the pot. Old stewing hens make the very best soup, not tender, young fryers. The chicken may be stuffed, or not, and the pot vegetables are similar to those of the *pot-au-feu*. Sometimes veal shanks are added for a wonderful viscosity in the broth.

It's important to remember that French meat and poultry soups are always—without any exception, I believe—full meal dishes, very serious ventures. They comprise at least two courses (first the broth is eaten and then the solids), with *les restes* used frugally over the following few days. Besides cabbage, *potées* quite often include

dried beans. Potatoes and turnips provide the starch for a *pot-au-feu*. French cooks often like to offer noodles (or pasta of some kind) with a *poule-au-pot*.

In many French cookbooks, the directions for serving soup indicate that a soup tureen seems to be a standard item for many households. As these grand two-course soups are *the* meal, they are presented with much ceremony, as befits them.

Ingredients list:

1¼ CUPS (ABOUT ½ POUND) RED OR WHITE DRIED BEANS

6½ QUARTS WATER

½ POUND LEAN BACON, DICED

1 MEDIUM-SIZED ONION, CHOPPED

1 TABLESPOON JUNIPER BERRIES WRAPPED IN CHEESECLOTH OR ENCLOSED IN TEA BALL

½ POUND GERMAN-STYLE FRESH SAUSAGES

1 HEAD SAVOY CABBAGE, CUT INTO 6 WEDGES

4 YOUNG, SLENDER CARROTS, PEELED AND HALVED CROSSWISE

4 MEDIUM-SIZED WAXY POTATOES, PEELED AND QUARTERED

3 CELERY STALKS, HALVED CROSSWISE

6 SMALL PORK CHOPS

1 TEASPOON SALT

FRESHLY GROUND BLACK PEPPER

6 THICK SLICES FRENCH BREAD, TOASTED IN THE OVEN

ASSORTED MUSTARDS

Old World charm lives on. This enduring potée, so fragrant and so full of compound flavors, takes us back to another time. It is also theatrical. Choucroûte garni, the famed Alsatian dish of sauerkraut with sausages, ham, pork, and potatoes, brings sighs of pleasure (and often disbelief) when it is presented to famished family and friends, and this dish evokes almost the same response. But this potée is much lighter than a choucroûte garni, although I do use the term lighter with hesitation.

Two items are essential to this dish: an assortment of mustards (an old-fashioned whole-grain mustard, a dark German Dusseldorf, and maybe a Dijon-style blend) and a nicely chilled Alsatian Riesling.

Rinse the beans, then place in a bowl and cover generously with cold water. Soak the beans overnight. The following day, drain, place in a heavy saucepan, and add 4 quarts of the water. Bring to a boil and cook over high heat for 10 to 12 minutes. Reduce the heat to medium-low and cook for 45 minutes. Drain and reserve.

Sauté the bacon pieces in a heavy 4-quart soup pot over medium heat, stirring often, until crisp, 5 to 7 minutes. Remove the bacon with a slotted spoon, drain on paper towels, and reserve.

Pour off all but 2 tablespoons of the bacon fat from the pot. Add the onion and cook over low heat, stirring occasionally, until softened, about 5 minutes. Add the reserved beans, 2 quarts of the water, and the juniper berries to the soup pot. Bring to a boil over high heat and cook for 10 to 12 minutes. Reduce the heat to very low, cover partially, and simmer, stirring occasionally, until the beans are almost tender, about 30 minutes.

Prick the sausages randomly with the tip of a knife. Add the sausages, all the vegetables, the pork chops, and the salt to the pot. Simmer, uncovered, over low heat until the pork chops are tender, 45 to 60 minutes.

Using a slotted utensil, remove the meats, cabbage, carrots, potatoes, and celery from the soup pot and arrange on a heated platter. Cut the sausages to yield 6 pieces in all. Moisten with a little of the broth. Remove the juniper berries and discard. Add the remaining ½ quart (2 cups) water to the pot if needed to thin. Taste and add salt if needed and black pepper to taste.

Place the toasted bread slices in heated soup plates and ladle the broth and beans over the bread slices. Sprinkle with crisp bacon and accompany with the platter of meats and vegetables. Pass the mustards at table.

GOOD SOUP AND GOOD HEALTH With nearly everyone aware of the hazards of eating too much animal fat, I find there is no inherent quarrel between the use of fat in authentic French soup recipes and its cautioned use by the cooks of today. Many rustic farm soups were prepared with a minimum of meat, as a little had to stretch a long way. The peasants that prepared these soups often ate them three times a day. The variety of soups made with assorted pigs' parts or with anything that grew and was edible demonstrates not only a hardworking, struggling people, but also their continued and watchful frugality. These situations were not unique to France, obviously, but they are vital to my story.

It was not unusual for a farm family to exist for one year on the meat from one hog. This hog, traditionally enormous and fat by our standards, was usually butchered in the coldest part of winter (for optimum sanitation). Every single part of the animal (to the distaste of many modern cooks) was preserved, whether salted, smoked, or made into sausage. Little of it was eaten fresh. Pork fat was vital for the amount of calories needed for the work that was required. But, as the year on the farm rolled on, less and less pork was available, and the meat was carefully rationed.

In the southwestern regions, where goose and duck were preserved in confits for later uses, the rendered confit fat was added stingily to soups, a little spoonful at a time. A celebratory soup used a few pieces of the confit itself.

In most cases, the farmhouse kitchen soups in this chapter have been adapted to modern tastes. Nearly all the recipes yield six servings, and I have limited the amount of fat used. I use the traditional fat to give the dish its authenticity and then remove what is unnecessary. The flavor stays, while the fat goes.

le pays Basque

GARLIC, SAUSAGE, and RED PEPPER SOUP

BARATXURI SALDA

MAKES 6 SERVINGS

½ POUND SPICY FRESH SAUSAGES

3 RED BELL PEPPERS

1 TABLESPOON FRUITY OLIVE OIL

8 TO 10 CLOVES GARLIC, FINELY MINCED

PINCH OF *PIMENT D'ESPELETTE* (PAGE 120) OR CAYENNE PEPPER

2 QUARTS WATER

1 TEASPOON SALT

RED WINE VINEGAR

GARLIC *CROÛTES* (PAGE 79)

Although many variations of this brightly colored Basque soup exist, they all have a resounding amount of fresh garlic. If you want to make a more filling dish, whisk an egg or two into a froth and stir vigorously into the boiling soup. Alternatively, you might poach eggs separately and add them to the soup; the sausage and eggs are a good combination. Set out a cruet of fine red wine vinegar with the soup, as it is the custom for diners to add a trickle of vinegar at table.

Remove the casings from the sausages and crush the meat with a fork.

Trim and seed the red bell peppers and cut them into narrow, short ribbons about 1 inch long by ¼ inch wide.

Heat the olive oil in a heavy 4-quart soup pot over very low heat. Add the garlic, sausage meat, and bell peppers and sauté, stirring often with a wooden spoon, until the sausage is browned, about 10 minutes. Drain off any excess fat from the pot. Add the *piment d'Espelette* or cayenne pepper, water, and salt and bring to a boil over high heat. Reduce the heat to low and simmer, uncovered, for 20 minutes. The garlic and bell pepper ribbons should be softly tender.

Taste and add more salt, and *piment d'Espelette* or cayenne if needed. Ladle into heated soup plates and pass the vinegar and *croûtes* at table.

"WOODEN LEG" SOUP (*POTAGE À LA JAMBE DE BOIS*)

Because this soup is described in eighteenth-century cuisine, I think it is imperative to include it in this book, which looks at the evolution of French soups. The selection translated here is attributed to the writings of Grimod de la Reynière, a well-known gourmet and bon vivant, who lived in Paris following the Revolution. His recipe:

"One takes a leg of beef, which can be cut into 2 pieces of about a foot each, and puts them in a pot with a good broth, a piece of beef, and cold water. After cooking, the pot is skimmed, seasoned with salt and whole cloves. One adds 2 or 3 dozen carrots, a dozen onions, 2 dozen celery roots, a dozen turnips, 1 chicken, and an old partridge. Put the pot on the fire early in the morning and cook it slowly so your bouillon will be the finest. Take then a piece of veal, about 2 pounds, sweat it in the pot, and moisten with your bouillon. When it has been degreased you will add 2 celery roots and cook for 1 hour before serving. The bouillon will be finished and have a good taste when you take some bread, which has been dried and cut into slices, and add it to your bouillon and simmer. When that is finished, you will put the soup in soup plates and garnish it with all sorts of vegetables from the pot. Add a veal bone to the pot to moisten and serve it very hot."

STUFFED CABBAGE IN SAVORY BROTH (*SOUPE AU POULE VERTE*)

Green chicken (*poule verte*) soup? No, this isn't even a chicken soup at all. It's a plump green bundle of stuffed cabbage that does look for all the world like a green chicken simmering in the pot.

Prepare a ham-bacon-cabbage stuffing, carefully enclose it in overlapping dark green Savoy cabbage leaves, tie it all up, and create a chicken-shaped package. The cabbage parcel is poached and the resulting broth is deeply flavored, by its own aromatics as well as the ingredients of the cabbage filling. The broth is traditionally served at the side of the stuffed-cabbage main dish. Another option would be to reserve the broth for another meal and serve only the stuffed cabbage and potatoes also cooked in the broth. This unusual dish is extremely filling but not particularly rich. Rye bread and an assortment of mustards are the typical accompaniments.

CHICKEN, HAM, and SAUSAGE KETTLE

POTÉE CHAMPENOIS

MAKES **6** MAIN-COURSE SERVINGS

2 CUPS (ABOUT ¾ POUND) DRIED WHITE BEANS SUCH AS NAVY OR GREAT NORTHERN

6 QUARTS WATER

2 OUNCES SALT PORK

¾-POUND PIECE SMOKED HAM WITH BONE

6 MEDIUM-LARGE CHICKEN THIGHS

3 YOUNG, SLENDER CARROTS, PEELED AND COARSELY CHOPPED

3 TURNIPS, PEELED AND COARSELY CHOPPED

1 SMALL HEAD SAVOY CABBAGE, CORED AND COARSELY CHOPPED

2 FRESH PORK SAUSAGES, EACH ABOUT 6 OUNCES

4 MEDIUM-SIZED WAXY POTATOES, PEELED AND CUT LENGTHWISE INTO EIGHTHS

SALT

FRESHLY GROUND BLACK PEPPER

Potée champenois is a good choice when preparing a one-pot meal for people with different meat preferences, for it has a selection for everyone. The cooks of Champagne prepare their traditional potée with pork and cabbage, of course, but also include one entire chicken, which they simmer with the other savory components. I have adapted the recipe by substituting chicken thighs for the whole chicken. The dark thigh meat adds deeper flavor, is a little more manageable during preparation, and may be served in the soup plate on the bone. The dish then becomes a knife-fork-and-spoon soup. If the occasion is more formal, you can always remove the chicken thigh bones in the kitchen.

The chalky soil of Champagne may be perfect for raising fine grapes, but it makes the work of farming more arduous. Dishes as robust as this potée have been essential.

Rinse the beans, then place in a bowl and cover generously with cold water. Soak the beans overnight. The following day, drain, place in a heavy saucepan, and add 3 quarts of the water. Bring to a boil and cook over high heat for 10 to 12 minutes. Drain and reserve.

Although not necessary, it is traditional to blanch the salt pork and the ham in a large amount of boiling water for 2 to 3 minutes and then drain. This step will reduce the saltiness of the finished soup.

Combine the reserved beans and the remaining 3 quarts of water in a heavy 6-quart soup pot. Bring to a boil over high heat, reduce the heat to medium, and skim off any foam that rises to the surface. Cook for 10 to 12 minutes. Add the salt pork, ham, and chicken thighs, reduce the heat to low, cover partially, and simmer for 1 hour, stirring occasionally and skimming as necessary. The beans should be nearly tender.

Add the carrots, turnips, and cabbage and return to a boil over high heat. Reduce the heat to low and cook for 15 minutes, stirring gently. Add the sausages and potatoes and cook until the potatoes are tender, about 20 minutes. Taste and add salt if needed and black pepper to taste.

Transfer the meats to a carving board. Remove the skin from the chicken thighs (and the bones, if desired) and place 1 thigh in each of 6 heated soup plates. Cut the salt pork into small dice, and cut the ham and sausages into chunks. Add the meats to the soup plates. Ladle the soup over the meats and serve immediately.

Champagne - le Nord

FLEMISH CHICKEN and CREAM SOUP

WATERZOOI de POULET

MAKES **6** TO **8** SERVINGS

Keep waterzooi in mind when you have family or friends you wish to treat or to dazzle, for it is the ultimate cream and chicken soup. Using chicken broth to cook chicken imparts the most intense flavor imaginable. It's possible to use water instead, of course, but I do recommend using broth for this opulent soup.

1 CHICKEN, 3 TO 3½ POUNDS, PREFERABLY FREE RANGE

6 FRESH PARSLEY SPRIGS, LEAVES FINELY MINCED AND STEMS RESERVED

2 TABLESPOONS UNSALTED BUTTER

2 CELERY STALKS, THINLY SLICED

3 SLENDER LEEKS, WHITE AND PALE GREEN PARTS ONLY, THINLY SLICED

1 MEDIUM-SIZED ONION, STUCK WITH 2 WHOLE CLOVES

1 CUP DRY WHITE TABLE WINE

6 CUPS CHICKEN BROTH

1 TEASPOON SALT

¼ TEASPOON FRESHLY GRATED NUTMEG

¾ CUP HEAVY CREAM

4 EGG YOLKS

PINCH OF FRESHLY GROUND WHITE PEPPER

CROÛTONS (PAGE 79)

Rinse the chicken well. Cut into 6 pieces: 2 legs, 2 thighs, 2 half breasts. Reserve (or freeze) the giblets, wings, and back for making broth. Tie the fresh parsley stems together with kitchen string. Reserve the minced leaves.

Spread 1 tablespoon of the butter on the bottom of a heavy 6-quart soup pot or other large, deep pot. Scatter the celery and leek pieces, the parsley-stem bundle, and the onion in the center. Sprinkle the wine over all. Cut out a circular piece of parchment paper (or aluminum foil) the size of the pot's diameter and butter one side. Cut a small hole in the center of the paper "lid" for steam to escape and place the paper, buttered-side down, on top of the vegetables.

Put the soup pot over very low heat and allow the vegetables to simmer for 20 minutes so they will release their moisture. Discard the round paper, place the pieces of chicken on top of the vegetables, and pour the chicken broth over the entire contents. Add the salt and nutmeg, bring to a boil over high heat, reduce the heat to very low, cover, and allow the chicken and vegetables to cook, stirring occasionally so the chicken cooks evenly, for 1¼ hours. The chicken should be very tender. After the chicken has cooked for 1 hour, place a tureen in a 250°F oven to preheat.

With tongs or a slotted spoon, remove the chicken pieces from the pot. Allow to cool briefly and pull or cut the chicken meat from the bones, then remove the skin. Cut the chicken meat into bite-sized pieces and place in the preheated soup tureen, cover with its lid or aluminum foil, return to the oven, and keep hot. Discard the chicken skin and bones. Remove the fresh parsley stems and whole onion from the soup pot and discard.

Put the cream, the egg yolks, the minced parsley leaves, and the remaining 1 tablespoon butter, cut into tiny pieces, in a bowl. Mix thoroughly with a whisk. Slowly add a ladleful of the hot soup to the bowl, whisking constantly. Carefully pour the contents of the bowl into the soup pot while whisking constantly. Place over very low heat and continue to whisk without letting the soup come to a boil. Taste for seasoning and add more salt if needed and the white pepper.

Pour the hot soup over the chicken in the soup tureen and serve immediately. Accompany with the *croûtons*.

3 POUNDS OXTAILS

1 POUND BONELESS LAMB SHOULDER, IN ONE PIECE, TRIMMED OF EXCESS FAT

1 POUND BEEF SHORT RIBS

1 PIG'S FOOT OR KNUCKLE (OPTIONAL)

2 TABLESPOONS GOOD-QUALITY LARD

WATER TO COVER MEAT IN THE POT BY 1 INCH (ABOUT 4 QUARTS)

1 TABLESPOON SALT

1 LARGE ONION, COARSELY CHOPPED

1 SMALL HEAD SAVOY CABBAGE, CORED AND CUT INTO 1-INCH DICE

3 YOUNG, SLENDER CARROTS, PEELED AND CUT INTO ¾-INCH-THICK SLICES

3 SLENDER LEEKS, WHITE AND PALE GREEN PARTS ONLY, CUT INTO ½-INCH-THICK SLICES

3 TURNIPS, PEELED AND QUARTERED

6 SMALL, SPICY FRESH SAUSAGES

FRESHLY GROUND BLACK PEPPER

Champagne–le Nord

POT of OXTAILS and MIXED MEATS

QUEUE de BOEUF en HOCHEPOT FLAMANDE

MAKES 8 TO 10 MAIN-COURSE SERVINGS

If there was ever a recipe that evoked a Brueghel painting, this is it. All those satisfied roly-poly peasant men with rosy-cheeked maids have just polished off a big bowl of Flemish hochepot. I'm sure of it.

Of course, it is a dish of enormous proportions, but it is native to Flanders, a region in the north of France and, accordingly, one full of work-sustaining calories. For simplicity of service, I suggest that the vegetables and meats be cut into smaller pieces than is traditional and served within broth, made even more succulent with the oxtails.

Soak the oxtails in cold water to cover for 15 minutes, then rinse and drain. Thoroughly dry the oxtails and the rest of the meats, to aid in the browning procedure.

Melt the lard in a heavy 10-quart soup pot over medium heat. Sauté the oxtails, lamb, beef ribs, and the pig's foot or knuckle (if using), stirring often, until all the surfaces are thoroughly browned, 12 to 15 minutes. Add water to cover by 1 inch and the salt and bring to a boil. Reduce the heat to very low and simmer for 2 to 2½ hours, skimming away impurities from the surface as often as necessary. The meats should be tender. If not, simmer for an additional 20 to 30 minutes.

Add the onion, cabbage, carrots, leeks, turnips, and sausages and cook until the vegetables are tender and the sausages are cooked through, about 20 minutes. Taste and add more salt if needed and black pepper to taste.

Using tongs or a slotted utensil, transfer all the meats to a cutting board. Cut the sausages and lamb into 1-inch pieces. Pull or cut the meat from the oxtails, the short ribs, and the pig's foot or knuckles (if used), and discard the bones. Return the meat pieces to the pot and simmer for 2 to 3 minutes to heat thoroughly.

Ladle the soup into heated soup plates and serve at once.

GEOGRAPHY RULES When Caesar reported on the three divisions of Gaul, we assume he was not commenting on the three major branches of French cooking as defined by the use of three essential cooking fats, butter, olive oil, and pork or goose fat. Within France, so many variations exist in the countryside that there is no question but that these differences would be reflected in the local cooking. The climate is just as varied. The cool, damp north requires and produces foods that are distinguished from those of the warm, sunny Mediterranean provinces.

We look first at the soil to see how the geography of a place shapes and defines its cooking. What grows in a particular area not only feeds its people but also nourishes its animals. The rich, lush pastures of much of northern France (generally north of the Loire River) favor cattle raising, but a cow would starve in the rugged, rocky lands of southeastern France. There, without much encouragement, sturdy olive trees flourish. The cooler climate in northern regions, like Normandy, Brittany, and Atlantic coastal Charentes, is agreeable for butter making, whereas the hot weather in Provence is ideal for the ripening of olives. Olive trees also need the respite of a chilly winter, which Provence provides, too. In contrast, the central and southwest terrains of France, as well as northeastern Alsace, support a limited agriculture. These farms produce hogs and geese, and the fat used by cooks is lard or goose fat. Hogs do not need rich pasturage to be sustained, and geese, the so-called hogs of poultry, are nourished by the smallest amount of grain of any fowl.

When anyone thinks of French cuisine, he or she usually thinks of butter and cream. But this only holds true for the region that lies north of an uneven line that stretches across the country. Here, the people have created methods of preserving their milk supply. In Normandy, where cows graze on green grasslands, the milk is churned into pale, sweet butter and formed into some of the finest cheeses in France. The Normans' next-door neighbors, the Bretons, prefer their butter to be lightly salted, but there is no cheese-making tradition in Brittany. All of the provinces in the domain of butter make delicious, tender pastries, however.

On the other hand, in the southeast, local olive oil is much more than a cooking medium. Because of its distinctive flavor, it is a specific ingredient found in most of the dishes of the region. The late food writer Waverley Root said of the importance of the oddly shaped crinkled olive tree: "It looks like death but to the countries where it grows, it sometimes literally means life." There have been times when the impoverished actually made a meal of olives.

The people of France, having taken root throughout their variegated countryside, appropriately and creatively cook with the products that are at hand—an essential fusion of geography and cuisine.

4 TO 4½ POUNDS BEEF WITHOUT BONES SUCH AS RUMP, CHUCK, OR TOP ROUND

1 POUND BEEF BONES, INCLUDING BONES WITH MARROW

5 TO 6 QUARTS WATER

1 TEASPOON COARSE SALT

2 LARGE ONIONS, EACH STUCK WITH A FEW WHOLE CLOVES

6 YOUNG, SLENDER CARROTS, PEELED AND CUT INTO 2-INCH PIECES

4 TURNIPS, PEELED AND HALVED LENGTHWISE

4 SLENDER LEEKS, WHITE AND PALE GREEN PARTS ONLY, CUT INTO 2-INCH PIECES

2 CELERY STALKS, CUT INTO 2-INCH PIECES

1 SMALL CLOVE GARLIC

6 MEDIUM-SIZED WAXY POTATOES, BOILED OR STEAMED AND KEPT WARM (OPTIONAL)

FRESHLY GROUND BLACK PEPPER

CROÛTONS (PAGE 79; OPTIONAL)

GRATED GRUYÈRE CHEESE (OPTIONAL)

Ile-de-France

BEEF in ITS BROTH with VEGETABLES

POT-au-FEU

MAKES **6** TO **8** MAIN-COURSE SERVINGS

If there is a soup that is more essentially French than the pot-au-feu, I do not know what it could be. The name, "pot on the fire," is simplicity itself. Yet the name doesn't really describe the dish, or its contents, at all. It suggests that at one time it was the soup, the only soup extant. It is so old that its origins go back to the moment when a vessel for holding liquid was discovered. Since then, meat began to be cooked in water, rather than only directly over the fire on a primitive spit or grill. Very little about this dish, mankind's first soup, has changed since those long-ago days.

If the name pot-au-feu *is unadorned and simple, so is the soup's preparation. Beef, water, and aromatic vegetables are cooked to tenderness. In the street markets of France (particularly in Paris), I have found little bundles of leeks, carrots, celery, onions, and turnips tied with coarse string for home cooks' pot-au-feu. After simmering for a few hours, the broth is served as a first course, generally followed by the beef and maybe the marrowbones. There has been a lot of experimenting with this dish, but the basics remain deliciously the same.*

All people have their soups.
France alone possesses le pot-au-feu.
—**FRENCH WRITER** E. Auricoste de Lazarque

Place the beef meat and bones in a heavy 10-quart soup pot. Add water to cover, bring to a boil over high heat, reduce the heat to medium, and simmer for about 5 minutes. With a slotted spoon, remove the beef and bones, discard the water, and rinse out the pot. Return the meat and bones to the pot, add 5 quarts of the water, the coarse salt, and the whole onions and slowly bring to a boil over high heat. Reduce the heat so that the water barely simmers and skim until no more scum appears. Replace with water any of the cooking broth that is lost due to skimming. Cover partially and simmer gently until the meat is tender, 3 hours or more. Add additional water as needed to keep the meat covered at all times.

At the end of the cooking time, place a serving platter and 1 soup plate for each guest in a 250°F oven.

Add the carrots, turnips, leeks, celery, and garlic to the soup pot and simmer until the vegetables are tender, about 30 minutes. The addition of the vegetables may make it necessary to skim away additional foam from the surface. If you are using potatoes, do not add them to the pot, as they tend to sully the broth.

Using a slotted utensil or tongs, remove the meats and vegetables from the broth and arrange on the heated platter. Add the potatoes to the platter, if using. Cover with aluminum foil and return to the oven to keep warm.

AT AN ELEGANT MARKET NEAR THE PALACE OF VERSAILLES IN THE ILE-DE-FRANCE, THE WINDOW OF A *BOUCHER* ADVERTISES MEAT SPECIALTIES.

Skim off the fat from the surface of broth. Strain the broth through a fine-mesh sieve and return to the pot. Bring to a simmer, then taste and add more salt if needed and the black pepper to taste. Remove the foil covering the platter and moisten the meats and vegetables with a little of the hot broth. Re-cover and keep warm until serving.

Ladle the broth into heated soup plates and accompany with more coarse salt. Serve with *croûtons* and grated cheese, if desired. Serve the meat and vegetables as a second course.

145 SOUPS *from* THE FARMHOUSE KITCHENS: MEAT AND POULTRY

Languedoc

CATALAN HOLIDAY STEW

ESCUEDELLA de NADAL

MAKES **10** TO **12** MAIN-COURSE SERVINGS

I cannot think of any simmering soup that fills my house with a more amazing blend of aromas than this dish. It is an unqualified Spanish-French treasure. French-speaking cooks call it écuelle de Noël and create it as a Christmas feast. Despite all the ingredients, it is not that complicated to assemble, and the completed dish is spectacular. The vegetable-laden broth and tender, juicy meats, including a huge, plump meatball (pilota), add up to a meal perfect for a celebration.

For the *pilota:*

1 TABLESPOON OLIVE OIL

1 LARGE ONION, FINELY CHOPPED

6 OUNCES GROUND LEAN PORK

6 OUNCES GROUND LEAN VEAL OR TURKEY

6 OUNCES GROUND LEAN BEEF

1 EGG, LIGHTLY BEATEN

2 CLOVES GARLIC, FINELY MINCED

1 TEASPOON SALT

FRESHLY GROUND BLACK PEPPER

¼ CUP FINELY CHOPPED FRESH PARSLEY

For the soup:

1 HAM HOCK, ABOUT ¾ POUND

1 POUND BONELESS LAMB SHOULDER, IN ONE PIECE, TRIMMED OF EXCESS FAT

6 OUNCES FRESH HAM RIND OR SALT PORK RIND

4 TO 5 QUARTS WATER

1 CHICKEN, 2½ TO 3 POUNDS, CUT INTO 8 PIECES (RESERVE THE BACK FOR MAKING CHICKEN BROTH)

2 WHOLE DUCK BREASTS

¼ TEASPOON SAFFRON THREADS, STEEPED IN ¼ CUP HOT WATER

2 CLOVES GARLIC, FINELY MINCED

2 TEASPOONS SALT

6 MEDIUM-SIZED WAXY POTATOES, PEELED, AND COARSELY CHOPPED

3 MEDIUM-SIZED TURNIPS, PEELED AND COARSELY CHOPPED

6 YOUNG, SLENDER CARROTS, PEELED AND COARSELY CHOPPED

1 SMALL HEAD SAVOY CABBAGE, CORED AND COARSELY CHOPPED

6 CELERY STALKS, COARSELY CHOPPED

2 LARGE TOMATOES, PEELED, SEEDED AND CHOPPED

5 TABLESPOONS LONG-GRAIN WHITE RICE

FRESHLY GROUND BLACK PEPPER

To prepare the *pilota,* heat the olive oil in a 10-inch skillet over medium heat and add the onion. Sauté, stirring often, until lightly golden, 8 to 10 minutes. Remove from the heat. In a large bowl, combine the pork, veal or turkey, beef, cooked onion, egg, garlic, salt, pepper, and parsley and mix well. Form into a large, compact sausage-shaped meatball. Roll up in a large piece of plastic wrap, twisting the ends carefully to enclose securely.

Put the ham hock, lamb, *pilota,* and ham rind or salt pork rind in a heavy 10-quart soup pot. Add 4 quarts of the water and bring to a boil over high heat. Skim off any scum from the surface. Reduce the heat to very low, cover partially, and simmer for 1 hour, continuing to skim as necessary.

Add the chicken, duck, saffron and water, garlic, and salt and continue to simmer, partially covered, for 30 minutes longer. Place a large platter, a soup tureen (or large casserole), and a soup plate for each guest in a 250°F oven.

Add the potatoes, turnips, carrots, cabbage, and celery to the pot, cover, and cook over low heat for 10 minutes. Add the tomatoes and rice, re-cover, and cook until all the vegetables and the rice are tender, about 20 minutes longer. Taste and add more salt if needed and black pepper to taste. Thin with as much of the remaining 1 quart water as needed to achieve a good consistency.

Using tongs or a slotted utensil, remove the meats and the *pilota* from the pot and place on a cutting board. Remove the plastic wrap from the *pilota* and slice. Slice the meat from the ham hock and discard the bone. Finely dice the ham rind or salt pork rind and return it to the soup pot. Slice the lamb, and bone and slice the duck breasts. Arrange the sliced meats and chicken pieces on the heated platter. Pour the soup and vegetables into the heated soup tureen. Carry the platter of meats, the soup tureen, and the heated soup plates to the table and serve immediately.

Languenoc

SAUSAGE and ROOT VEGETABLE SOUP with HAM-and-BACON GRIDDLECAKES

AZINAT

MAKES **6** SERVINGS

1 HAM HOCK, ABOUT ¾ POUND

3½ QUARTS WATER

½ POUND FRESH PORK SAUSAGES (SEE RECIPE INTRODUCTION)

5 YOUNG, SLENDER CARROTS, PEELED AND CUT INTO CHUNKS

1 MEDIUM-SIZED ONION, COARSELY CHOPPED

1 CLOVE GARLIC, FINELY MINCED (OPTIONAL)

2 TURNIPS, PEELED AND CUT INTO CHUNKS

½ TEASPOON SALT

1 LARGE HEAD SAVOY CABBAGE, CORED, COARSE RIBS REMOVED, AND CUT INTO 2-INCH CHUNKS

4 MEDIUM-SIZED WAXY POTATOES, PEELED AND CUT LENGTHWISE INTO EIGHTHS

FRESHLY GROUND BLACK PEPPER

3 HAM-AND-BACON GRIDDLECAKES (RECIPE FOLLOWS)

6 THICK CROÛTES MADE FROM COARSE COUNTRY BREAD (PAGE 79)

Azinat calls for a French sausage prepared with pork rind (couenne). It is similar to the Italian sausage known as cotechino, *and if that is available in your markets, by all means use it in this soup. Any fresh pork sausage that you like will be appropriate in this robust, country dish.*

The griddlecakes (rouzoles), which are made especially for this soup, are so unusual that I prefer to highlight them. I cut the cakes into wedges and serve them on a side plate. The French cut them into chunks and serve them in the soup itself.

Put the ham hock and 2 quarts of the water in a heavy 4-quart soup pot and bring to a boil over high heat. Reduce the heat to low, cover, and simmer gently for 1 hour. Add the sausages, carrots, onion, garlic, turnips, salt, and 1 quart of the water and bring to a boil over high heat. Reduce the heat to low and simmer for 30 minutes, stirring occasionally. It may be necessary to skim away a little foam from the surface from time to time.

Add the cabbage and potatoes to the soup pot and continue to cook until the potatoes are tender, about 20 minutes. Taste and add more salt if needed and black pepper to taste. The griddlecakes may be cut and added to the soup at this point or served on the side.

Place a *croûte* in each heated soup plate. Ladle the hot soup over the bread and serve immediately.

HAM-and-BACON GRIDDLECAKES
ROUZOLE

THREE 7-INCH GRIDDLECAKES

8 THICK SLICES FIRM WHITE BREAD (ABOUT $\frac{1}{2}$ POUND), CRUSTS REMOVED AND CUT INTO CUBES

1 CUP MILK

$\frac{1}{2}$ POUND LEAN BACON, WELL CHILLED

1 SLICE SMOKED HAM, ABOUT $\frac{1}{2}$ POUND, WELL CHILLED

3 EGGS

2 CLOVES GARLIC, FINELY MINCED

3 TABLESPOONS FINELY CHOPPED FRESH MINT

3 TABLESPOONS FINELY CHOPPED FRESH PARSLEY

$\frac{1}{2}$ TEASPOON SALT

$\frac{1}{4}$ TEASPOON FRESHLY GROUND BLACK PEPPER

These savory pancakes, with a crisp, tender texture and a rich, smoky flavor, are unusual. What makes them special is the surprise of fresh mint, an herb not often found in French cooking—perfect here in combination with the heady garlic. While these rouzoles are an essential ingredient in an authentic azinat, *I think they would make a wonderful breakfast or brunch dish themselves, served sizzling from the pan with corn muffins and chilled maple-poached apples.*

It may even be advantageous to place the bacon and the ham in the freezer for half an hour or so. The bacon can be very wiggly when you try to chop it. The colder it is, the easier the cutting will be.

Soak the bread in the milk in a bowl for 15 minutes. While the bread is soaking, cut off a small piece of the bacon and reserve. Finely mince the remaining bacon and all the ham using a very sharp, heavy knife. Whisk the eggs in a large mixing bowl until completely blended. Gently squeeze the excess milk from the bread. Add the bread, bacon, ham, garlic, herbs, salt, and black pepper to the eggs. Mix together well. Refrigerate for 30 minutes.

Lightly grease a 7- or 8-inch sauté pan by slowly rendering the reserved piece of bacon over very low heat, swirling it around to coat the cooking surface. Pour about 1 cup of the batter into the center of the sauté pan, smoothing the top with a wooden spoon until it is a flat, round cake about $\frac{1}{2}$ inch thick and 7 inches in diameter. Cook over very low heat until the first side is golden brown, about 5 minutes. (*Roussir*, "to singe" or "scorch," may have given the name to this dish.) With a wide spatula, gently turn over the cake and cook until the second side is also golden brown, about 5 minutes. If you do not have a wide spatula, slip the cake out onto an 8-inch plate, and then flip it over onto the reverse side into the sauté pan, to cook the second side. Transfer the cooked cake to a heated plate. Repeat to make 2 more cakes. Serve hot.

Loire

BARREL MAKERS' VEAL and RED WINE SOUP

MATELOTE des TONNELIERS

MAKES **6** SERVINGS

2 POUNDS BONELESS VEAL BREAST OR SHOULDER, CUT INTO 1-INCH CUBES

¼ CUP UNSALTED BUTTER

2 MEDIUM-SIZED ONIONS, FINELY CHOPPED

3 YOUNG, SLENDER CARROTS, PEELED AND SLICED

3 TABLESPOONS ALL-PURPOSE FLOUR

1 BOTTLE (750 ML) CHINON OR BOURGUEIL OR OTHER FINE DRY RED WINE

6 TO 7 CUPS WATER

1 BOUQUET GARNI (6 FRESH PARSLEY STEMS, 2 BAY LEAVES, 2 FRESH THYME SPRIGS TIED IN 1 LARGE CELERY STALK)

1 TEASPOON SALT

FRESHLY GROUND BLACK PEPPER

¼ CUP CHOPPED FRESH PARSLEY

12 *CROÛTES* (PAGE 79)

How can you go wrong with a soup that is essentially made with veal and a great red wine? You can't. It is an uncommon dish for friends and family when you want to treat them to veal and yet be economical. There are California Cabernet Francs that are good to use here, and it's fun to sample a number of them to find one you like, for the soup and for its accompaniment.

When most of us think of wines and the Loire Valley, we recall the versatile and fresh whites, but excellent red wines also exist that should not be overlooked. Loire reds, like the Chinon or Bourgueil in this recipe, are made from the high-quality juicy red Cabernet Franc grape. This grape is often over shadowed by its well-regarded cousin, the Cabernet Sauvignon.

The French word matelote ("sailor's wife") usually indicates a freshwater fish soup made with red or white wine. This matelote is unusual because it calls for an inexpensive cut of veal combined with the wine. The tonneliers, or "barrel makers," (coopers), are craftsmen who have had steady work for centuries turning out barrels for French wine makers.

RIGHT: A TONNELIER AT WORK MAKING WINE BARRELS IN THE CAHORS REGION OF SOUTH-WESTERN FRANCE.

Trim off any fat and membranes from the veal. To remove any impurities, blanch the cubes in boiling salted water for 5 minutes. Drain.

Melt the butter in a heavy 4-quart soup pot over medium heat. Add the onions and carrots and cook, stirring occasionally, until golden, 8 to 10 minutes. Add the flour and stir thoroughly over low heat for a few minutes. (There is no need to cook the mixture of flour and fat, the *roux*, further at this time, as the long simmering of the soup will eliminate any raw flour taste.) Pour in the wine and 6 cups of the water and whisk together to combine completely. Add the veal, bouquet garni, and salt and bring to a boil over high heat. Reduce the heat to very low, cover, and simmer until the veal is tender, 1½ hours.

When the veal is tender, discard the bouquet garni. Taste and add more salt if needed and black pepper to taste. If necessary, thin with as much of the remaining 1 cup water as needed to achieve a good consistency and heat thoroughly. Ladle the soup into heated soup plates, garnish with the chopped parsley, and serve immediately. Pass the *croûtes* at table.

BEEF, SAUSAGE, HAM, and RABBIT SOUP

POTÉE SARTHOISE

MAKES **8** MAIN-COURSE SERVINGS

2 POUNDS BEEF CHUCK OR TOP RIBS

5 QUARTS WATER

1 BOUQUET GARNI (6 FRESH PARSLEY STEMS, 2 BAY LEAVES, 2 FRESH THYME SPRIGS TIED IN 1 LARGE CELERY STALK)

2 MEDIUM-SIZED ONIONS, EACH STUCK WITH 1 WHOLE CLOVE

1 TEASPOON SALT

1-POUND PIECE SAUSAGE WITH PISTACHIO NUTS (RECIPE FOLLOWS)

½ POUND SMOKED SAUSAGES SUCH AS KIELBASA OR KNOCKWURST

½ POUND SMOKED HAM

1 HEAD SAVOY CABBAGE, CORED AND CUT INTO 10 WEDGES

3 CELERY STALKS, CUT INTO 3-INCH LENGTHS

5 YOUNG, SLENDER CARROTS, PEELED AND CUT INTO 3-INCH LENGTHS

3 TURNIPS, PEELED AND QUARTERED

1 RABBIT, 3 TO 3½ POUNDS, CUT INTO 8 PIECES

5 MEDIUM-SIZED WAXY POTATOES, PEELED AND QUARTERED

FRESHLY GROUND BLACK PEPPER

The addition of the rabbit in a country dish such as this is not at all unexpected, and it adds immeasurably to its succulence. Lavish with complex flavors, the broth of the potée is delectable and the platter of meats is memorable. All of the meats (and the cabbage) are perfect with a vigorous mustard passed during the meal.

French food writer Robert Courtine has written that a potée "always holds a mirror up to the soil that has produced it. The pasture, the pigsty, the poultry run, and the kitchen garden are its very being."

This is an interpretation of a recipe as suggested by M. Courtine.

Put the beef and water into a heavy 10-quart soup pot. Bring to a boil over high heat and add the bouquet garni and onions. Reduce the heat to low, cover partially, and cook at a bare simmer for 30 minutes. Skim the surface carefully, removing any scum that appears, and replace with water any liquid lost during skimming. Season with the salt and add both kinds of sausages and the ham. Simmer for additional 15 to 20 minutes.

Add the cabbage, celery, carrots, turnips, and rabbit and simmer until the rabbit is almost completely cooked, about 45 minutes longer. Place a soup tureen and 8 soup plates in a 250°F oven.

Add the potatoes to the soup pot and cook until they are tender, 15 to 20 minutes. Using a slotted utensil, remove the beef, sausages, and ham from the pot and place on a cutting board. Carve the meat into chunks. Skim off any excess fat from the surface of the soup. Taste and add more salt if needed and black pepper to taste. Return the meat pieces to the pot and reheat thoroughly.

Ladle the steaming *potée* into the heated soup tureen and place the heated soup plates on the table. Carry the tureen to the table and serve immediately.

1 POUND BONELESS LEAN PORK SHOULDER

½ POUND PORK FAT

½ CUP PISTACHIO NUTS

¼ TEASPOON FRESHLY GRATED NUTMEG

¼ TEASPOON GROUND ALLSPICE

1½ TEASPOONS SALT

½ TEASPOON FRESHLY GROUND WHITE PEPPER

½ TEASPOON FRESHLY GROUND BLACK PEPPER

3 TABLESPOONS COGNAC OR OTHER FINE BRANDY

1 POUND COARSELY GROUND TURKEY

SAUSAGE with PISTACHIO NUTS
SAUCISSES aux PISTACHES
TWO 12-INCH-LONG SAUSAGES,
ABOUT 2½ POUNDS
TOTAL WEIGHT

I have adapted the old recipe for these sausages by substituting lean ground turkey for some of the pork without sacrificing the traditional flavor. Leftover cooked sausage may be chilled, cut diagonally into ¼-inch slices, and served as an appetizer with assorted mustards.

Cut the pork shoulder into 1-inch chunks, removing any membrane and gristle. Cut the pork fat into 1-inch chunks. Finely chop the pistachio nuts either with a sharp, heavy knife or in a food processor. Mix the nuts with the spices, salt, peppers, and brandy in a small bowl. Divide this mixture in half.

Place one-half of the pork and the pork fat in a food processor with half of the pistachio mixture. Pulse until the mixture is coarsely ground. Turn out into a bowl. Repeat with the remaining pork, pork fat, and nut mixture. Add to the bowl along with the ground turkey and mix well.

To test for seasoning, form a tiny meatball of the mixture and sauté in a small sauté pan over medium heat until cooked through. Alternatively, place the meatball on a small plate in a microwave, cover with a paper towel, and cook thoroughly. Cool briefly and taste. Adjust the seasoning of the mixture if necessary.

Instead of using pork casings, I use plastic wrap for enclosing the sausages. Place a 20-inch long piece of plastic wrap on a work surface. Spoon the sausage mixture into a pastry bag fitted with a 1-inch plain tip (or without a tip at all). Pipe out half of the mixture into an even log 12 inches long and 1 inch in diameter onto the plastic wrap, positioning it about 2 inches from one edge. Roll the plastic wrap and the sausage log up like a jelly roll, twisting the ends of the plastic wrap tightly and then knotting them. Repeat with the remaining sausage mixture to make a second sausage. (The sausages may be used immediately or they can be frozen for up to 4 months.)

Fill a very large skillet or a shallow roasting pan three-fourths full of water. Bring to a boil over high heat, reduce the heat to low, and add the wrapped sausage. Simmer for about 20 minutes to cook thoroughly. Remove the sausage from the water and let cool, then remove the plastic wrap.

LAMB, TOMATO, and CHICKPEA SOUP

SOUPE de MOUTON SENDERENS

MAKES **6** MAIN DISH SERVINGS

The esteemed Alain Senderens, of Restaurant Lucas-Carton in Paris, has always drawn inspiration from the roots of gastronomy. He named his first restaurant L'Archestrate as a tribute to the Roman epicure. In the 1990s, he became involved in a personal quest to research and document the foods, products, and cooking of the regions of France. He has contributed this soup recipe, which is one of the most unusual I've encountered. The ingredients are vivid and varied, but it is the intelligent way M. Senderens has constructed the dish that gives it authority. The Provençaux have prepared a thick, traditional country soup, soupe courte, using the mothers of their well-fed Sisteron lambs. The following dish has its culinary echoes in that "mutton" soup.

½ CUP DRIED WHITE BEANS SUCH AS NAVY OR GREAT NORTHERN, RINSED AND SOAKED OVERNIGHT IN WATER TO COVER GENEROUSLY

4 QUARTS WATER

1½ POUNDS LAMB SHORT RIBS, CUT INTO LARGE PIECES

SALT

FRESHLY GROUND BLACK PEPPER

4 TABLESPOONS OLIVE OIL, OR AS NEEDED

1 CAN (15 OUNCES) CHICKPEAS, WELL RINSED AND DRAINED, OR 2 CUPS DRAINED COOKED CHICKPEAS

2 TEASPOONS COARSE SALT

1 BOUQUET GARNI (3 FRESH PARSLEY STEMS, 1 BAY LEAF, 8 TO 10 FRESH THYME SPRIGS TIED IN 1 LEEK LEAF)

1 RED BELL PEPPER

1 GREEN BELL PEPPER

1 LARGE ONION, FINELY CHOPPED

4 CLOVES GARLIC, FINELY MINCED

½ POUND TOMATOES, PEELED, SEEDED, AND COARSELY CHOPPED

PINCH OF SAFFRON THREADS, STEEPED IN ½ CUP HOT WATER

4 OR 5 FRESH MINT LEAVES, CUT INTO NARROW RIBBONS

2 BUNCHES THYME FLOWERS (STEMS REMOVED), OR FRESH LEMON THYME SPRIGS

2 SMALL ZUCCHINI, SEEDED AND CUT INTO ½-INCH DICE

Drain the white beans, place in a heavy saucepan, and add 1 quart of the water. Bring to a boil and cook over high heat for 10 to 12 minutes. Reduce the heat to medium-low and cook for 45 minutes. Drain and reserve.

Season the lamb pieces with 6½ pinches of salt and 10 turns of the pepper grinder. Toss and roll the lamb pieces so that they are well seasoned on all sides.

Put a heavy iron pot on the heat and add 2 tablespoons of the olive oil. When it is quite hot, add the lamb pieces and brown well. Make sure all facets of the meat become golden brown. Remove the lamb with a skimmer, drain on paper towels, and reserve.

Rinse and dry the pot and return it to the stove top. Add the reserved white beans and the chickpeas, the reserved lamb, 2 quarts of the water, and the coarse salt to the pot. Add sev- eral turns of the pepper grinder and the bouquet garni. Bring to a boil over high, reduce the heat to low, and simmer for 45 minutes. During cooking, skim away any fat that rises to the surface.

Meanwhile, one at a time, spear the bell peppers on a long-handled fork and hold over the flame of a gas burner until blistered on all sides. If you do not have a gas stove, roast under a broiler. Set aside until cool enough to handle, then peel away the skin. Remove the stems, cut the bell peppers in half, and scrape out the interior membranes and seeds. Cut the bell peppers into ½-inch dice and reserve.

In a second soup pot, heat the remaining 2 tablespoons olive oil over medium heat. Sauté the onion, stirring often, for 3 minutes. Do not let the onion color. Add the garlic, toma- toes, bell peppers, 5 pinches of salt, 8 turns of the pepper grinder, saffron and water, mint leaves, thyme flowers or sprigs, and 1½ cups of the water. Bring to a boil over high heat, reduce the heat to low, and cook until the vegetables are very tender, about 30 minutes. Add the zucchini during the last few minutes of cooking. If the mixture begins sticking, add a little olive oil.

When the lamb is tender, remove the excess fat from the surface with a ladle. Add the tomato mixture and 1½ cups of the water to the lamb and beans and bring to a boil over high heat. Reduce the heat to low and simmer for 5 minutes to cook the zucchini and blend the flavors. Thin with as much of the remaining 1 cup water as needed to achieve a good consistency.

Remove the bouquet garni and discard. Taste and add more salt if needed and black pep- per to taste. Serve immediately in heated soup plates.

SAUSAGE, SAGE, and GARLIC SOUP

RATE-RATE

MAKES 6 SERVINGS

12 TINY, SPICY FRESH SAUSAGES SUCH AS *CHIPOLATAS*

2 TABLESPOONS OLIVE OIL

1 LARGE ONION, FINELY CHOPPED

12 FRESH SAGE LEAVES, OR 1 TABLESPOON DRIED SAGE

4 CLOVES GARLIC, FINELY MINCED

6 PLUM TOMATOES, PEELED, SEEDED AND COARSELY CHOPPED

6 CUPS WATER

SALT

FRESHLY GROUND BLACK PEPPER

FRESHLY GRATED NUTMEG

6 THIN SLICES FRENCH BREAD, TOASTED IN OVEN

6 TABLESPOONS GRATED GRUYÈRE CHEESE

In late summer when tomatoes are ripe and garden sage will soon have to be dried for winter, this is an ideal soup to assemble. In Provence, sage is thought to be beneficial to good health, as an old adage illustrates: "He who has sage in the garden, does not need a doctor." Even so, often bay leaves are used instead of sage. People in Aix-en-Provence make a meal of this soup by adding a poached egg to each bowl.

Food writer Robert Courtine inspired my version of rate-rate. He writes that this was one of the favorite soups of the Provençal writer Frédéric Mistral. In Trésor de Félibrige, Mistral advises adding freshly grated nutmeg to this soup. Mistral also wrote a periodic newsletter for his fellow Provençal writers. He named it, as one might imagine, Aïoli.

Gently prick each sausage a few times with the tip of a sharp knife. Brown the sausages on all sides in a preheated 400°F oven or in a nonstick skillet on the stove top.

Heat the olive oil in a heavy 4-quart soup pot over medium heat. Sauté the onion, stirring occasionally, until softened, about 5 minutes. If using fresh sage, cut 6 of the leaves into narrow ribbons. (Reserve the remaining 6 leaves for garnish.) Add the sage ribbons, garlic, tomatoes, water, and salt and black pepper to taste to the pot. If using dried sage, crumble it into the pot. Bring to a boil over high heat, reduce the heat to low, and simmer for 5 minutes. Add the sausages and cook until the flavors are blended and the sausages are completely cooked, an additional 5 minutes. Taste and add salt and black pepper if needed and nutmeg to taste.

Place the toasted bread slices in bottom of heated soup plates and sprinkle each with 1 tablespoon of the grated cheese. Ladle the hot soup over the cheese toasts and garnish each bowl with a whole sage leaf, if desired. Serve immediately.

TOP RIGHT: AT ARLES, SYMBOLS IN STONE INDI-CATE AN ANCIENT PROVENÇAL BUTCHER SHOP.

BOTTOM RIGHT: SPRING-BORN LAMB IN THE HILLS NORTH OF PROVENCE.

VEAL SOUP with SORREL and TOMATOES
POTAGE DAUPHINOISE

MAKES **6** MAIN-COURSE SERVINGS

The smooth creaminess of tender beans cooked in veal stock sounds wonderful. Add to that sweet tomatoes, tart sorrel, and the region's famed heavy cream and you have mountain cookery at its finest. At the outset, the dish may sound quite rich. It is not. The foundation flavoring of veal is intense, but the soup, especially with the morsels of fresh tomatoes and snippets of sorrel, becomes a bright and lively mosaic of colors and tastes.

The Dauphiné region of eastern France is acclaimed for the its cream-soaked potato casserole, gratin dauphinoise. This potage dauphinoise *is just as satisfying. Sometimes it is called* la soupe de Tullins, *after a tiny village west of Grenoble.*

For the veal broth:

2 POUNDS MEATY VEAL SHANKS

4 QUARTS WATER

3 ONIONS, HALVED AND EACH HALF STUCK WITH 1 WHOLE CLOVE

2 CARROTS, PEELED AND CUT INTO LARGE CHUNKS

2 LEEKS, CUT INTO LARGE CHUNKS

1 BOUQUET GARNI (6 FRESH PARSLEY STEMS, 2 BAY LEAVES, 2 FRESH THYME SPRIGS TIED IN 1 LARGE CELERY STALK)

1 TEASPOON SALT

For the soup:

½ CUP DRIED WHITE BEANS SUCH AS NAVY OR GREAT NORTHERN, RINSED AND SOAKED OVERNIGHT IN WATER TO COVER GENEROUSLY

1 QUART WATER

6 TABLESPOONS UNSALTED BUTTER

3 MEDIUM-SIZED ONIONS, FINELY CHOPPED

3 YOUNG, SLENDER CARROTS, PEELED AND DICED

2 LEEKS, WHITE AND PALE GREEN PARTS ONLY, SLICED

3 TOMATOES, PEELED, SEEDED, AND CHOPPED

1 TEASPOON SALT

2 QUARTS RESERVED VEAL BROTH

1 CUP CRÈME FRAÎCHE

1 CUP SORREL LEAVES, STEMS REMOVED AND LEAVES CUT INTO SHORT, NARROW RIBBONS

FRESHLY GROUND BLACK PEPPER

12 VERY THIN *CROÛTES* (PAGE 79)

To prepare the broth, put the veal shanks and water in a heavy 10-quart soup pot and bring to a boil over high heat. Reduce the heat to a bare simmer and skim off any scum from the surface. Add the onions, carrots, leeks, bouquet garni, and salt and simmer, uncovered, for 2 hours, continuing to skim any scum from the surface

Meanwhile, drain the beans, place in a heavy saucepan, and add the 1 quart water. Bring to a boil and cook over high heat for 10 to 12 minutes. Reduce the heat to medium-low and cook for 45 minutes. Drain and reserve.

When the broth is ready, lift out the veal shanks, let cool, and refrigerate for another use. Strain the broth through a fine-mesh sieve and discard the vegetables and bouquet garni. Measure the broth, add water as needed to make 2 quarts, and reserve.

Melt 4 tablespoons of the butter in a heavy 4-quart soup pot over medium-low heat. Add the onions, carrots, and leeks and cook, stirring often, until golden, about 20 minutes. Stir in the reserved beans, tomatoes, salt, and the reserved broth. Bring to a boil and cook for 10 to 12 minutes over high heat. Reduce the heat to low and simmer until the vegetables are tender, about 30 minutes.

Remove the pot from the heat and stir in the crème fraîche, mixing thoroughly. Add the sorrel, black pepper to taste, and additional salt if needed. Simmer very briefly, swirl in the remaining 2 tablespoons of butter, then ladle into a heated soup tureen or directly into heated soup plates. Accompany with the *croûtes*.

NOTE: Slice the meat from the chilled veal shanks and serve with a tangy vinaigrette and coarse salt.

Sud-ouest

CHICKEN-in-the-POT
POULE-au-POT

MAKES 6 MAIN-COURSE SERVINGS

Everyone's comfort food: chicken-in-the-pot. Once you've said that, you've about said it all. Alas, if the chicken we buy today were as full of the running-around-the barnyard-herbage that chickens of a generation or two ago were, imagine the real comfort possible. So, the ultimate quality of the dish is determined by the chicken. Avoid supermarket birds at all costs, instead buying from a supplier who carries free-range poultry. Even though I live in a small, remote town, after a few phone calls, I can now buy them. Kosher butchers are another good source of chicken (see Sources).

For the soup:

2 POUNDS MEATY VEAL SHANKS

4 QUARTS PLUS 1 CUP WATER

2 MEDIUM-SIZED YELLOW ONIONS, HALVED AND EACH HALF STUCK WITH 1 WHOLE CLOVE

2 SLENDER LEEKS, WHITE AND PALE GREEN PARTS ONLY, QUARTERED

2 CELERY STALKS, QUARTERED

6 YOUNG, SLENDER CARROTS, PEELED AND QUARTERED

1 BOUQUET GARNI (6 FRESH PARSLEY STEMS, 2 BAY LEAVES, 2 FRESH THYME SPRIGS TIED IN 1 LARGE CELERY STALK)

1 ROASTING CHICKEN, ABOUT 5 POUNDS, LIVER RESERVED

6 MEDIUM-SIZED SAVOY CABBAGE LEAVES

VINEGARED GREEN BEANS (RECIPE FOLLOWS)

For the chicken stuffing:

¾ POUND RYE, WHOLE-WHEAT, OR DENSELY TEXTURED WHITE BREAD, CRUSTS REMOVED

1 CUP MILK

1 TABLESPOON RENDERED GOOSE FAT OR CHICKEN FAT OR GOOD-QUALITY LARD

2 CLOVES GARLIC, FINELY CRUSHED

3 SHALLOTS, FINELY CHOPPED

1 CHICKEN LIVER, FROM THE CHICKEN, FINELY CHOPPED

¼ POUND BAYONNE-STYLE HAM OR PROSCIUTTO, BOTH LEAN AND FAT, VERY FINELY CHOPPED

3 EGGS, WELL BEATEN

¼ CUP CHOPPED FRESH PARSLEY

½ TEASPOON SALT

FRESHLY GROUND BLACK PEPPER

CAYENNE PEPPER

FRESHLY GRATED NUTMEG

Put the veal shanks and 4 quarts of the water in a heavy 10-quart soup pot and bring to a boil over high heat. Reduce the heat to low and skim from time to time until no more foam rises to the surface. Add the remaining 1 cup water at this point. It will cause a small amount of remaining material to be sloughed off. Skim a final time and add the onions, leeks, celery, carrots, and bouquet garni. Simmer, uncovered, for 2 hours. While the veal is simmering, rinse the chicken and cut off any excess fat. Reserve.

To prepare the stuffing, cut the bread in tiny cubes or crumble it. Place in a bowl, add the milk and let soak for 5 minutes. Firmly squeeze out the excess milk, and put the soaked crumbs in a large bowl. Heat the fat in a small sauté pan over low heat. Add the garlic and shallots and cook, stirring occasionally, until softened, 5 to 7 minutes. Add the liver and ham and cook for 2 minutes. Transfer the contents of the pan to the bowl of soaked crumbs. Add the eggs, parsley, salt, and the black pepper, cayenne pepper, and nutmeg to taste. Mix all the ingredients together extremely well. Reserve 1½ cups of the stuffing and refrigerate.

Fill the chicken cavity with the remaining stuffing and truss the chicken with string, tying the legs together and the wings close to the body. (It's a good idea to tie an extra piece of string to the legs in order to lift the chicken out of the pot when it's cooked.) When the veal has simmered for 2 hours, add the chicken to the pot, cover, and simmer over very low heat for about 2 hours longer.

Meanwhile, blanch the cabbage leaves in salted, boiling water for 1 minute. Remove, drain, and rinse in cool water. Pat the leaves dry. Place one-sixth of the reserved stuffing on each leaf and roll up into a small packet. Reserve the packets.

After the chicken has cooked for 1½ hours, add the cabbage rolls to the pot and cook for the remaining 30 minutes of cooking time. Place a large platter and 6 soup plates in a 250°F oven to heat.

To check if the chicken is fully cooked, lift it from the broth and insert the tip of a small, sharp knife into the thickest part of the thigh. The chicken is ready to eat if the escaping juices run clear. Remove the trussing strings and carve the bird into serving pieces. Place on the heated platter along with the stuffing. Remove the cabbage rolls from the pot, and arrange around the chicken pieces on the platter. Moisten the rolls and the chicken with some of the hot broth. Cover the platter with aluminum foil and return to the oven to keep warm.

Remove the veal shanks from the pot and refrigerate for another meal. Strain the cooking broth through a fine-mesh sieve and reheat briefly. Ladle into the heated soup plates and serve immediately accompanied with the chicken, the cabbage rolls, and the green beans.

NOTE: Slice the veal from the shanks and serve at another meal with mayonnaise and cornichons.

(RECIPE CONTINUES)

VINEGARED GREEN BEANS
CONFITURE de HARICOTS VERTS

2 QUARTS WATER

½ POUND GREEN BEANS

½ CUP RED WINE VINEGAR

1 CLOVE GARLIC, HALVED

2 THIN SLICES JALAPEÑO CHILE

The French never cease to amaze me. If there is a more palliative dish than poule-au-pot, *what could it be? Even understanding that, they take the flavors of this faultless dish to a deeper level. They add a variety of incomparable accompaniments: angel hair pasta to the intense chicken broth, a piquant tomato* concassée *beside the delicate chicken meat. In the southwestern Quercy region, they snip off some tender tendrils of the new growth in the vineyards and preserve them in a spicy vinegared elixir. Most of us don't have access to a vineyard, but vinegared green beans give an approximate, if not actually authentic, sense of the impact vine tendrils can offer a* repas.

If God give me life, I shall see to it that no laborer in my kingdom lacks the wherewithal for a chicken in his pot.

—Henri IV

Bring the water to boil in a saucepan. While waiting for the water to reach a boil, trim the stem ends of the beans. Plunge the beans into the boiling water and cook until crisp-tender, 3 to 4 minutes.

Meanwhile, combine the vinegar, garlic, and chile slices in a wide, shallow bowl. Drain the beans and add to the vinegar mixture. Toss and let cool. Stand the beans upright in a glass jar and pour the vinegar mixture into the jar. Cover and refrigerate until serving.

RIGHT: THE DISTINCTIVE FREE-RANGE CHICKENS FROM THE BRESSE REGION (*POULETS DE BRESSE*), RAISED UNDER STRICTLY DEFINED RULES, ARE GIVEN ADDITIONAL NOURISHMENT OF CORN AND BUCKWHEAT.

Sud-ouest

VEGETABLE SOUP
with HAM and PRESERVED DUCK
GARBURE et CONFIT

MAKES 6 MAIN-COURSE SERVINGS

½ CUP DRIED NAVY BEANS

5 QUARTS WATER

1 SMOKED HAM HOCK

2 TABLESPOONS FAT FROM CONFIT OR GOOD-QUALITY LARD

2 MEDIUM-SIZED WHITE ONIONS, COARSELY CHOPPED

4 YOUNG, SLENDER, CARROTS, PEELED AND CUT INTO 1-INCH CHUNKS

3 SMALL TURNIPS, PEELED AND EACH CUT INTO 6 WEDGES

2 MEDIUM-SIZED WAXY POTATOES, PEELED AND EACH CUT INTO 8 WEDGES

2 CLOVES GARLIC

1 BOUQUET GARNI (6 FRESH PARSLEY STEMS, 2 BAY LEAVES, 2 FRESH THYME SPRIGS TIED IN 1 LARGE CELERY STALK)

½ SMALL HEAD SAVOY CABBAGE, CORED, COARSE RIBS REMOVED, AND LEAVES CUT INTO WIDE RIBBONS

1 POUND FRESH PORK SAUSAGES SUCH AS SWEET ITALIAN

6 SMALL TO MEDIUM PIECES PRESERVED DUCK (RECIPE FOLLOWS)

SALT

FRESHLY GROUND BLACK PEPPER

6 THICK *CROÛTES* (PAGE 79)

Garbure, *one of the best-known French regional soups outside of France, has, like all regional soups, many variations. However, the cooks on the farms of Béarn and Gascony insist on a few "musts": the indispensable ham bone with some small amount of ham still attached (*trébuc*), a morsel (at least) of preserved duck or goose (*confit*), hunks of country bread, and an abundance of seasonal vegetables. No wonder many other cooks around the world know about this dish.*

Eric Mariottat of Bon-Encontre, a village near Agen in the heart of Gascony, has shared his recipe for this soup. He believes that a good Buzet, a full-flavored local red wine, is the choice to drink with this soupe paysanne. *A charming custom in garbure regions unites the soup and the wine.*

The art of swirling a little red wine in the bottom of the bowl with the last of the broth is called faire goudale *in this corner of Gascony. A local bit of wisdom advises "a well-made* goudale *takes money from the doctor's pocket." Current medical research confirms the Gascon's belief in the benefits of red wine in the daily diet.*

LEFT: IN GASCONY, THE FRENCH HONOR FEARLESS D'ARTAGNAN, THE CONSUMMATE GASCON AND PROTECTOR OF DUMAS'S *LES TROIS MOUSQUETAIRES*.

Rinse the beans, then place in a bowl and cover generously with cold water. Soak the beans overnight. The following day, drain, place in a heavy saucepan, and add 1 quart of the water and the ham hock. Bring to a boil over high heat and cook for 10 to 12 minutes. Reduce the heat to low, cover partially, and cook for 45 minutes. Drain and reserve the beans and the ham hock.

Melt the fat from the confit or the lard in a heavy 6-quart soup pot, over medium heat. Sauté the onions, stirring often, until they begin to take on color, 8 to 10 minutes. Add the carrots, turnips, potatoes, drained beans and ham hock, garlic, bouquet garni, and the remaining 4 quarts water. Bring to a boil over high heat; reduce the heat to low, and simmer, stirring occasionally, for 30 minutes.

Add the cabbage, sausages, and preserved duck pieces to the soup pot and cook until the cabbage is tender, about 30 minutes. Season with salt and black pepper to taste.

Remove the bouquet garni and discard. Transfer the duck, sausages, and ham hock to a cutting board and cut up, discarding the bones. Return the pieces to the soup and simmer the soup for a few minutes until piping hot.

Place the *croûtes* in heated soup plates, ladle in the hot soup, and serve immediately.

(RECIPE CONTINUES)

PRESERVED DUCK
CONFIT de CANARD

8 PIECES

1 DUCK

1 CUP WATER

2 TABLESPOONS KOSHER SALT FOR EACH POUND TRIMMED DUCK

2 TEASPOONS BLACK PEPPERCORNS

1 TABLESPOON FINELY CHOPPED GARLIC

1 BAY LEAF

1 FRESH THYME SPRIG, OR 1 TEASPOON DRIED THYME

4 TO 6 CUPS RENDERED DUCK FAT

GOOD-QUALITY LARD, IF NEEDED

When the farmers of France began to fatten geese and ducks in order to sell their greatly enlarged livers (foie gras) profitably, local cooks evolved a way to preserve for long keeping (confiter) the fowl that remained. Goose and duck meat was salted and sealed in its own fat. Although with modern refrigeration there is no need to continue this culinary safekeeping, pieces of preserved goose and duck are so succulent and unique that no one would consider stopping the practice. For an incomparable flavor in soups and braised dishes, confit is an authentic and vital ingredient.

If you wish to prepare a goose confit, the ingredients are in proportion to the weight of the goose, which is approximately double that of a duck.

Rinse the duck well and cut it up into 8 pieces (2 leg-thigh pieces, 4 breast pieces, 2 wings). Cut off the wing tips. Remove the skin from the back and reserve the back, gizzard, neck, and wing tips for freezing or for making duck broth. Remove any other loose pieces of skin and collect *all* loose fat.

To use the fat of duck—the loose fat as well as the fat attached to the skin—in order to preserve the meat, it must first be melted. Cut the skin and fat into tiny dice. (This procedure is made quicker and safer if the skin and fat pieces are almost frozen before cutting and if the surface of the cutting board is dried often.) Place in a heavy saucepan, add the water, and cook over very low heat until the fat turns clear and the skin pieces become a pale gold and float to the surface. The water will prevent the fat from burning. Pour through a sieve lined with a double layer of dampened cheesecloth, cool, and refrigerate.

Rinse the duck pieces and dry thoroughly. Place on a rack and allow to air-dry while you prepare the preserving-salt mixture.

Weigh the duck pieces and place approximately 2 tablespoons salt for each pound of fowl in a large bowl. Crush the peppercorns in a heavy plastic bag by smashing with the bottom of a heavy saucepan. Add the pepper to the salt and mix well. Add 1 tablespoon of the salt mixture to the chopped garlic on the cutting board and mix together completely. Add the garlic mixture, bay leaf, and thyme to the salt-pepper mixture. Toss the duck pieces in the salt mixture, cover tightly with plastic wrap, and refrigerate for 24 hours.

The following day, melt enough of the rendered duck fat in a very heavy 6-quart pot to yield 4 to 6 cups. If there is insufficient fat, add lard as needed to yield enough volume to immerse the duck pieces completely in liquid fat.

Rinse the salt mixture off the duck pieces under cold running water. Dry completely. Allow to air-dry on a rack for 20 to 30 minutes. Carefully place the duck pieces into the melted fat and cook over *very* low heat, turning the pieces occasionally, for at least 1½ to 2 hours. The fat must never come to a boil, as it would fry the pieces. The duck will be completely cooked when the tip of a knife or a skewer is inserted and the juice that runs out is not touched with any color.

Remove the duck pieces from the fat and drain. Continue to simmer the fat barely over low heat until there is no more moisture evaporating. (This vapor is visible above the surface of the fat.) This procedure can take as long as 15 to 20 minutes. The step is vital to cook out any remaining meat juices that may be present in the fat, as they could eventually cause spoilage. Pour this fat through a sieve lined with a doubled layer of dampened cheesecloth.

Pour a layer of the warm fat into a glass or glazed ceramic pot and add a layer of duck pieces, skin-side down. Cover with more melted fat. Repeat with all the pieces, covering each layer with fat. Refrigerate the pot with the confit in order to solidify the fat, then cover with plastic wrap and refrigerate overnight. Refrigerate the remaining fat.

The following day, melt about 1 cup of the remaining fat and pour it into the pot to create a sealing layer. Cover the pot and place in your basement or a cool pantry. If there is room in your refrigerator, store the confit there.

THE OCCITANE Many French food writers refer to the large southwestern corner of France, which includes the old provinces of Gascony, Béarn, Auvergne, Languedoc, Rouergue, Roussillon, and the Basque Country, as the Occitane. *Garbure* is typical of that entire region, where many people lived year in and year out at a poverty level, often too poor to own simple soup porringers, even though soup was the foundation of their cuisine. Consequently, many families built tabletops of thick walnut slabs (walnut trees were plentiful!) into which they carved a shallow bowl, *un creux dans le bois* (hollow in the wood), for each member of the family. Often their soup spoons were made of wood as well. Many regional museums exhibit these poignant glimpses of another time.

CHAPTER FIVE

*An autumn menu: wild mushrooms, girolles,
coulemelles, mousserons, gathered in the
moist woods, sautéed in butter for several
minutes; some boiled chestnuts and an apple.*
—Colette, *PRISONS ET PARADIS*

SOUPS *from*

THE STREAMS AND WOODLANDS: GAME AND WILD DELICACIES

LEFT: *CHAMPIGNON DE BOIS* NEAR CAHORS IN
SOUTHWESTERN FRANCE IN OCTOBER.

A NATURAL CLOSENESS TO THE LAND

France is an angler's paradise. One Sunday years ago, while driving along the Saône River in Burgundy, I saw entire families, *mère*, *père*, and *all* the children, plus lawn chairs, coolers, and everything needed for an afternoon of fishing, spread out mile after mile on the riverbanks. That scene attests to the prominence of freshwater fish dishes in France, dishes taken from the Seine, the Loire, and the Rhône. A careful look at a map shows the intricate tracery of the rivers and streams tumbling out of the many mountainous regions. Hundreds of waterways marked in blue look like fanciful lacework spread over the *entire* nation. The French will eat any kind of river fish from the tiniest *ablette* to the largest salmon.

Local fishermen have always snagged fish and shellfish from icy mountain lakes and tributaries. These are often prepared in *matelotes*, fish soups simmered with white or red wine depending on the region. In the Loire, *matelotes* are made with a Cabernet Franc; in Lorraine, *vin gris*, a local rosé from the Moselle, is used, and so on.

Whether called crawdads in Indiana, mudbugs in Louisiana, or *écrevisses* in France, rich, sweet crayfish are appreciated the world over, and the French can claim more recipes for crayfish soups than any other country's cooks. Crayfish are reasonably easy to catch, but they are time-consuming to prepare. Like anything else that is a little painstaking, the rewards are particularly enjoyable. Previously abundant, crayfish have become difficult to find, so most are now imported. The same availability problem occurs with snails. What was once an excellent source of protein and, ironically, often a food for the poor, has now become even more *recherché*.

In addition to the treasures found in lakes and rivers, France is literally jumping with wild game and game birds. After the Revolution, when hunting laws changed to free peasant hunters from any game levy to the court, Frenchmen took to *la chasse* in numbers. There are now more licensed hunters per capita in France than in any other European nation.

Game presents a cook with problems: there are a limited number of choices in cooking game. It is quite lean and thus has a tendency to be tough, so it requires marinating, interlacing with strips of fat, or long, slow moist cooking. Preparing a soup with game is a fitting solution: a soup tenderizes as it simmers with savory aromatics. An added advantage to this method is its economy, as only a small amount of game gives its unique flavor to an entire pot of soup. Always frugal, the French prepare soups with the *restes* (leftovers) of their roast wild boar, venison, and pheasant, and bless them with the name of Saint Hubert, patron saint of hunters.

In the plant-based realm, France is a forager's paradise. Wild mushrooms flourish literally in every corner of the country. Chestnut trees, with their prized nuggets, are plentiful as well. Whether plucking spring dandelion leaves or harvesting wild nettles, there is always a seasonal aspect to the foray—a harmony with nature that is inescapable. This may or may not be a throwback to our cultural memory as hunters-gatherers. A natural closeness to the land and its untamed treasures gives a satisfaction that nothing in the marketplace can offer: the best of frugality, a genuine *bon marché*.

RIGHT: A LONE *PÊCHEUR* TRIES HIS LUCK AT AN ALPINE LAKE NEAR THE ITALIAN BORDER.

4 DOZEN CANNED SNAILS

¼ CUP UNSALTED BUTTER

1 MEDIUM-SIZED ONION, FINELY CHOPPED

3 YOUNG, SLENDER CARROTS, PEELED AND FINELY SLICED

2 SLENDER LEEKS, WHITE AND PALE GREEN PARTS ONLY, HALVED LENGTHWISE AND THINLY SLICED

2 QUARTS CHICKEN BROTH

10 CLOVES GARLIC, FINELY MINCED

1 TEASPOON SALT

1 ½ CUPS CRÈME FRAÎCHE, OR ¾ CUP EACH SOUR CREAM AND HEAVY CREAM

FRESHLY GROUND BLACK PEPPER

½ CUP FINELY CHOPPED FRESH CHERVIL OR PARSLEY

SMALL *CROÛTONS* (PAGE 79)

Alsace Lorraine

GARLIC CREAM SOUP with SNAILS

SOUPE d'ESCARGOTS à la CRÈME d'AIL

MAKES **6** SERVINGS

I first sampled this garlicky snail soup at La Providence, a tiny Parisian restaurant, and the chef readily gave me the recipe. Even though it is on a busy Paris street, the restaurant is like a typical wine bar (winstub) in the Alsace and its cooking is sincere and faithfully regional. The succulent snails were so tender that they literally melted in the mouth. The vegetables were cut into very small pieces, so that a single spoonful of soup delivered a sampling of all its flavors. The original recipe requires four-dozen snails, which is more than ample; that number may be adjusted according to appetites.

Rinse the canned snails thoroughly and drain. Melt the butter in a heavy 4-quart soup pot over low heat. Add the onion, carrots, leeks, and snails and cook until the vegetables have softened, about 5 minutes. Add the broth, garlic, and salt, bring to a boil over high heat, reduce the heat to low, cover partially, and simmer until the garlic is soft and tender, about 30 minutes.

Add the crème fraîche to the pot, mix thoroughly, and return the soup to a boil. Taste and add more salt if needed and black pepper to taste. Ladle into heated soup plates, sprinkle with chervil or parsley, and serve immediately. Pass the little *croûtons* at table.

THE PROVENÇAL SUN, BLISTERING IN SUMMER AND PERSISTENT IN WINTER, TAKES ITS TOLL ON BUILDING FACADES. AT ARLES—THE QUIN-TESSENCE OF OLD PROVENCE—PAINT HAS GRADUALLY FADED AND PEELED FROM A HOTEL PORTE, LEAVING A SOFTENED TEXTURAL COLLAGE.

Auvergne

STINGING NETTLE and POTATO SOUP

SOUPE d'ORTIES

MAKES **6** SERVINGS

6 LARGE HANDFULS OF NETTLE LEAVES (ABOUT ½ POUND)

4 TABLESPOONS UNSALTED BUTTER

1 MEDIUM-SIZED ONION, CHOPPED

1 ½ POUNDS MEDIUM-SIZED WAXY POTATOES (ABOUT 6), PEELED AND THINLY SLICED

6 CUPS WATER

1 TABLESPOON WHITE WINE VINEGAR

1 TEASPOON SALT

6 FRESH CORIANDER LEAVES (OPTIONAL)

2 CUPS MILK

¼ TEASPOON FRESHLY GROUND BLACK PEPPER

THIN *CROÛTES* (PAGE 79)

The exceptional flavor of this healthful soup is so unique that I hardly know how to describe it. It is definitely untamed. Only long sleeves, gloves, and sharp scissors are needed to gather a flavorful and unusual soup ingredient. I usually find nettles in places where there is a lot of moisture and the vegetation is lush. However, when I asked George, my good neighbor who loves taking long walks, where he finds nettles, he told me: "I don't find nettles. They find me."

Wash the nettle leaves by putting them in a large bowl and adding cold water. Swish the leaves around in the water with a wooden spoon or spatula. Remove the leaves from the water with tongs, place them in a colander, and discard the dirty water. Repeat the rinsing at least 3 or 4 times, until the water is clear and clean. Reserve.

Melt 3 tablespoons of the butter in a heavy 3-quart saucepan over medium heat. Sauté the onion, stirring often, until translucent but not colored, 3 to 4 minutes. Add the nettle leaves, potatoes, water, vinegar, salt, and coriander and bring to a boil over high heat. Reduce the heat to low, cover, and simmer until the potatoes are thoroughly cooked and extremely soft, about 15 minutes.

Working with 1 or 2 ladlefuls at a time, purée the soup in a blender until satinlike, processing each batch for at least 30 to 40 seconds until smooth and adding a little of the 2 cups milk to achieve a creamy result if necessary. Return the purée to the saucepan and add the remaining milk. Bring the soup to a simmer. Taste and add more salt if needed and the black pepper. Do not allow the soup to boil.

Swirl in the remaining 1 tablespoon butter. Ladle into heated soup plates and accompany with the *croûtes*.

NOTE: In the spring, when dandelions first creep above ground, the French look forward to picking the young leaves and tossing them in salads. They also use them to prepare a dandelion soup (*soupe de pissenlits au printemps*) that is made exactly like this nettle soup. To prepare it, simply substitute small, well-washed dandelion leaves for the nettle leaves.

Franche-Comté

WILD MUSHROOM and HAZELNUT SOUP

SOUPE aux ORONGES FRANC-COMTOISE

MAKES **6** SERVINGS

1 ¼ POUNDS FRESH *ORONGES* (SEE RECIPE INTRODUCTION)

¼ POUND FRESH *MOUSSERONS* OR WHITE BUTTON MUSHROOMS

3 TO 4 TABLESPOONS UNSALTED BUTTER

1 ½ CUPS CHOPPED ONIONS

2 TEASPOONS SALT

6 TO 7 CUPS CHICKEN BROTH, HOMEMADE OR LOW-SODIUM CANNED

6 TABLESPOONS LONG-GRAIN WHITE RICE

FRESHLY GROUND BLACK PEPPER

¼ CUP FINELY CHOPPED FRESH CHERVIL OR PARSLEY

½ CUP HAZELNUTS, TOASTED, PEELED AND COARSELY CHOPPED (SEE NOTE)

The appeal of the Franche-Comté, a region in eastern France tucked between Burgundy and Switzerland, lies in its unusual wines, aged cheeses, crayfish from mountain streams, abundant game, and exhilarating scenery. The gentle Jura Mountains are handsome, and deep forests cover nearly half the region. The wild mushrooms and hazelnuts in this dish celebrate the bounty of the Jura woodlands.

Occasionally, the English word hazelnut (noisette, or "little nut," in French) is replaced by the word filbert, in honor of Saint Philibert, whose birthday is celebrated August 22 when the nuts begin to ripen. Whatever the name chosen for the nut, earthy mushrooms paired with buttery hazelnuts create a one-of-a-kind soup.

To my knowledge, the oronge (Aminita caesarrae), a wild mushroom, is not found in the United States, nor is the small mousseron (Tricholoma georgil), which is the origin of the English word mushroom. Use any fresh wild mushroom that is available for the oronge, either from your market or from your own foraging discoveries. What is needed is the earthy delicacy of forest-floor flavors that wild mushrooms possess.

Clean the mushrooms by wiping carefully but do not use any water. Cut off any stem bases that contain soil, then cut the mushrooms into thin slices; reserve 18 slices for garnish.

Melt 3 tablespoons of the butter in a heavy 4-quart soup pot over low heat. Add the onions and cook, stirring often, until they are translucent but not colored, about 10 minutes. Add the mushrooms and additional butter if needed and cook over low heat until the mushrooms have yielded all their moisture, 10 to 12 minutes. Add the salt, 6 cups of the chicken broth, and the rice and bring to a boil over high heat. Reduce the heat to low, cover, and cook, stirring occasionally, until the rice is very tender, about 1 hour.

Working with 1 or 2 ladlefuls at a time, purée the soup in a blender or food processor, processing each batch for at least 40 seconds until smooth. Add more liquid from the pot as necessary to create a smooth purée. Return the purée to the soup pot and add as much of the remaining 1 cup broth as needed to achieve a good consistency. Reheat gently to serving temperature.

Taste and add more salt if needed and black pepper to taste. Stir in the chervil or parsley. Ladle into heated soup plates and garnish with the reserved mushroom slices and a sprinkling of hazelnuts.

NOTE: To toast and skin hazelnuts, spread out the whole nuts on a baking sheet and toast in 350°F oven until fragrant and beginning to darken, 8 to 10 minutes. Remove the nuts from the oven and spread them out onto a double layer of paper towels. Wrap up the warm nuts in the towels and rub thoroughly between your palms to remove the skins. Peel away any skins that still remain after the rubbing.

FRESHWATER FISH SOUP with WHITE WINE

PÔCHOUSE VERDUNOISE

MAKES **6** MAIN-COURSE SERVINGS

I have limited the choices of freshwater fish to those most likely to be available in the fish markets in this country. Depending on where you live, eel can be a problem to find. As its flavor, texture, and juiciness are incomparable, it is worth the search. The delicate lightness of the dish is reflected in the French expression for freshwater fish: eau douce, or "sweet water."

Describing how a dish tastes is one of the greatest challenges for a writer. Portraying flavors and aromas with language is often so difficult that we use settings and situations from a lifetime of memories to try and approximate that experience for the reader. We have to use mere words to describe the senses of smell and taste. My first encounter with the remarkable pôchouse resulted in the following notes, written quickly à table and then tucked away: My sweet fish soup tasted of "the perfume of country air after a thorough and protracted rainfall, clean and natural . . . like the bluegills of my childhood caught in Wisconsin lakes."

1 EEL, ABOUT 1 POUND, CLEANED AND SKINNED (SEE NOTE)

1 POUND PIKE OR LAKE PERCH

1 POUND STRIPED BASS

1 POUND RAINBOW TROUT

1 BAY LEAF

1 SMALL FRESH THYME SPRIG, OR 1 TEASPOON DRIED THYME

3 FRESH PARSLEY SPRIGS

3 CLOVES GARLIC, FINELY MINCED

2 MEDIUM-SIZED ONIONS, CHOPPED

5 TO 6 CUPS WATER

1 TABLESPOON UNSALTED BUTTER

1 TABLESPOON ALL-PURPOSE FLOUR

1 BOTTLE (750 ML) VERY DRY WHITE BURGUNDY SUCH AS ALIGOTÉ OR DRY CALIFORNIA CHARDONNAY

1 TEASPOON SEA SALT

⅛ TEASPOON FRESHLY GROUND WHITE PEPPER

12 GARLIC *CROÛTES* (PAGE 79)

Prepare the eel as directed and cut crosswise into 1½-inch-thick slices. Clean and scale any whole fish as necessary and cut off the heads and tails. Discard the tails. Cut the whole fish crosswise into 1½-inch-thick slices. Cut any other fish into 1½-inch-thick slices as well. Rinse the fish pieces and fish heads well.

Put the fish heads, bay, thyme, parsley, garlic, and onions in a heavy 4-quart stainless-steel soup pot with 4 cups of the water. Bring to a boil over high heat, reduce the heat to medium, and simmer, uncovered, for about 20 minutes. Strain through a fine-mesh sieve; you should have about 3 cups. Reserve the fish broth.

Melt the butter in a 1-quart saucepan over low heat. Add the flour and whisk together to make a white roux, stirring and cooking for about 3 minutes. Whisk in 2 cups of the reserved fish broth and bring to a simmer over low heat, stirring often, until a rich, lightly thickened fish sauce forms, 3 to 4 minutes. Remove from the heat and reserve.

Rinse out the 4-quart pot and add the fish slices. Pour the white wine, the remaining 1 cup fish broth, and 1 cup of the water over the fish. Place over medium heat, bring to a low simmer, and poach the fish, keeping the liquid at a constant gentle simmer, until cooked through. This may take 15 minutes. Using a slotted spoon, remove the fish pieces and divide evenly among 6 heated soup plates. Cover each plate with foil to keep the fish hot for a few moments while you complete the soup.

Add the reserved fish sauce to the fish poaching liquid and bring to a lively boil, whisking vigorously. Add as much of the remaining 1 cup water as needed to thin to a good consistency. Add the salt and white pepper, then taste and adjust the seasoning. Ladle the soup over the fish in the soup plates and garnish each serving with *croûtes*. Serve immediately.

NOTE: It is imperative that you have your fishmonger skin and clean the eels. Rinse the body cavities thoroughly and drain. With a small sharp knife or kitchen shears, clip off the tiny bones at the sides of the backbones.

PHEASANT POT-au-FEU

POT-au-FEU au FAISAN d'ARDENNES

MAKES **6** MAIN-COURSE SERVINGS

Here is an unexpected treat: a down-to-earth pot-au-feu prepared with an elegant game bird. Nonetheless, the final presentation is not homey at all. It is as refined as the slowly simmered pheasant is juicy and flavorful. The root vegetables in the soup pot, especially the celery root, create a game broth that has a deep, distinctive flavor.

2 PHEASANTS, CUT INTO SERVING PIECES

¼ CUP UNSALTED BUTTER

1 BOUQUET GARNI (6 FRESH PARSLEY STEMS, 2 BAY LEAVES, 2 FRESH THYME SPRIGS TIED IN 1 LARGE CELERY STALK)

2 MEDIUM-SIZED ONIONS, EACH STUCK WITH 2 WHOLE CLOVES

1 TEASPOON DRIED MARJORAM

8 FRESH BASIL LEAVES, FINELY MINCED, OR 1 TEASPOON DRIED BASIL

2½ TO 3 QUARTS WATER

1 TEASPOON SALT

6 YOUNG, SLENDER CARROTS, PEELED

4 SMALL TURNIPS, PEELED

1 SMALL HEAD SAVOY CABBAGE, CORED

½ CELERY ROOT, PEELED

2 SLENDER LEEKS, WHITE AND PALE GREEN PARTS ONLY, THINLY SLICED

½ TEASPOON FRESHLY GROUND BLACK PEPPER

¼ CUP FINELY MINCED FRESH PARSLEY

CROÛTONS (PAGE 79)

COARSE SALT

6 MEDIUM-SIZED WAXY POTATOES, STEAMED AND KEPT WARM

Rinse the pheasant pieces and pat dry. Melt the butter in a heavy 6-quart soup pot over medium heat. Add the pheasant pieces and cook until they are golden brown on all sides, about 15 minutes. It's important that the pheasant pieces are nicely browned so that the finished soup will have an appetizing amber color. Add the bouquet garni, onions, herbs, 2 ½ quarts of the water, and the salt and bring to a boil over high heat. Reduce the heat to very low and simmer, uncovered, for 45 minutes, skimming off any scum from the surface of the liquid as necessary. Add water to replace any liquid removed by skimming.

Cut the carrots, turnips, cabbage, and celery root into large, attractive chunks and add them and the leeks to the pot. Bring to a boil over high heat, reduce the heat to low and simmer, uncovered, until the vegetables and pheasant are tender, about 45 minutes more, again skimming as necessary. Place a platter and 6 soup plates in a 250°F oven.

Remove the bouquet garni and discard. Taste and add more salt if needed and the black pepper. Add as much of the remaining ½ quart (2 cups) water as needed to thin the broth to a good consistency.

With a slotted utensil, lift out the pheasant pieces and arrange on the heated platter. Surround with the vegetables and moisten with some of the hot broth. Cover with foil and return to the warm oven until serving.

Strain the cooking broth through a fine-mesh sieve and return it to the pot. Reheat to serving temperature, then ladle into the heated soup plates. Sprinkle with the parsley and accompany with *croûtons*.

Follow the broth course by presenting the platter of pheasant and vegetables. Accompany with coarse salt and the steamed potatoes.

CELERY ROOT Inventive French cooks and their contented families and guests adore celery root. There is scarcely a bistro menu in France that does not offer *céleri-rave rémoulade* (celery root in a spirited mustardy-mayonnaise sauce), or a *grand-mère* who does not, when winter nears, whip up a warm and comforting *purée de céleri-rave*.

Corse

CHESTNUT and PANCETTA SOUP

SOUPE de CHÂTAIGNES CORSE

MAKES 6 SERVINGS

1 POUND FRESH CHESTNUTS, OR ½ POUND CANNED WHOLE
PEELED CHESTNUTS, COARSELY CHOPPED

¼ POUND PANCETTA, WELL CHILLED

OLIVE OIL, IF NEEDED

2 CUPS FINELY CHOPPED ONIONS

2 FENNEL STALKS, INCLUDING LEAVES, TRIMMED AND
THINLY SLICED (LEAVES RESERVED)

2½ QUARTS WATER

1 TEASPOON SALT

½ TO 1 CUP MILK

FRESHLY GROUND BLACK PEPPER

Three ingredients essential in Corsican cuisine, chestnuts, fennel, and pancetta, are found in this soup, and I particularly like the results. Chestnuts, rich and sweet at the same time, have an unusual affinity for the anise taste of fresh fennel, and both are enhanced by the savor of pancetta. The pancetta is an example of the unique flavor of the local charcuterie that, with other pork dishes, depends on Corsican pigs' running free to graze. Corsica is covered with chestnut trees, and the easily found chestnuts provide tasty rations for the pigs. In the mountains northeast of Ajaccio, the capital, are found chestnut forests and a village, Castagniccio, that takes its name from Castanea sativa, *"sweet chestnut."*

It's vitally important to find true pancetta (lightly salted, dried pork) for this dish, as it delivers a flavor that is intense and incomparable, and only a small amount is needed to add that unique taste. The Corsicans may have many varieties from which to choose but finding an imported pancetta is difficult, if not impossible, for American cooks. Domestic pancetta, however, is available and worth ordering from your butcher.

If using fresh chestnuts, slit on the flat side with a knife tip and place in a saucepan with cold water to cover. Bring to a boil over high heat and cook for 20 minutes. Remove from the heat. Remove only a few chestnuts at a time from the hot water and set aside until they have cooled slightly and can be handled. (Chestnuts are easier to peel when still warm.) Remove both the outer shells and the inner furry coating. Set the peeled chestnuts aside. If using canned chestnuts, drain and set aside.

Cut the chilled pancetta into fine dice. Brown the pancetta in a heavy 4-quart soup pot over medium heat, stirring often, until thoroughly crisp, 8 to 10 minutes. Remove with a slotted spoon and drain on paper towels. Reserve.

Discard all but 2 tablespoons of the pancetta fat from the pot. If the pancetta, which is usually lean, does not yield 2 tablespoons of fat, add olive oil. Return the pot to very low heat and sauté the onions and fennel, stirring often, until softened and very lightly colored, 10 to 12 minutes.

Add 2 quarts of the water, the chestnuts, and the salt to the pot and bring to a boil. Reduce the heat to low, cover partially, and cook, stirring occasionally, until the fennel is tender, about 30 minutes.

Working with 1 or 2 ladlefuls at a time, purée the soup in a blender or food processor, adding a little milk as needed to each batch to ease the processing, until extremely smooth, 30 to 40 seconds for each batch. Return the purée to the pot and bring to a boil over high heat. Reduce the heat to low and simmer for 2 to 3 minutes to blend the flavors. Taste and add more salt if needed and black pepper to taste. If the soup seems too thick, add as much of the remaining ½ quart (2 cups) water as needed to thin to a good consistancy. Ladle into heated soup plates and sprinkle with the reserved pancetta pieces and chopped fennel leaves.

NOTE: I like the unpuréed version of this soup, too. Simply omit the processing, adjust the seasoning and serve sprinkled with the reserved pancetta and fennel leaves.

FENNEL Fennel *(fenouil)*, a bulb vegetable with dark green feathery leaves, has an anise scent and nestled symmetrical ribs. The strings are more pronounced than in celery and should be removed before cooking. Eaten raw or cooked, fennel is found in markets in the fall and winter, and I have seen it labeled "anise." It adds its subtle, but distinctive flavor to soups, most often in those in Provence and Corsica.

CHESTNUTS—IN BLOSSOM? In April. And in Paris, yes. And throughout much of France, particularly in the south. Chestnuts also blossom in the cooking of regional France. Traditionally, starch-rich chestnuts were a dietary staple of the poor of Europe. (Carbohydrates make up between one-eighth and one-fifth of the content in most nuts, but in the chestnut the amount is more than double that.) In *Père Goriot*, novelist Honoré Balzac illustrates the poverty of one French family: "The household consumes more boiled chestnuts than bread. . . ."

The chestnut is also a remarkably adaptable foodstuff that can be roasted, boiled, grilled, or simmered into a substantial soup. Writer Roger Lallemand recounts a moving recipe for a humble chestnut soup, *nouzillards au lait*, from the Anjou region. It reads as harsh as the life must have been: "In the winter . . . it was often the evening meal in the country. Simply cook the chestnuts in salted water, shell them, and put them in a bowl. Pour on fresh milk, hot or cold, to the brim and eat it with a spoon." The nutrient-rich chestnut is also often dried, ground into flour, and used for baking healthful chestnut-flour breads and cakes and for making porridges.

The chestnut's versatility is illustrated best on the island of Corsica, where the acutely poor ate chestnuts in every imaginable way. Whole chestnuts were often stored in peasant homes in a large drawer. While today, we open the fridge to find something to eat, a Corsican would "look in his drawer." French writer Jean Lorrain describes a scene between a tourist and a Corsican *paysan*. "How do I live?" responded the Corsican. "By the bread from a tree and the wine from a rock." (*De pain de bois et de vigne de pierre.*) The bread was, of course, made from chestnut flour, and the "wine" was spring water flowing down the rocks of the Corsican mountains.

Two words for chestnut, *marron* and *châtaigne*, exist in the French language. (The word *chestnut* is derived from *châtaigne*.) Chestnut trees are now cultivated in France specifically for their large chestnuts, the *marrons*, that have one kernel. Older, wilder chestnut trees produce the smaller *châtaignes*, which have two small kernels.

Alsace Lorraine

FROGS' LEGS in WATERCRESS CREAM

SOUPE des GRENOUILLES HAEBERLIN

MAKES **6** SERVINGS

¼ CUP UNSALTED BUTTER

18 PAIR SMALL FROGS' LEGS

1 SHALLOT, FINELY MINCED

¼ CUP LONG-GRAIN WHITE RICE

6 TO 7 CUPS WATER

1 BOTTLE (750 ML) ALSATIAN SYLVANER (SEE RECIPE INTRODUCTION)

1 TEASPOON SALT

4 CUPS WATERCRESS LEAVES, OR 2 CUPS EACH WATERCRESS AND SORREL LEAVES

2 EGG YOLKS

2 CUPS CRÈME FRAÎCHE OR HEAVY CREAM

PINCH OF FRESHLY GROUND WHITE PEPPER

If you have never tried frogs' legs, or if you have only eaten them fried (as they are usually prepared), this recipe is a revelation. Flavored by both the tender bones and meat of the legs, the sumptuous cream soup delivers the meat, lean and moist, simmered to exceptional tenderness.

It is also a beautiful soup. The watercress leaves cannot completely purée due to their short cooking time. This retains their fresh flavor and the vivid color as well. The soup becomes a pale green flecked with dark green bits.

Sylvaner wine is sometimes difficult to find in the United States, but often a nice, crisp Alsatian white of Pinot Blanc grapes is blended with some Sylvaner. That wine is perfect for this soup and for sipping, too.

Melt the butter in a heavy 4-quart soup pot over medium heat. Add the frogs' legs and shallot and cook, stirring gently, until the shallot is softened, 5 to 7 minutes. Add the rice, 6 cups of the water, the wine, and the salt and bring to a boil over high heat. Reduce the heat to low and simmer, uncovered, until the rice is very tender, about 30 minutes.

Meanwhile, place a small baking pan in a 250°F oven. Remove the stems from the watercress (and sorrel) leaves. Reserve a few watercress leaves for garnish. Add the leaves to the pot and simmer for 5 minutes more.

Take the frogs' legs out of the pot and remove the meat from the bones. Cut into bite-sized pieces. Discard the bones and place the meat in the preheated baking pan. Cover the pan with aluminum foil and return to the oven. Working with 1 or 2 ladlefuls at a time, purée the soup in a blender or food processor, processing each batch 30 seconds until very smooth. Return the purée to the soup pot and reheat.

Whisk together the egg yolks and crème fraîche in a small bowl. Whisk in a ladleful or two of the hot puréed soup. Slowly add the egg mixture to the soup while whisking constantly. Add the reserved meat from the frogs' legs and as much of the remaining 1 cup water as needed to achieve a good consistency. Reheat gently over medium-low heat for 2 to 3 minutes. Do not allow to boil.

Taste and add more salt if needed and the white pepper. Serve in heated soup plates and garnish with the reserved watercress leaves.

WILD MUSHROOM SOUP

Dordogne

SOUPE de CÈPES CORRÈZIENNE

MAKES **6** SERVINGS

1 POUND FRESH CÈPE MUSHROOMS

3 TABLESPOONS RENDERED GOOSE OR DUCK FAT OR UNSALTED BUTTER

3 SHALLOTS, FINELY CHOPPED

2 QUARTS WATER

3 CLOVES GARLIC, FINELY MINCED

1 TEASPOON SALT

FRESHLY GROUND BLACK PEPPER

CROÛTONS (PAGE 79)

Wherever there are dense old-growth forests, we find—or we hope to find—wild mushrooms. The Corrèze département of the Limousin, which borders the Dordogne on the northeast, is noted for being well provided in the spring and autumn with the Boletus edulis, or earthy cèpe. If you are lucky enough to have foraged and found, or bought at the market, a cache of these prized mushrooms, also known as porcini, preparing this soup is a tempting treat for your guests. With only a pound of the fresh wild mushroom treasures, you can make six people deliriously happy.

With dried mushrooms widely available, a close likeness to the fresh flavor of the cèpe is possible year-round. In fact, some prefer the concentrated dried cèpe flavor to the fresh. If you would like to try this soup with dried mushrooms, a recipe follows the fresh version.

Clean the mushrooms by wiping carefully, but do not use any water. Separate the caps from the stems, and cut off any stem bases that contain soil. Cut the stems into tiny dice and the caps into very thin slices. Place a baking pan in a 250°F oven.

Melt 1½ tablespoons of the goose or other fat in a heavy 4-quart soup pot over medium heat. Add the sliced mushroom caps and cook until golden, 10 to 12 minutes. Shake the pan or stir so that the pieces cook evenly. Transfer the mushrooms to the heated baking pan, cover with aluminum foil, and reserve in a warm oven.

Add the shallots and the remaining 1½ tablespoons goose or other fat to the soup pot and sauté over low heat, stirring occasionally, until the shallots are lightly colored, about 8 minutes. Add the diced mushroom stems, cover, and cook, stirring constantly, for 2 to 3 minutes. Add the water, garlic, and salt and bring to a boil over high heat. Reduce the heat to low, cover, and simmer until the mushroom stems are tender, about 45 minutes.

Return the reserved mushroom cap pieces to the pot. Taste and add more salt if needed and black pepper to taste. Alternatively, before adding the reserved mushroom caps, working with 1 or 2 ladlefuls at a time, pass the soup through a food mill or purée the soup in a blender or food processor, processing each batch for at least 30 seconds. Return the purée to the pot, add the reserved mushroom caps, cover, and cook over low heat for 10 minutes to blend the flavors, then season.

Ladle immediately into heated soup plates and accompany with the *croûtons*.

THE FRENCH OBTAIN WILD MUSHROOMS
EITHER BY HUNTING FOR THEM IN THEIR SPE-
CIAL, SECRET LOCATIONS OR BY BRINGING
THEM HOME FROM A MARKET, WHERE OTHER
FORAGERS SUPPLY A VARIETY OF AUTUMN
CHOICES.

VARIATION WITH DRIED CÈPES: Soak 3 ounces dried cèpes in 1 quart lukewarm water for 20 minutes. Drain, reserving both the cèpes and water. Add enough water to the reserved soaking liquid to measure 2 quarts.

Melt 1½ tablespoons rendered goose or duck fat or unsalted butter in a heavy 4-quart soup pot over medium heat. Sauté 3 shallots, finely chopped, until softened, for 2 to 3 minutes, stirring often. Add the reserved water, reserved cèpes, 1 teaspoon salt, and 3 cloves garlic, finely minced. Bring to a boil over high heat, reduce the heat to low, cover, and simmer for 30 minutes. Purée in a blender or food processor, 2 or 3 ladlefuls at a time, until smooth. Return to the pot and reheat, simmering for 1 to 2 minutes. Taste and add more salt if needed and black pepper to taste. Garnish with *croûtons* (page 79).

6 TABLESPOONS UNSALTED BUTTER

30 CRAYFISH (SEE PAGE 101)

3 MEDIUM-SIZED ONIONS, FINELY CHOPPED

4 YOUNG, SLENDER CARROTS, PEELED AND THINLY SLICED

1 SHALLOT, FINELY CHOPPED

2 CLOVES GARLIC, FINELY MINCED

¼ CUP ALL-PURPOSE FLOUR

2 CUPS *VIN JAUNE D'ARBOIS* OR CHÂTEAU-CHALON (SEE OPPOSITE)

1 TEASPOON SEA SALT

6 PLUM TOMATOES, PEELED, SEEDED, AND CHOPPED

2 QUARTS WATER

1 BOUQUET GARNI (6 FRESH PARSLEY STEMS, 2 BAY LEAVES, 2 FRESH THYME SPRIGS TIED IN 1 LARGE CELERY STALK)

2 EGG YOLKS

¾ CUP CRÈME FRAÎCHE OR HEAVY CREAM

¼ TEASPOON FRESHLY GROUND WHITE PEPPER

6 LEMON WEDGES

Franche-Comté

CRAYFISH SOUP with GOLDEN WINE

SOUPE d'ÉCREVISSES COMTOISE

MAKES 6 SERVINGS

The flavor, texture, and appearance of this soup are opulent. It is one of the real treasures of French regional cooking. It gave me my first opportunity to track down and taste the renowned, often mysterious "golden wine," Château-Chalon.

If you can't find crayfish, you can use the same number of medium-sized shrimp for this recipe. When the soup is prepared with shrimp, the flavor is more delicate but equally tempting and the procedure is exactly the same.

Melt the butter in a heavy 4-quart soup pot over medium heat. Add the crayfish, onions, carrots, and shallot, stirring often, until lightly colored, 6 to 8 minutes. Add the garlic and flour and cook, stirring constantly, until the flour is absorbed and produces a golden paste, 3 to 4 minutes.

Add 1½ cups of the wine, the sea salt, tomatoes, water, and bouquet garni and bring to a boil over high heat, stirring constantly. Reduce the heat to low and simmer, uncovered, for 10 minutes. Scrape the bottoms and sides of soup pot with a rubber spatula and stir.

Using a slotted utensil, remove the crayfish from the soup pot and pull off the heads and claws. Take the crayfish meat out of the tails and reserve. Put the heads, claws, and tail shells in a heavy plastic bag and crush as finely as possible with a rolling pin or other heavy object. Return the crushed shells to the soup, bring to a boil over high heat, reduce the heat to low, and simmer, uncovered, for 30 minutes to intensify the flavors.

Pour the broth through a sieve lined with a double layer of dampened cheesecloth. Return the strained broth to the pot and place over low heat.

In a small bowl, whisk together the egg yolks and crème fraîche or cream. Whisk in a ladleful or two of the hot soup. Slowly add the egg mixture to the soup pot while whisking constantly. Add the remaining ½ cup wine and taste, adding more salt if needed and the white pepper. Add the reserved crayfish meat and reheat completely, but do not allow to boil.

Ladle into heated soup plates and garnish with the lemon wedges. Serve immediately.

THE BEAUTIFUL, TERRACED VINEYARDS OF
THE WINE COMMUNE CHÂTEAU-CHALON IN THE
FRANCHE-COMTÉ.

GOLDEN WINE In the Jura region of the Franche-Comté, wine makers bottle an unusual wine known as *vin jaune*—"golden wine"—that is seldom exported, although well loved on French soil.

While it is difficult to find any golden wines in the United States, occasionally one can locate a bottle of the finest, Château-Chalon. Château-Chalon is made from 100 percent Savagnin grape, and by French law must be aged in old barrels for no fewer than six years. Because the wine is powerful in flavor and alcohol, wine writer Oz Clarke has described it as "death-defying." To prepare this soup without the French golden wine, I would suggest using a *fino* sherry.

Loire

EEL, PRUNE, and RED WINE SOUP

BOUILLITURE d'ANGUILLES SAUMUROISE

MAKES **6** SERVINGS

2 CUPS BOILING WATER

24 PRUNES, PITTED

3 EELS, ABOUT 1 POUND EACH, CLEANED AND SKINNED (SEE NOTE ON PAGE 177)

ALL-PURPOSE FLOUR

½ CUP UNSALTED BUTTER

1 MEDIUM-SIZED ONION, FINELY CHOPPED

¾ POUND FRESH WHITE BUTTON MUSHROOMS, WIPED CLEAN, TRIMMED, AND SLICED

1 BOTTLE (750 ML) SAUMUR RED, A LOIRE RED, OR A CABERNET SAUVIGNON OR CABERNET FRANC

1 BOUQUET GARNI (6 FRESH PARSLEY STEMS, 2 BAY LEAVES, 2 FRESH THYME SPRIGS TIED IN 1 LARGE CELERY STALK)

3 CLOVES GARLIC, FINELY MINCED

1 TEASPOON SEA SALT

1½ CUPS COLD WATER

FRESHLY GROUND BLACK PEPPER

¼ CUP CHOPPED FRESH PARSLEY

CROÛTONS (PAGE 79)

It may seem an odd combination to pair any fish with prunes, even though both these ingredients are often found in medieval cooking. This soup is an affirmation that each—wine, eel, prunes, mushrooms—adds its unique flavor to the finished soup. The eel is especially appealing, with its white interior edged with traces of the garnet of the wine.

This dish is a classic in the Loire Valley as well as in all of France. It is almost as celebrated as the famed Loire pike with white butter sauce (brochet au beurre blanc). The Loire region has contributed a number of delectable fresh-water fish dishes to French cuisine: perch stuffed with sorrel or mushrooms, pike with shallot butter. These dishes are as full of complex flavors as the following recipe.

The eel, then, was cooked with care and served with distinction. It not only looked magnificent and smelt delicious, but when it was tasted, words could not be found to express its praise; and so it disappeared, body and sauce, down to the last particle.

—Brillat-Savarin, IN PRAISE OF EEL

Pour the boiling water over the prunes in a bowl and reserve.

Cut the eels crosswise into 2-inch pieces. Roll the pieces in flour and tap off the excess. Melt ¼ cup of the butter in an enameled or stainless-steel 6-quart soup pot over medium heat. Add the eel pieces and cook, turning the pieces over gently so they cook evenly, until lightly golden, about 10 minutes. Remove the eel with a slotted spoon and reserve.

Add the onion and mushrooms to the pot and sauté over medium heat, stirring often, until lightly colored, about 10 minutes. When the onion is golden, add the wine, bouquet garni, garlic, and salt. Reduce the heat to low, cover partially, and simmer for 15 minutes.

Return the eel to the soup pot, add the prunes and their soaking water, and the 1½ cups cold water. Cover partially and simmer over very low heat until the eel and prunes are tender, 15 to 20 minutes.

Using a slotted spoon, remove the eel to a heated shallow soup tureen and encircle with the prunes and mushrooms. Strain the soup through a fine-mesh sieve and return it to the pot, adding more water if needed to provide ample broth for each guest. Taste and add more salt if needed and black pepper to taste. Reheat until the soup is at serving temperature.

Swirl in the remaining ¼ cup butter and ladle the soup over the eel in the tureen. Sprinkle with the parsley and pass the *croûtons* at table.

2 POUNDS FRESH CHESTNUTS, OR 1 POUND CANNED WHOLE PEELED CHESTNUTS

1 POUND PEELED PUMPKIN FLESH

¼ CUP UNSALTED BUTTER

1 LARGE WAXY POTATO, PEELED AND SLICED

1 YOUNG, SLENDER CARROT, PEELED AND FINELY DICED

½ CELERY STALK, FINELY DICED

1 SLENDER LEEK, WHITE AND PALE GREEN PARTS ONLY, FINELY MINCED

1 SMALL ONION, FINELY DICED

1 CLOVE GARLIC, FINELY MINCED

1 BAY LEAF

6 CUPS BROTH FROM CHICKEN-IN-THE-POT (PAGE 160), OR HOMEMADE CHICKEN BROTH, OR AS NEEDED

1 TEASPOON SALT

6 CUPS MILK

FRESHLY GROUND BLACK PEPPER

FRESHLY GRATED NUTMEG

CROÛTONS (PAGE 79)

Sud-ouest

CHESTNUT and PUMPKIN SOUP

SOUPE de CHÂTAIGNES au CITROUILLE

MAKES 6 SERVINGS

I have used French whole peeled chestnuts, sold in jars and cans, for this soup. The product is not economical, but the chestnuts are choice, and the time saved considerable. If you are buying fresh chestnuts, buy domestic ones. They tend to break apart easily, so they are suitable for preparing soups like this that are to be puréed. Buy fresh chestnuts that are fat, hard to the touch, and have a brilliant skin.

This soup is ideal for family and guests in autumn and winter when chestnuts and pumpkins appear in the markets. Rich, colorful, and symbolic of harvest, this dish is an ideal opener for Thanksgiving dinner.

The Limousins eat chestnuts and they're not complaining.
—French Revolutionary Saint-Just,
A COLLEAGUE OF ROBESPIERRE

If using fresh chestnuts, slit on the flat side with a knife tip and place in a saucepan with cold water to cover. Bring to a boil over high heat and cook for 20 minutes. Remove from the heat. Remove only a few chestnuts at a time from the hot water and leave them until they have cooled slightly and can be handled. (Chestnuts are easier to peel when still warm.) Remove both the outer shells and the inner furry coating. Reserve some whole peeled chestnuts for garnish. If using canned chestnuts, drain well.

Cut the chestnuts into morsels. Cut the pumpkin into ¾-inch cubes; you should have 2 cups. Heat the butter in a heavy 4-quart soup pot over low heat. Add the chestnuts, potato, carrot, celery, leek, onion, garlic, and bay leaf and cook, stirring, until the butter is absorbed, 8 to 10 minutes. Add the pumpkin, 6 cups chicken broth, salt, and milk and bring to a boil over high heat. Reduce the heat to low, cover partially, and simmer for 20 minutes.

Remove the bay leaf and discard. Working with 1 or 2 ladlefuls at a time, purée the soup in a blender or food processor, processing each batch for 20 to 30 seconds until smooth. Strain the soup through a sieve; it should have the consistency of thick cream. If the soup is too thick, dilute with additional broth. Return the purée to the soup pot and reheat.

Taste and add more salt if needed and black pepper and nutmeg to taste. Ladle the soup into heated soup plates and garnish with the reserved whole chestnuts and *croûtons*.

Ingredients

1 RABBIT, 3 TO 3½ POUNDS, CUT INTO 8 SERVING PIECES

ALL-PURPOSE FLOUR

6 TABLESPOONS UNSALTED BUTTER

1 TEASPOON CURRY POWDER

1 POUND FRESH WHITE BUTTON MUSHROOMS

2½ QUARTS WATER

3 MEDIUM-SIZED ONIONS, FINELY CHOPPED

1 CLOVE GARLIC, FINELY MINCED

1 BOUQUET GARNI (6 FRESH PARSLEY STEMS, 2 BAY LEAVES, 2 FRESH THYME SPRIGS TIED IN 1 LARGE CELERY STALK)

1 TEASPOON SALT

1 FRESH ROSEMARY SPRIG, OR 1 TEASPOON DRIED ROSEMARY

8 FRESH BASIL LEAVES (OPTIONAL)

3 EGG YOLKS

1 CUP CRÈME FRAÎCHE, OR ½ CUP EACH HEAVY CREAM AND SOUR CREAM

FRESHLY GROUND BLACK PEPPER

The unusual use of curry, rosemary, and fresh basil adds a depth to a soup that is already supremely succulent with mush- rooms juices and cream. I was happy to learn once, when pressed for time, that this recipe can be made successfully in a slow cooker. After browning the rabbit on the stove top, cook it overnight in its liquid in a crock pot. Return it to the soup pot in the morning for finishing. It's exquisite.

Rinse the rabbit pieces, then dry well. Dust the rabbit pieces with flour. Melt 4 table-spoons of the butter in a soup pot over medium heat. Brown the rabbit pieces on all sides. While the rabbit is cooking, sprinkle the pieces with the curry powder.

Meanwhile, clean the mushrooms by wiping carefully, but do not use any water. Separate the caps from the stems, and cut off any stem bases that contain soil. Finely slice the stems and reserve. Select 6 nice mushroom caps for garnish. Thinly slice and reserve. Cut all the remaining mushroom caps into quarters and reserve. Place a small baking pan in a 250°F oven.

When the rabbit is nicely browned, add the water, onions, garlic, bouquet garni, salt, reserved mushroom pieces, rosemary, and basil, if using. Cover, reduce the heat to low, and simmer for 2 hours. The meat should fall off the bone at this time.

Melt the remaining 2 tablespoons butter in a sauté pan. Add the reserved sliced mush-rooms for garnish and cook lightly for 2 to 3 minutes. Remove from the pan and reserve.

When the rabbit is ready, remove the pieces from the pot, take the meat off the bone, and discard the bones. Put the rabbit meat in the baking pan, cover with aluminum foil, and place in the oven. Strain the cooking broth through a fine-mesh sieve, forcefully pressing against the solids in the sieve. Return the strained broth to the soup pot and add the reserved quartered mushroom caps. Cook over low heat for 5 minutes, then add the rabbit meat, stirring to heat thoroughly.

RABBIT AT MARKET ON RUE CLER IN THE
SEVENTH *ARRONDISSEMENT* IN PARIS.

In a small bowl, whisk together the egg yolks and crème fraîche (or heavy cream and sour cream). Whisk in a ladleful of the hot soup. Slowly add this mixture to the soup pot while whisking constantly. Taste and add more salt if needed and black pepper to taste. Be careful not to allow the soup to reach a boil.

Ladle into heated soup plates and garnish with the reserved sliced mushroom caps. Serve immediately.

> ### THE "AGE OF PREFERENCE"
> In the United States, most shoppers find farm-raised rabbits in supermarkets, and that's what we use unless we know a hunter. But old French recipes often offer their readers an interesting option. When preparing poultry and game dishes, French cooks are advised to choose a rabbit, or a hen, for example, of the "age of preference."

CHAPTER SIX

The guests were silent, constrained, and replaced their spoons after eating two spoon-fuls of onion soup, which lacked cheese. . . .
—Philippe Hériat, *LES GRILLES D'OR*,
ON CHRISTMAS EVE IN WORLD WAR II FRANCE

SOUPS *from*
THE DAIRY: CHEESE AND EGGS

LEFT: BREBIS, A CHEESE MADE FROM THE MILK OF EWES, IS USUALLY PRODUCED IN LIMITED AMOUNTS ON LOCAL FARMS AND IS TRADITIONALLY EATEN LOCALLY.

ENRICHING SOUPS WITH CHEESE AND EGGS

Whoever said about France that "Any nation that produces over 350 cheeses is incapable of self-government" undoubtedly provoked a political discussion. It may have been Winston Churchill or Charles de Gaulle; respected authorities continue to debate the quotation's origin. But unarguable is the overwhelming number, variety, and quality of the cheeses of France. It follows that good French cooks have added some of those cheeses to bowls or tureens of steaming soup, providing nourishment, texture, and flavor.

There are now, in 2002, well over 30 different cheeses in France that are distinguished enough to bear an AOC designation *(appellation d'origine de contrôlée)*, a French grading system in which wines, cheeses, and many other fine products are subject to meticulous production requirements, including rigid geographical boundaries, and precise labeling. Of course, problems are created in such a system, but on the whole the consumer usually wins. French cheese producers are threatened on another front, however. As the European Union (EU) continues to exert its power, cheese makers are gravely concerned with certain rules calling for standardizations that would forever change some of their wonderful and traditional cheeses.

Eggs are as critical to the French pantry as its celebrated cheeses. Cooks have long had the inclination to serve eggs, in some form or another, as a first course. Often *oeufs dur*— simply hard-cooked eggs, sometimes with mayonnaise— are seen on bistro menus as an opening option. Once on a cassoulet-tasting journey in southwestern France, a waiter in Carcassone suggested "something light"—"*une omelette*?"— as a first course. My companion and I were served omelets filled with buttery sautéed mushrooms. That "light" first course nearly ambushed the enjoyment of our complex cassoulet.

When French cooks combine their culinary genius for delicate egg cookery with their gift for inventive soups, the results are remarkable. Variations abound. Tempered, uncooked eggs are added to broth to thicken soups, while frothy uncooked eggs are stirred into simmering soup to create golden threads. Often clouds of whipped egg whites are poached in hot soups, while other soups contain perfectly poached whole eggs, either simmered in another liquid or poached in the soup itself. Some of these reviving and delectable dishes follow.

RIGHT: PLACE AU BEURRE—"BUTTER SQUARE"—
PUBLIC PLAZA IN THE PICTURESQUE TOWN
OF QUIMPER, IN BRITTANY, A REGION WITH A
TASTE FOR LIGHTLY SALTED BUTTER.

PLACE
AU BEURRE

Alsace Lorraine

BACON LARDONS and CHEESE SOUP

SOUPE au FROMAGE LORRAINE

MAKES **6** SERVINGS

¼ POUND LEAN BACON (4 OR 5 SLICES), WELL CHILLED AND CUT INTO ¼-INCH DICE

2 MEDIUM-SIZED ONIONS, FINELY CHOPPED

6 CUPS WATER OR VEGETABLE BROTH

1 TEASPOON SALT

FRESHLY GROUND BLACK PEPPER

6 THICK SLICES WHOLE-GRAIN COUNTRY BREAD

1 ½ CUPS GRATED GRUYÈRE CHEESE

6 TABLESPOONS HEAVY CREAM OR LOW-FAT SOUR CREAM

In this soup, bacon, the Lorraine cook's favorite ingredient, flavors the onions that are cooked in its fat, and then it is added as a crunchy topping. I like the harmonious flavor layering created here, a kind of soup version of the estimable quiche Lorraine. *The difference between the cuisine of Alsace and Lorraine? That of Alsace is more solid* (le plus solide), *states one French writer. This soup is decidedly "solid," but a great indulgence.*

On a good fire, a little kettle simmers tranquilly with a murmur of satisfaction. It is a little late to keep someone up for a marmite. *From time to time . . . its cover is agitated by the vapor . . . the hot, appetizing breath rises and it diffuses in all the room. Oh! The good aroma of a cheese soup!*

—Alphonse Daudet,
CONTES DU LUNDIS, HYMN TO CHEESE SOUP

Put the bacon in a large, heavy saucepan and cook over medium heat, stirring often, until the bacon morsels (*lardons*) become completely cooked and crisp, 4 to 5 minutes. Using a slotted spoon, remove the bacon from the pan and drain on paper towels.

Pour off all but 2 tablespoons of the fat from the pan and add the onions. Cook over very low heat, stirring constantly, until they are translucent and lightly colored, 8 to 10 minutes. Add the water or broth and the salt and bring to a boil over high heat. Reduce the heat to low, cover partially, and simmer for 45 minutes. Taste and add more salt if needed and black pepper to taste.

Place a slice of bread in the bottom of each of 6 heated soup plates. Spread equal portions of the grated cheese over the bread in each plate and top each with 1 tablespoon of cream or sour cream. Ladle the hot soup over the bread and sprinkle each serving with *lardons*. Serve immediately.

LEFT: *PAYSAN*—"COUNTRY"—BACON, SMOKED OVER WOOD, AT A MARKET IN ALSACE.

Auvergne

CHEESE and RYE BREAD SOUP

SOUPE CANTAL d'AUVERGNE

MAKES **6** SERVINGS

10 OUNCES CANTAL CHEESE

3 TABLESPOONS UNSALTED BUTTER

4 MEDIUM-SIZED ONIONS, FINELY CHOPPED

1 ½ QUARTS WATER OR VEGETABLE BROTH, BOILING

1 TEASPOON SALT

FRESHLY GROUND BLACK PEPPER

½ POUND STALE DARK RYE BREAD, VERY THINLY SLICED

1 CUP CRÈME FRAÎCHE OR HEAVY CREAM

Cantal is an ancient French cheese that is produced only from the milk of cows in the Auvergne. Lightly salted during production, it is formed into huge cylinders that become hard, similar to a Cheddar or a Gruyère. Its wonderfully sharp flavor mates well with dark bread (I prefer a pumpernickel), and it melts perfectly for this hearty soup. When buying Cantal and dark bread for this recipe, purchase some extra. The cheese is a good table cheese, delicious for nibbling with toasted dark bread.

Used by the French in many sauces, soups, and other savory and sweet dishes, crème fraîche is rich unpasteurized cream with a pronounced flavor. It is possible to buy it in some specialty shops and well-stocked supermarkets, but it is simple to make at home. By combining heavy cream with sour cream, buttermilk, or yogurt, the bacteria lost in pasteurizing is returned. For home preparation, whisk together 2 cups heavy cream with ¾ cup sour cream, buttermilk, or plain yogurt. Place in a container, cover, and leave in a warm place until thickened, for 8 hours or up to overnight. Once thickened, refrigerate until needed. While homemade crème fraîche does not have the authentic flavor of the French product, it is tangy and good to use, particularly in soups.

Carefully cut the cheese into very thin slices. Using a vegetable peeler may give you the thin slices needed here. Or you may grate the cheese.

Melt the butter in a heavy 4-quart soup pot over medium heat. Add the onions and cook, stirring occasionally, until they begin to color, 10 to 12 minutes. Add the boiling water or broth and the salt, reduce the heat to low, and simmer, uncovered, for 30 minutes. Taste and add more salt if needed and black pepper to taste. Meanwhile, preheat the oven to 325°F.

Using all the bread and cheese, layer the slices alternately in the bottom of a flameproof 3-quart earthenware casserole. Pour in the onion broth. Cover the casserole with its own lid or with aluminum foil, place in the oven, and bake until bubbling, about 30 minutes. (Individual ovenproof soup bowls may be used instead; baking time is then reduced to 15 minutes.)

Take the casserole out of the oven, and turn on the broiler. Remove the lid from the casserole and pour the crème fraîche or cream over the soup. Place under a broiler for a few minutes until golden brown, then serve immediately.

6 LARGE ONIONS, FINELY CHOPPED

6 TABLESPOONS UNSALTED BUTTER

½ CUP WATER

¼ CUP ALL-PURPOSE FLOUR

2 QUARTS WATER OR VEGETABLE, CHICKEN, OR BEEF BROTH, BOILING

SALT

FRESHLY GROUND BLACK PEPPER

6 SLICES COARSE COUNTRY BREAD

¼ POUND GRUYÈRE CHEESE, GRATED

With a classic, it's best to say very little. This version is adapted from a collection of authentic regional recipes edited by Alain Senderens. I like the safety net of adding a little water to cook with the onions while they are caramelizing. They still cook to a golden color, but you don't have to hover over the onions as usual. Senderens writes that this is "The soup of the wee hours of the morning for the Parisian noctambules after the theater, the nightclub, or a dinner with strong libations. The soup that invigorates those who have a gueule de bois." The French for hangover? A wooden mouth.

Put the onions, butter, and water in a heavy 3-quart soup pot. Place over low heat, cover, and simmer for 30 to 40 minutes, stirring as often as necessary to make sure the onions cook evenly. The onions should be a uniform deep gold.

Stir in the flour and cook, continuing to stir, until lightly colored without burning, 3 to 4 minutes. Very slowly add the boiling water or broth while stirring constantly, then cook an additional 15 minutes over low heat to blend the flavors. Meanwhile, preheat the oven to 450°F.

Add salt and black pepper to taste to the soup, then ladle the soup into 6 ovenproof soup bowls. Top each serving with a slice of bread and sprinkle evenly with the grated cheese. Place in the oven immediately and bake until the cheese has melted and browned, about 10 minutes. Carefully remove from the oven and serve at once.

¼ CUP DRIED WHITE BEANS SUCH AS NAVY OR GREAT NORTHERN

2 ½ QUARTS WATER

1 "BEAUTIFUL" HEAD SAVOY CABBAGE

4 YOUNG, SLENDER CARROTS, PEELED

2 TURNIPS, PEELED

2 TABLESPOONS UNSALTED BUTTER

1 LARGE ONION, FINELY MINCED

1 SLENDER LEEK, WHITE AND PALE GREEN PARTS ONLY, FINELY MINCED

1 CELERY STALK, FINELY MINCED

¼ POUND PROSCIUTTO OR OTHER AIR-CURED HAM, FINELY DICED

1 WHOLE CLOVE

1 BOUQUET GARNI (6 FRESH PARSLEY STEMS, 2 BAY LEAVES, 2 FRESH THYME SPRIGS TIED IN LARGE CELERY STALK)

2 MEDIUM-SIZED WAXY POTATOES, PEELED AND CUT INTO ¾-INCH CUBES

SALT

FRESHLY GROUND BLACK PEPPER

3 OUNCES ROQUEFORT CHEESE

CROÛTONS MADE WITH COARSE COUNTRY BREAD (PAGE 79)

CABBAGE and ROQUEFORT SOUP

SOUPE aux CHOUX et au ROQUEFORT
AMBASSADE d'AUVERGNE

Auvergne

MAKES 6 SERVINGS

Ambassade d'Auvergne, the fine Auvergnate restaurant in Paris, contributed this version of soupe aux choux *and I have retained some of the chef's wording. It is a colorful and unusual cabbage soup. The vegetables are cut into attractive morsels and are cooked until they are just tender but no longer. Finding nuggets of Roquefort hidden in the steaming, savory soup is a splendid surprise.*

If you are lucky enough to have a small piece of country ham on hand, do use it in this dish. It will spread its incomparable fragrance throughout the soup.

Rinse the beans, then place in a bowl and cover generously with cold water. Soak the beans overnight. The following day, drain, place in a heavy saucepan, and add 1 quart of the water. Bring to a boil and cook over high heat for 10 to 12 minutes. Reduce the heat to medium-low and cook for 30 minutes. Drain and reserve.

Cut the cabbage head through the stem end into quarters. Remove the coarse center ribs. Cut each quarter into 2 wedges, making a total of 8 cabbage pieces. Cut the carrots and turnips into *batonnets* (small sticks). Reserve the vegetables.

Melt the butter in a heavy 10-quart soup pot over low heat. Add the onion, leek, celery, and prosciutto and cook, stirring often, until the vegetables are golden, about 15 minutes. Add the remaining 1½ quarts water and bring to a boil over high heat. Add the reserved beans and cabbage, the clove and the bouquet garni, reduce the heat to low, and simmer, uncovered, for 15 minutes, stirring occasionally. Add the potatoes, carrots, and turnips, cover partially, and cook over medium heat, stirring occasionally, until all the vegetables are tender, about 15 to 20 minutes.

200 THE SOUPS *of* FRANCE

ROQUEFORT, A TANGY BLUE-VEINED CHEESE, IS
PRODUCED FROM EWE'S MILK AND IS MATURED
IN CHALKY CAVES UNIQUE TO THE VILLAGE OF
ROQUEFORT.

Remove the bouquet garni and discard. Add salt and black pepper to taste. Since the ham and Roquefort are quite salty, very little (if any) salt may be needed.

Divide the Roquefort evenly among the 6 heated soup plates. Ladle the hot soup over the cheese, sprinkle with the *croûtons*, and serve immediately.

Auvergne

GARLIC LOVERS' SOUP
with CHEESE and WHITE WINE
BILLOMOISE

MAKES **6** SERVINGS

20 WHOLE CLOVES GARLIC, UNPEELED

1 MEDIUM-SIZED ONION, HALVED

2 QUARTS WATER

1 TEASPOON SALT

2 OR 3 FRESH THYME SPRIGS

1 BAY LEAF

6 *CROÛTES* (PAGE 79)

¼ POUND CANTAL CHEESE, GRATED

¼ POUND UNSALTED BUTTER, AT ROOM TEMPERATURE

1 TABLESPOON ALL-PURPOSE FLOUR

2 EGG YOLKS, AT ROOM TEMPERATURE

1 TO 2 CUPS FRUITY WHITE WINE, AT ROOM TEMPERATURE

*Yes, twenty cloves of garlic, yet they surren-
der much of their pungency to long, gentle
cooking. The intense broth that results
is further enhanced by a fruity white wine.
Billom, an old medieval town in the
Auvergne that was once a thriving garlic
and spice market, has lent its name to this
potent soup.*

Place the unpeeled garlic cloves in a mortar and crush them with a pestle, or put them in a
small plastic bag and pound them with a rolling pin. Put the garlic, skins and all, in a heavy
4-quart soup pot and add the onion, water, salt, thyme, and bay leaf. Bring to a boil, reduce
the heat to low, cover partially, and simmer slowly for 30 minutes.

While the garlic simmers, place the *croûtes* on baking sheet and sprinkle with the grated
Cantal cheese. Reserve. Preheat the oven to 250°F and place 6 soup plates in the oven
to heat.

Put the butter in a bowl and mash with a wooden spoon until it is a soft paste. Add the flour
and egg yolks and combine thoroughly.

At the end of the garlic cooking time, strain the garlic broth through a fine-mesh sieve and
return it to the pot. Slowly, a few tablespoons at a time, add 1 to 1½ cups of the hot broth to
the butter-egg mixture, whisking to combine thoroughly. Off the heat, pour the egg-broth
mixture into the pot, stirring until the soup is creamy and thoroughly blended.

Remove the soup plates from the oven and increase the oven temperature to 400°F. When
the oven is fully preheated, place the baking sheet with the cheese-covered *croûtes* in the
oven for a few moments to melt the cheese.

Add the white wine to taste to the soup and place over low heat, stirring occasionally. Do
not allow the soup to boil. Taste and add more salt if needed.

When thoroughly heated, remove the soup from the heat. Place the cheese-glazed *croûtes* in
bottom of the heated soup plates and top with the hot soup. Serve immediately.

LEFT: VIOLET GARLIC AT A GREENGROCER'S
STALL ON MARKET DAY IN SOUILLAC IN THE
DORDOGNE REGION.

Bourgogne

CABBAGE SOUP with SAUSAGE-CHEESE TOASTS

SOUPE au SAUCISSON MORVANDELLE

MAKES 6 SERVINGS

½ CUP UNSALTED BUTTER, SOFTENED

2 MEDIUM-SIZED ONIONS, FINELY CHOPPED

1 SMALL HEAD SAVOY CABBAGE, CORED AND FINELY CHOPPED

1 TEASPOON SALT

2 QUARTS WATER

12 SLICES FRENCH BREAD, TOASTED

12 SLICES GARLIC SAUSAGE SUCH AS KIELBASA

2 CUPS GRATED GRUYÈRE CHEESE

FRESHLY GROUND BLACK PEPPER

There is a surprise when you ladle this soup into a heated soup tureen lined with the sausage toasts hot from the oven. When the broth contacts the blistering sausages, it sputters and sizzles. This is unexpected and entertaining, but the aroma of the garlic sausage is breathtaking, exactly as French food writer Roger Lallemand describes: "When the maîtresse de maison serves this redolent soup, she removes the cover of the tureen at table and exclaims: 'Vous parlez d'un fumet morvandiau!'" (Roughly translated: "Talk about garlic sausage!")

Melt ¼ cup of the butter in a heavy 4-quart soup pot over very low heat. Add the onions and cabbage, and cook, stirring often, until they begin to take on a golden color, 10 to 12 minutes. Add the salt and water and bring to a boil over high heat. Reduce the heat to low, cover, and simmer for 30 minutes.

Meanwhile, preheat the oven to 450°F. Place an ovenproof tureen or deep casserole in the oven to preheat.

Spread the slices of French bread with remaining ¼ cup butter and place a round of sausage on each. Sprinkle evenly with the cheese, completely covering the sausage and bread. Press down lightly on the sausage pieces. Put the cheese-sausage *croûtes* on a baking sheet and bake in the oven until cheese is melted and golden, 4 to 5 minutes.

Taste the soup and add more salt if needed and black pepper to taste. Put the hot *croûtes* in the bottom of the hot tureen or casserole and pour the cabbage-onion soup over them. Cover and serve.

ROQUEFORT-GLAZED ONION SOUP

GRATINÉE au ROQUEFORT

MAKES **6** SERVINGS

6 TABLESPOONS UNSALTED BUTTER, AT ROOM TEMPERATURE

3 MEDIUM ONIONS, FINELY CHOPPED

1 TABLESPOON ALL-PURPOSE FLOUR

2 QUARTS WATER

1 TEASPOON SALT

6 THICK SLICES STALE FRENCH BREAD

1/4 POUND ROQUEFORT CHEESE, AT ROOM TEMPERATURE

1/2 CUP ARMAGNAC OR COGNAC

PINCH OF FRESHLY GRATED NUTMEG

1/2 TEASPOON FRESHLY GROUND BLACK PEPPER

3/4 CUP GRATED GRUYÈRE CHEESE

Here the traditional bistro favorite, onion soup gratinée, is given an unusual elegance. Onions are cooked to translucence, strained, and only their heady essence is used for the broth with the added refinement of Armagnac (or Cognac). A surprising blend of two cheeses—pungent Roquefort and nutty Gruyère—caps this extraordinary elixir.

It carries with it the strong odor of the earth, and the aroma of the prairies, and it seems its presence is a window open on distant country fields.

—Curnonsky, ON ROQUEFORT CHEESE

Melt 4 tablespoons of the butter in a heavy 4-quart soup pot over medium-low heat. Sauté the onions, stirring often, until golden, 12 to 15 minutes. Sprinkle the onions with the flour and stir thoroughly. Whisk in the water and salt and bring to a boil over high heat. Reduce the heat to low and simmer, uncovered, for 15 minutes. Meanwhile, preheat the oven to 400°F.

Thinly spread the bread slices on both sides with the remaining 2 tablespoons butter. Sauté over medium heat in a sauté pan until crisp and golden on both sides, 5 to 7 minutes total. Spread one side of each slice of golden toast with the Roquefort cheese and reserve.

Pour the onion broth through a fine-mesh sieve, pressing on the solids firmly with a wooden spoon. Return the broth to the soup pot, add the Armagnac or Cognac and the nutmeg, and reheat to serving temperature over medium heat. Taste for seasoning and add salt if needed and the black pepper.

Divide the hot broth among 6 ovenproof soup bowls and top with the Roquefort toasts. Sprinkle with the Gruyère cheese and place in the oven. When the cheeses are melted and golden, in 5 to 8 minutes, carefully remove the hot soup bowls from the oven and serve immediately.

HERBED SOUP
with AGED CHEESE

SOUPE au VIEUX BROCCIU

MAKES 6 SERVINGS

½ POUND AGED BROCCIU CHEESE

3 QUARTS WATER

¼ CUP FRUITY OLIVE OIL

2 MEDIUM-SIZED ONIONS, FINELY CHOPPED

1 CLOVE GARLIC, FINELY MINCED

1 TEASPOON SALT

¼ POUND THIN PASTA, BROKEN INTO 1-INCH PIECES

1 CUP SHORT RIBBONS SWISS CHARD

¼ CUP FINELY CHOPPED FRESH MINT

FRESHLY GROUND BLACK PEPPER

The fragrances that rush from a steaming bowl of this soup are hard to describe. They are a result of an alliance of garlic, which usually holds its own, balmy mint, and bold cheese. Add that exuberant perfume to the visual appeal of this soup—straw-colored pasta, golden cheese nuggets, dark green speckles—and you have a memorable Corsican dish.

Brocciu (or broccio) is an unusual Corsican cheese that is eaten fresh, aged, and at stages in between. Available fresh year-round, in winter brocciu is produced from the milk of sheep and in the summer from the milk of goats. The taste of aged brocciu slightly resembles that of Parmigiano-Reggiano. As the Corsican cheese may be difficult to track down in your market, a good Parmigiano-Reggiano may be used.

Put the cheese in a large bowl with 1 quart of the water. Let it soak it for 1 hour. Drain, cut into ½-inch cubes, and reserve.

Heat the olive oil in a heavy 4-quart soup pot over medium heat. Sauté the onions, stirring occasionally, until golden, 10 to 12 minutes. Add the remaining 2 quarts water, the garlic, and the salt to the pot and bring to a boil over high heat. Reduce the heat to low and simmer, uncovered, for 10 minutes, cooking the onions to tenderness.

Bring back to a boil and add the pasta and cheese. Cook, stirring occasionally, until the pasta is al dente, about 10 minutes. Quickly stir in the Swiss chard and mint and mix well.

Taste and add more salt if needed and black pepper to taste. Ladle the soup into heated soup plates and serve immediately.

LEFT: BESIDES THEIR ADAPTABLE BROCCIU CHEESE, CORSICANS ENJOY AN ARTISANAL CHEESE WITH A SPRIG OF FERN IMPRESSED INTO ITS SURFACE KNOWN AS *"A FILETTA"*— THE FERN—EITHER OF GOAT'S MILK (*CHEVRE*) OR EWE'S MILK (*BREBIS*).

207 SOUPS *from* THE DAIRY: CHEESE AND EGGS

Provence

GARLIC and SAGE BROTH with CHEESE

AÏGO BOULIDO

MAKES **6** SERVINGS

¼ CUP FRUITY OLIVE OIL

12 CLOVES GARLIC, FINELY MINCED

2 QUARTS WATER

1 FRESH SAGE SPRIG (SEE NOTE)

1 FRESH THYME SPRIG (SEE NOTE)

2 BAY LEAVES

1 TEASPOON SALT, OR TO TASTE

FRESHLY GROUND BLACK PEPPER

6 THICK SLICES FRENCH BREAD, TOASTED

1 CUP GRATED PARMIGIANO-REGGIANO CHEESE

Perhaps only the French would have the nerve to call a soup aïgo boulido, "boiled water," and in Provence they have done just that. The soup, which is also known as eau bouille (in French), is eaten not only in Provence, but also in one form or another all over France. There is scarcely a cookbook, old or new, that does not offer at least one version of aïgo boulido.

Because this soup is water, albeit with plenty of garlic and some fresh herbs, it is very often taken "the morning after." This fragrant soup is also given to infants at the time of their weaning, and because of its bold, reviving, and curative nature, it is traditionally served to convalescents. There is a jaunty Provençal saying, "The boiled water saves the life." Everybody else enjoys this soup as well because it is invigorating and as easy to make as boiling water.

Heat the olive oil in a heavy 4-quart soup pot over low heat. Sauté the garlic, stirring often, until it is softened, but has not colored, 10 to 12 minutes. Add the water and herbs and bring to a boil over high heat. Reduce the heat to low and simmer, uncovered, for 15 minutes.

Remove the herbs from the soup pot and discard. Add the salt and black pepper to taste. Place a slice of the bread in each of 6 heated soup plates. Ladle the hot soup over the bread and serve immediately. Pass the cheese at table.

NOTE: It is essential to use fresh herbs in this soup. A mixture of chopped fresh basil and parsley lends fragrance and can be substituted for the fresh thyme and sage.

Rhône-Alpes

ALPINE CHEESE-GLAZED ROOT VEGETABLE SOUP

SOUPE SAVOYARDE

MAKES **6** SERVINGS

1 SMALL CELERY ROOT, PEELED

1 SLENDER PARSNIP, PEELED

1 SLENDER SALSIFY ROOT, PEELED

2 SMALL TURNIPS, PEELED

2 MEDIUM-SIZED WAXY POTATOES, PEELED

3 YOUNG, SLENDER CARROTS, PEELED

6 OUNCES BACON, CUT INTO $\frac{1}{3}$-INCH DICE

1 MEDIUM-SIZED ONION, FINELY CHOPPED

1 TEASPOON SALT

1 $\frac{3}{4}$ QUARTS WATER

1 CUP MILK, HEATED

$\frac{1}{2}$ TEASPOON FRESHLY GROUND BLACK PEPPER

6 THICK SLICES FRENCH BREAD, TOASTED

6 TABLESPOONS GRATED BEAUFORT OR GRUYÈRE CHEESE

In this and many French recipes, it is customary to sprinkle bread slices with cheese, place the bread in bottom of a soup plate, and ladle on the hot soup. In soupe savoyarde, *I prefer to toast French bread, heap it with Gruyère cheese, float it on the soup, and glaze it in a hot oven. I sprinkle crisp bacon morsels over the molten cheese and serve the soup immediately. Also known as oyster plant, salsify, a long, slender root vegetable popular in France but less so in the United States, is in markets from late spring into winter. This is a particularly inviting dish—its aroma alone will give your family and friends the appetite of a rugged mountaineer.*

Cut the celery root, parsnip, salsify, turnips, potatoes, and carrots into small sticks and reserve. Sauté the bacon in a heavy 4-quart soup pot over medium heat, stirring often, until crisp, 4 to 5 minutes. Using a slotted spoon, remove the bacon pieces, drain on paper towels, and reserve. Preheat the oven to 350°F.

Pour off all but 2 tablespoons of the fat from the soup pot. Add the onion and sauté over very low heat, stirring often, until lightly colored, about 8 minutes. Add the salt, reserved vegetables, and water and bring to a boil over high heat. Reduce the heat to medium, cover partially, and cook until all the vegetables are tender, about 20 minutes. Add the hot milk and stir until well blended. Taste and add more salt if needed and the black pepper.

Sprinkle the bread slices evenly with the grated cheese. Ladle the soup into ovenproof bowls, top with the cheese-topped bread slices, and place in the oven until the cheese has lightly browned, 10 to 12 minutes. Carefully remove from the oven, scatter the reserved bacon over the cheese, and serve immediately.

ONION and GARLIC SOUP

OUILLAT BÉARNAISE

MAKES **6** SERVINGS

6 TABLESPOONS RENDERED GOOSE FAT OR GOOD-QUALITY LARD

3 MEDIUM-SIZED ONIONS, FINELY CHOPPED

4 CLOVES GARLIC, FINELY MINCED

2 QUARTS VEGETABLE BROTH OR WATER SAVED FROM COOKING GREEN BEANS, FAVA BEANS, ASPARAGUS, OR DRIED PEAS

6 FRESH PARSLEY STEMS

2 BAY LEAVES

2 FRESH THYME SPRIGS, OR 1 TEASPOON DRIED THYME

1 TEASPOON SALT

2 EGGS

2 TO 3 TEASPOONS RED WINE VINEGAR

FRESHLY GROUND BLACK PEPPER

CROÛTONS (PAGE 79)

Since ouillat *is surprisingly light yet full of flavor, I think it would be a good choice for serving in punch cups to guests before a large buffet. Given its delicate yellow color, its lingering perfume, and the fact that it is one of the most ancient of French soups, the soup represents a warm welcome to your friends.*

Heat 4 tablespoons of the goose fat or lard in the bottom of a heavy 4-quart soup pot over medium heat. Sauté the onions and garlic, stirring often, until lightly colored, 10 to 12 minutes. Add the vegetable broth or water, parsley stems, bay leaves, thyme, and salt and bring to a boil over high. Reduce the heat to low, cover partially, and simmer for 20 minutes.

Place the eggs in a large mixing bowl, add the vinegar, and whisk thoroughly to mix well. Slowly pour the boiling soup through a fine-mesh sieve into the egg mixture while whisking constantly. Return the soup to the pot and reheat over very low heat. Do not allow the soup to reach a boil.

Taste and add more salt if needed and black pepper to taste. Ladle into heated soup plates and pass the *croûtons*.

Sud-ouest

GARLIC SOUP with EGG
TOURIN BLANCHI

MAKES 6 SERVINGS

3 TABLESPOONS FRUITY OLIVE OIL

24 CLOVES GARLIC, PEELED BUT LEFT WHOLE

2 TABLESPOONS ALL-PURPOSE FLOUR

2 QUARTS WATER OR WATER SAVED FROM COOKING GREEN BEANS

1½ TEASPOONS SALT, OR TO TASTE

⅓ CUP BROKEN THIN PASTA (1-INCH PIECES)

2 EGGS

2 TO 3 TEASPOONS RED WINE VINEGAR

FRESHLY GROUND BLACK PEPPER

One of the better-known soups in which eggs are featured is this aromatic classic from the Quercy region of the Southwest. It is a pungent garlic soup enriched with egg yolk for color and flavor and garnished with fluffy poached egg white. Often tourins *are served with* croûtes *afloat. This version includes a little pasta instead.*

Although it is a thrifty tradition to prepare this soup with water saved from cooking green beans, I prefer it prepared with clear water. The whole garlic cloves are cooked to liquidity, the exact consistency for removing from the soup and spreading on thick chunks of French bread, which I highly recommend.

Recipes for this soup vary widely. Thin croûtes *are often used instead of pasta, added to the bottom of the bowl and then covered with the hot soup.*

Heat the olive oil in a heavy 4-quart soup pot over low heat. Sauté the garlic cloves lightly, stirring often, for about 3 minutes. The garlic should not color or it will become bitter. Stir in the flour with a wooden spoon and cook, stirring, for 2 to 3 minutes.

Pour in a small amount of the water, stirring well to make a liaison that is uniform and without lumps. Add the remaining water and the salt and bring to a boil over high heat. Reduce the heat to low, cover, and simmer for 20 to 30 minutes. The garlic will be fully cooked and tender.

Remove the cover, return the soup to a boil over high heat, and add the pasta. Reduce the heat to low and simmer for about 8 minutes, stirring occasionally.

Separate the whites and yolks of the eggs. With the broth over very low heat, gently slide the egg whites into the barely quivering liquid and poach for 2 or 3 minutes only. Do not overcook. Remove the egg whites with a skimmer and, when cool enough to handle, divide among 6 heated soup plates.

In another bowl, dilute the egg yolks with the wine vinegar. Add a little hot broth to the egg yolk mixture, stirring constantly. Add the egg mixture to the soup and "blanch" quickly (hence, the French word *blanchi*). Place over low heat and simmer until the soup thickens. The flour will prevent the egg yolk from curdling.

Remove from the heat, taste, and add a little black pepper. Ladle the soup into the plates over the poached egg-white pieces. Serve very hot.

Broths

VEGETABLE BROTH
BOUILLON des LÉGUMES
ABOUT 2 QUARTS

What constitutes a good vegetable broth is an array of full-of-flavor vegetables. This recipe is an up-to-date version of what many old French vegetable soup recipes advised: use water left over from cooking green beans, fava beans, or any single vegetable or combination of vegetables. For your stock, use aromatics (carrot, onion, celery), some fresh herbs, and whatever vegetable scraps you have in your fridge. I personally do not include vegetables from the cabbage family in vegetable broth because of their unique, strong flavors. The following recipe is merely a guideline.

1 LARGE LEEK, WHITE AND ALL BUT 1 TO 2 INCHES OF DARK GREEN PARTS, THINLY SLICED

6 CARROTS, PEELED AND CUT INTO 1-INCH CHUNKS

6 LARGE LOVAGE OR CELERY STALKS, COARSELY CHOPPED

2 ONIONS, UNPEELED, QUARTERED

½ HEAD GARLIC, UNPEELED, CRUSHED

¼ POUND FRESH MUSHROOMS, COARSELY CHOPPED, OR 1 CUP CHOPPED MUSHROOM STEMS

6 FRESH THYME SPRIGS, OR 1 TEASPOON DRIED THYME

1 BUNCH FRESH PARSLEY STEMS

12 BLACK PEPPERCORNS

Put all the ingredients except the peppercorns in a heavy 4-quart soup pot and add cold water to cover by a few inches. Bring to a boil, reduce the heat to low, cover, and simmer for 45 minutes. Uncover, add the peppercorns, and simmer, uncovered, for 30 minutes to intensify the flavor. Strain through a fine-mesh sieve, pressing firmly on the solids with the back of a spoon to extract as much flavor as possible. Refrigerate for up to 3 days, or freeze for up to 3 months.

FISH BROTH
FUMET de POISSONS
ABOUT 1 QUART

If you buy your fish whole and bone them at home, you have the frames necessary for making this broth. If not, ask your fish-monger to give you leftover frames and heads to use as the basis of your fish fumet. From beginning to end, the process takes only 45 minutes, most of which time you can be busy with something else. But it makes such a difference to have a good fish broth available in your freezer for seafood dishes and sauces as well as soups.

3 POUNDS FISH FRAMES AND HEADS

1 TO 2 CUPS SHRIMP SHELLS AND CRAB SHELLS (OPTIONAL)

1 MEDIUM-SIZED ONION, CHOPPED

1 CELERY STALK, SLICED

1 YOUNG, SLENDER CARROT, PEELED AND SLICED

1 LEEK, WHITE AND PALE GREEN PARTS ONLY, THINLY SLICED

1 BOUQUET GARNI (6 FRESH PARSLEY STEMS, 2 BAY LEAVES, 1 FRESH THYME SPRIG TIED IN A BUNDLE)

9 CUPS WATER

1 CUP DRY WHITE WINE

Rinse the fish frames and heads repeatedly in plenty of cold running water to remove any traces of blood or viscera. Combine the fish frames and heads, the shellfish shells (if using), the vegetables, bouquet garni, and water in a heavy stainless-steel or enameled 6-quart soup pot.

Place the pot over low heat, bring to a boil, and reduce the heat to a bare simmer. Do not stir, but remove any scum as it comes to the surface. Keep the heat very low and continue to skim. When no more scum appears, add the wine. This may generate additional scum, which should then be removed. Continue to simmer, removing any scum as it appears, for a total of 20 minutes.

Remove the large bones with tongs and discard. Pour the broth through a fine-mesh sieve lined with a double layer of dampened cheesecloth into a glass, ceramic, or stainless-steel container.

Chill the broth as fast as you can by placing the container in a large bowl of ice and stirring the broth often until it cools to room temperature. Then store in the coldest part of your refrigerator. If you wish to freeze the broth, pour it into suitably sized containers. My preference is to use self-sealing 1-quart plastic bags. I label the bags with a felt marker, fill them three-fourths full, seal them, and lay them horizontally in the freezer. After the broth is frozen, the bags can be stacked.

3 POUNDS BEEF SHIN BONES, BUTCHER-CUT INTO SMALL PIECES

3 POUNDS BEEF NECK BONES, BUTCHER-CUT INTO SMALL PIECES

1 POUND PIGS' FEET, BUTCHER-CUT INTO SMALL PIECES (OPTIONAL)

2 TABLESPOONS VEGETABLE OR MILD OLIVE OIL

6 CARROTS, PEELED AND COARSELY CHOPPED

2 LARGE ONIONS, COARSELY CHOPPED

2 CELERY STALKS

1 TEASPOON DRIED LEAF THYME

3 FRESH PARSLEY STEMS

1 LARGE BAY LEAF

BROWN BEEF BROTH

ABOUT 3 QUARTS

Traditionally, the soups in this cookbook would not have been prepared with broths, which were inventions of classical chefs. When beef broth was needed, leftover broth from a pot-au-feu (page 144) was used. When chicken broth was called for, it was leftover broth from a poule-au-pot (page 160). Now, however, we rely on homemade or canned broth. Here's how to make beef and chicken broths in your kitchen. Both broths will keep in the refrigerator for 3 days or in the freezer for 3 months. If you refrigerate the broths and do not use them within 3 days, bring them to a boil and then chill. They will once again keep for 3 days.

Because the bones are oven-roasted for making the beef broth, resulting in a dark rich-colored broth, it is referred to as "brown." Because poultry bones are usually not browned in that way, the resulting broth is lighter, "blond." In classic French cuisine, however, veal stock is made both ways: a brown version (roasted bones) and a "white" (nonroasted).

Preheat the oven to 450°F. Place the beef bones and pigs' feet, if using, in a baking pan and sprinkle them with the oil. Place the bones in the oven and roast, turning them as needed so that they are all evenly exposed to the heat, until they are nicely browned, about 30 minutes. Once the bones are browned, examine them for any scorched spots and scrape the spots off.

Put the browned bones in a 10-quart soup pot and add water to cover by 2 inches. Bring to a boil, then reduce the heat until the water just simmers. Remove the scum as it appears. Continue to skim away the scum until it no longer rises to the surface. Add water to replace any liquid you have removed by skimming.

Add the vegetables and herbs and bring to a boil again over high heat. Reduce the heat to low and skim as necessary. Cover partially and cook at a bare simmer for 12 hours to give the broth the necessary strength and richness.

Remove from the heat and skim the fat from the surface. With tongs, remove the larger pieces of bones from the pot and discard. Line a fine-mesh sieve with a double layer of dampened cheese-cloth and strain the broth into a glass, ceramic, or stainless-steel container. Chill the broth as fast as you can by placing the container in a large bowl of ice and stirring the broth often until it cools to room temperature. Then refrigerate or freeze as desired.

BLOND CHICKEN BROTH

ABOUT 2 QUARTS

There are times when using canned chicken broth can't be avoided. We all need to open a can now and then, whether we like it or not. But taste still matters, so here is a quick way to liberate a canned chicken broth from its commercially dull flavor.

Open at least 4 cans of low-sodium chicken broth and empty them into a large saucepan or soup pot. There's no reason to fiddle with this for any less volume. Add a dozen fresh parsley stems (always save those in a sealed plastic bag in your freezer), a few fresh thyme sprigs (or about 1 teaspoon dried), a bay leaf, a few black peppercorns, a finely chopped medium-sized onion, a chopped carrot, a chopped celery stalk, and any fresh herbs you like. Fresh herbs give a clean, bright flavor to the broth. Bring to a boil over high heat, reduce the heat to low, and barely simmer for 20 to 30 minutes. Sometimes I like the brightness that results from adding a lemon half and simmering it for 10 minutes or so. Usually I strain this through a fine-mesh sieve lined with super-absorbent paper toweling. Use this broth right away or store it for 3 days in the refrigerator.

5 POUNDS CHICKEN WINGS AND BACKS

1 ONION, QUARTERED

1 SLENDER LEEK, WHITE AND PALE GREEN PARTS ONLY, SLICED

2 YOUNG, SLENDER CARROTS, PEELED AND CHOPPED

1 CELERY STALK AND LEAVES, CHOPPED

6 FRESH PARSLEY STEMS

2 FRESH THYME SPRIGS

3 CLOVES GARLIC, CRUSHED (OPTIONAL)

Rinse the chicken parts and place in a heavy 4-quart soup pot with water to cover by 2 inches. Bring to a boil over high heat, reduce the heat to low, and skim off the scum as it rises to the surface. Simmer over very low heat, skimming as necessary until no more scum appears. Add water to replace any liquid you have removed by skimming.

Add the vegetables, herbs, and garlic, if using, and bring to a boil again over high heat. Reduce the heat to low and skim as necessary. Cover partially and cook at a bare simmer for 4 hours to give the broth the necessary strength and richness.

Remove from the heat and skim the fat from the surface. Finish according to directions for Brown Beef Broth (page 213).

Bibliography: Cookbooks

Most of these books focus on the cuisine of a particular region. A few are included that cover all the regions of France.

Barberousse, Michel. *Cuisine basque d'hier et d'aujourd'hui.* Biarritz: TIKI, Éditeur, 1989.

Bardon, Chanal. *La Sologne à table.* Éditions Dominique Labarrière: Beaugency, 1982.

Bernadoc, Christian. *La cuisine de foix et du couserans.* Paris: Denoël/Résonances, 1982.

Bisson, Marie. *La cuisine normande.* Paris: Solar, 1978.

Caron, Michel, and Ned Rival. *Dictionnaire des potages.* Paris: Éditions de la Pensée Moderne, 1964.

Carréras, Marie-Thérèse. *Les bonnes recettes du pays catalan.* Paris: Presses de la Renaissance, 1979.

Ceccaldi, Marie. *Recettes recuelles cuisines du terroir.* Paris: Denoël, 1980.

Charreton, Bernard. *La bonnes cuisine des régions.* Montrouge: SOFRES, 1978.

Claustres, Francine. *Connaître la cuisine du Languedoc.* Bordeaux: Sud-Ouest, 1990.

Combrat, Henry. *Gastronomie du terroir.* Pau: Les Charmilles, 1989.

Conseil National des Arts Culinaires. *Inventaire du patrimoire culinaire de la France.* Paris: Albin Michel, 1995.

Contour, Alfred. *Le cuisiner bourguignon.* Marseilles: Laffitte Reprints, 1980.

Costantini, Simone. *La gastronomie corse.* Bastia: Edizioni di U Muntese, 1965.

Couffignal, Huguette. *Cuisine rustique alsace.* Forcalquier: Robert Morel, 1970.

Courtine, Robert J., and Jean Desmur. *Anthologie de la littérature gastronomique.* Paris: Éditions de Trévise, 1970.

———. *Il etait une fois. . . des recettes.* Paris: Flammarion, 1984.

———. *La cuisine des terroirs.* Lyons: La Manufacture, 1989.

Croze, Austin de. *Les plats régionaux de France.* Luzarches: Daniel Morcrette, 1923.

Drischel, Jean-Pierre. *Histoire et recettes de l'Alsace gourmande.* Toulouse: Privat, 1988.

Dussourd, Henriette. *Les secrets des fermes au coeur de la France.* Paris: Berger-Leorault, 1982.

Escuriguan, Maïte. *Manuel de cuisine basque.* Bayonne: Jean Curutchet, 1988.

Frederick, Robert. *Les cuisines de terroir.* Paris: Dargaud, 1986.

Galé, Anne-Marie. *Connaître la cuisine basque.* Bordeaux: Sud-Ouest, 1990.

Gault-Millau. *Les trois cuisines de France.* Paris: Larousse-Laffront, 1991.

Gracia, Marie-Claude. *La cuisine de passion.* Toledo, Spain: Éd. Oliver Orban, 1989.

Guillemand, Colette. *Les carnets des cuisinières de Bourgogne, de Bress, et de Franche-Comté.* Paris: Chez Berger-Levrault, 1983.

———. *La fourchette et la plume.* Paris: Carrere, 1988.

Hermann, Marie-Thérèse. *La cuisine paysanne de Savoie.* Paris: Éditeur Philippe Sers, 1982.

Jeunet, André, and Ginette Hell-Girod. *Les recettes de la table franc-comtoise.* Strasbourg: Libraire Istra, 1974.

Karsenty, Irène. *La cuisine de Savoie-Dauphiné: cuisines de terroir.* Paris: DeNoël, 1981.

Kocher, Joseph. *La toques blanches d'Alsace.* Strasbourg: Dernière Nouvelles d'Alsace, 1980.

Kohler, Irene. *La cuisine alsacienne.* Paris: Solar, 1974.

LaBars, Yvonne, and Geneviève LaBars. *Ludvennig-cuisine et traditions Bretagne en pays pagan.* Saint-Germain-Lembron: Éditions CREER, 1980.

Lallemand, Roger. *La vraie cuisine du Berry, de la Champagne, d'Alsace, du Franche-Comté, de la Lorraine, du Nivernais, du Morvan, de la Bresse.* Series published by Jacques Lanore of Paris and Quartier Latin of La Rochelle, from 1967.

———. *Les pot-au-feu.* Marseille: Jeanne Laffitte, 1984.

Lazarque, Auricoste de. *Cuisine Messine.* Nancy: Sidot, 1927.

Leveillé, Jeanne, and Philippe Guéroult. *La cuisine des Charentes et du Poitou.* Paris: Denoël, 1984.

Martin, Loïc. *La cuisine du nord et de Picardie.* Paris: DNP/La Voix du Nord, 1981.

Mathiot, Ginette. *À table avec Edouard Pomiane.* Paris: Albin Michel, 1975.

Palay, Simin. *La cuisine du pays (Armagnac, pays basque, Béarn, Bigorre, Landes).* Pau: Éditions Marrimpouey Jeune, 1970.

Pascale, Pynson. *La France à table.* Paris: Éditions La Dècouverte, 1987.

Philippe-Levatois, Jeanne. *Cuisine traditionelle de Poitou et de Vendee.* Poitiers: Le Bouquiniste, 1979.

Philliport, Henri. *Cuisine de provence.* Paris, Éditions Albin Michel, 1977.

Poilâne, Lionel. *Faire son pain.* Paris: Dessain et Tolva, 1982.

Poulain, Jean-Pierre. *Limousin gourmand.* Toulouse: Privat, 1984.

Poulain, Jean-Pierre, and Jean-Luc Rowyer. *Toulouse: Histoire et Recettes de la provence et du comté de Nice.* Privat, 1987.

Progneaux, J.-E. *Recettes et specialities gastronomiques charentaises.* La Rochelle: Quartier Latin, 1974.

Reboul, J.-B. *La cuisinière provençale.* Marseilles: Éditeur Tacussel, 1895.

Rey-Billeton, Lucette. *Les bonnes recettes du soleil.* Editions Aubanel, 1984.

Reynal, Charlou. *Mes recettes du terroir.* Evreux: Olivier Orban, 1986.

Rivovre, Éliane de, and Jacquette Rivoure. *La cuisine landaise.* Paris: Denoël, 1980.

Rogaglia, Suzanne. *Margaridou—cuisinière au pays d'Auvergne.* Nonette: Éditions CREER, 1977.

Saint-Ange, E. *La bonne cuisine.* Paris: Larousse, 1929.

Scotto, Elizabeth. *Encyclopédie de la cuisine française.* Paris: CIL, 1983.

Sloimovici, A. *Ethnocuisine de la Bourgogne.* Guillon: Éditions de Cormarin, 1976.

Vignaud, Jean-Claude. *Les cuisines de terroir.* Paris: Dargaud, 1986.

Walther, Doris, and Annie Walther. *Cuisines du terroir. Cuisine d'Alsace.* Paris: Denoël, 1983.

Bibliography: Quotations

BOOKS

Brillat-Savarin, Jean Anthelme. *Physiologie du goût*. Paris: Bibliothèque-Charpentier, 1907.

Colette. *Prisons et paradis*. Paris: Ferenczi, 1932.

Curnonsky (Maurice Saillard). *Souvenirs littéraires et gastronomiques*. Paris: Albin Michel, 1958.

———. *Recettes des provinces de France*. Paris: Les Productions de Paris, 1959.

Daudet, Alphonse. *Contes du Lundis*. Paris: Nelson Éditeurs, 1933.

———. *Premier voyage, premier mensonge*. Paris: Flammarion, 1898.

Dumas, Alexandre. *Le vicomte de Braglelonn*. Paris: Calmann Lévy, 1895.

Erckmann, Émile, and Alexandre Chatrian. *Contes vosgiens*. Paris: J. Hetzel et Cie, 1977.

Foyot, Charles. *Odeurs de forêt et fumets de table*. Paris: Privas, 1963.

Genevoix, Maurice. *Trente mille jours*. Paris: Seuil, 1980.

Hériat, Philippe. *Les grilles d'or*. Paris: Gallimard, 1957.

Hugo, Victor. *Voyage au Rhin*. Paris: Laffont, 1987.

La Fontaine, Jean de. *Oeuvres complète*. Paris: Gallimard, 1948.

Mercier, Louis-Sébastien. *Tableau de Paris*. Philadelphia: J.B. Lippincott, 1933.

Perec, Georges. *Cahier des charges de la vie, mode d'emploi*. Paris: CNRS Éditions, 1933.

Sabatier, Robert. *Les noisettes sauvages*. Paris: Albin Michel, 1974.

Tendret, Lucien. *La table au pays de Brillat-Savarin*. Paris: Éditions Rabalais, 1972.

Verlaine, Paul. *Oeuvres poétiques complètes*. Paris: Éditions Vialetay, 1955.

Zola, Émile. *Le ventre de Paris*. Paris: Bookking International, 1995.

PERIODICALS

Cuisine et vins de France, 1967 to 1973, 11 issues per year.

Le pot-au-feu, revue de cuisine, June 12, July 10, September 25, and October 9, 1926.

Sources

SEEDS AND PLANTS

Herb seeds and vegetable plants:
The Cook's Garden
P.O. Box 5335, Londonderry, VT 05148
800-457-9703
www.cooksgarden.com

Herb seeds (chervil, lovage, nettle):
Johnny's Selected Seeds
Foss Hill Road, Albion, ME 04910-8731
207-437-4301
Fax 207-437-2165
www.johnnyseeds.com

Herb seeds and vegetable plants:
Shepherd's Garden Seeds
30 Irene Street, Torrington, CT 06790-6658
860-482-3638
www.shepherdseeds.com

MEATS AND POULTRY

Free-range chicken:
Empire Kosher
www.empirekosher.com

Whole duckling, parts, carcasses, and fat:
Culver Duck Farms, Inc.
12215 C R. 10
P.O. Box 910, Middlebury, IN 46540
800-825-9225
www.culverduck.com

Duck, confit, pheasant, and rabbit:
D'Artagnan
280 Wilson Avenue, Newark, NJ 07105
800-DARTAGNAN
www.dartagnan.com

OTHER PRODUCTS

Herbs and spices (dried):
Penzey's Spices
P. O. Box 933
W19362 Apollo Drive, Muskego, WI 53105
800-741-7787
www.penzeys.com

Buckwheat flour, chickpea flour, *fleur de sel Guérande* (French sea salt):
The Baker's Catalogue
King Arthur Flour
P.O. Box 876, Norwich, VT 05055
800-827-6836
800-777-4434
www.bakerscatalogue.com

Crepe pans (5 ½ inch to 10 ¼ inch):
Bridge Kitchenware
214 East 52nd Street, New York, NY 10022
800-274-3435
www.bridgekitchenware.com

Piment d'Espelette (Basque red pepper):
Williams-Sonoma
P.O. Box 7456, San Francisco, CA 94120-7456
877-812-6235
www.williams-sonoma.com

Country hams, imported cheeses, and other fine foods:
Dean & Deluca
560 Broadway, New York, NY 10012
877-826-9246
www.deandeluca.com

Specialty produce:
Frieda's, Inc.
800-241-1771
www.friedas.com

Imported and domestic cheeses:
Murray's Cheeses
257 Bleeker Street, New York, NY 10014
888-692-4339
www.murrayscheeses.com

French wine and food sources:
SOPEXA
Directories of French Exporting Enterprises
www.winesoffrance.com

Wild mushrooms and unusual produce:
Marché aux Délices
P.O. Box 1164, New York, NY 10028
888-547-8471
www.auxdelices.com

Bread from France by mail order:
Poilâne
8, Rue Cherche-Midi, Paris 75006, France
Fax 01 45 44 99
www.commerce@poilane.com

INDEX

TABLE OF EQUIVALENTS

The exact equivalents in the following tables have been rounded for convenience.

LIQUID/DRY MEASURES

U.S.	METRIC
1/4 teaspoon	1.25 milliliters
1/2 teaspoon	2.5 milliliters
1 teaspoon	5 milliliters
1 tablespoon (3 teaspoons)	15 milliliters
1 fluid ounce (2 tablespoons)	30 milliliters
1/4 cup	60 milliliters
1/3 cup	80 milliliters
1/2 cup	120 milliliters
1 cup	240 milliliters
1 pint (2 cups)	480 milliliters
1 quart (4 cups, 32 ounces)	960 milliliters
1 gallon (4 quarts)	3.84 liters
1 ounce (by weight)	28 grams
1 pound	454 grams
2.2 pounds	1 kilogram

OVEN TEMPERATURE

FAHRENHEIT	CELSIUS	GAS
250	120	1/2
275	140	1
300	150	2
325	160	3
350	180	4
375	190	5
400	200	6
425	220	7
450	230	8
475	240	9
500	260	10

LENGTH

U.S.	METRIC
1/8 inch	3 millimeters
1/4 inch	6 millimeters
1/2 inch	12 millimeters
1 inch	2.5 centimeters

METRIC MILK PAILS AT MARKET IN THE
PROVENÇAL TOWN OF CARPENTRAS.